Mastering

Microsoft Intune

Your Ultimate Step-by-Step Guide to Modern Device
Management, Streamlining Your IT Operations and
Enhancing Data Security with Ease

TABLE OF CONTENTS

CHAPTER ONE

EVERYTHING ABOUT MICROSOFT INTUNE

Overview of Microsoft Intune

With Microsoft Intune, you can manage PCs, mobile devices, and mobile apps all from a cloud-based platform. It gives enterprises management over their devices and secures their data without requiring hardware to be installed on-site. No matter what operating system a device is running, businesses can use Microsoft Intune to control desktops, smartphones, and tablets. The ability of Microsoft Intune to provide a seamless and consistent user experience across all devices is among its best features. Users can easily access corporate tools and apps, while businesses may implement security measures and safeguard confidential information. Administrators can limit who has access to certain apps and files, making sure that only individuals with the proper authorization can see or modify private information. To protect devices and data from potential threats, Microsoft Intune also offers a plethora of security measures. By requiring encryption, passcodes, and remote wiping, this enables businesses to ensure that data remains protected even in the event of a device being lost or stolen.

Additionally, Intune provides real-time tracking and reporting so that managers can quickly identify any unusual activity and take action to lower risks. Microsoft Intune simplifies app management in addition to offering robust security measures. To guarantee that consumers have access to the latest versions, organizations can utilize it to share and update apps across various devices. Additionally, Intune is compatible with both private and public app stores, allowing companies to choose the app distribution method that best suits their needs. Microsoft Intune's compatibility with other Microsoft services, such as Office 365 and Azure Active Directory is one of its great features. Businesses can effortlessly manage user IDs and resource access with this relationship, all the while guaranteeing consistent user experiences across Microsoft platforms.

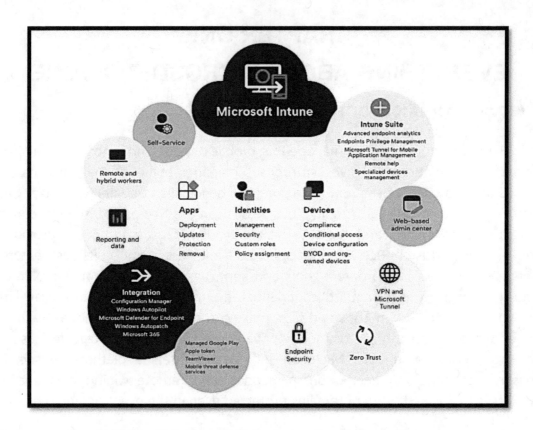

Comprehending Microsoft Intune's Advantages

Businesses can benefit greatly from Microsoft Intune if they wish to manage and safeguard their devices and data.

- **Centralized Management:** From a single console, setting up and managing policies, devices, and apps is simple. This facilitates and improves management.
- **Security Policy Enforcement:** Ensure that, even on non-company-owned devices, security standards are adhered to and data is protected. Establish and put into practice standards like password requirements, data encryption, and app limits to guarantee data security.
- **Flexible Device Management:** Manage circumstances involving both company-owned and "bring your own device" (BYOD) devices. Allow many distinct device ownership models while maintaining control over corporate data and applications.
- **Advanced Threat Protection:** You can be shielded from emerging internet threats by features like mobile threat protection and restricted access. To

protect private data, there must be constant monitoring for potential security threats and quick response.

- ↓ **Comprehensive App Management:** You can facilitate the installation and use of apps by implementing comprehensive app management. To ensure that every employee has access to the newest features and versions, apps are simple to share and upgrade across devices. Employee productivity increases as a result, and IT teams find it simpler to manage apps.
- ↓ **Adaptable Licensing choices:** From a variety of adaptable licensing choices, you can select the one that best suits your requirements. For both small and large businesses, Intune provides alternatives that scale to meet the demands of the organization.

Microsoft Intune features

Improved Functionalities for Advanced Analytics

With the help of this program, you may query specific cloud-controlled Windows devices for device data in real-time using the standard Kusto Query Language (KQL) syntax. It enhances the visibility of previously gathered inventory data in Intune. It becomes even more beneficial by providing managers with more information about the configuration and condition of the device by creating a live link to the device and asking queries in real-time. **Note:** Microsoft Intune Advanced Analytics is available as a stand-alone add-on or as a component of the Intune Suite.

The new Advanced Analytics add-on and the Intune Suite will both get the new features, which include Device inquiry and battery health reports. Finding anomalies, viewing device histories, and viewing the entire range of devices are some of these features. Real-time, detailed data from device questions can be used by IT administrators, security specialists, and support workers to gain deeper insight into the hardware configurations and functionality of devices. This enables them to react to threats and other issues promptly.

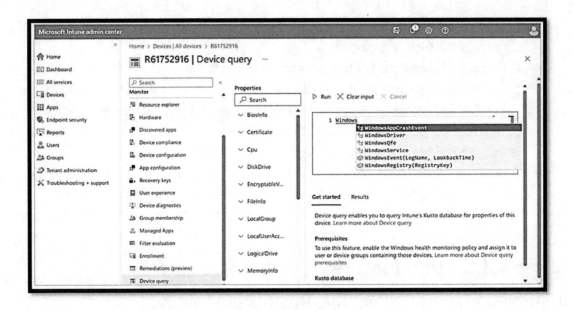

The Advanced Analytics Battery Health Report is currently accessible to the general public (GA). The updated report helps IT professionals manage their assets better by providing them with more information, preventing expensive downtime, and offering purchasing guidance. In order to assist IT managers in promptly identifying hardware issues, such as a dead battery that has to be changed before the warranty expires, this report also incorporates license device scores.

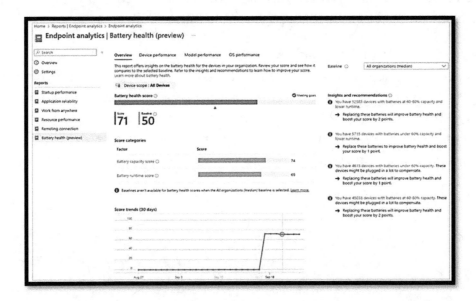

| Endpoint analytics | Startup performance | Work From Anywhere | **Battery health (preview)** | Device timeline |

Review battery health score for this device. Refer to insights and recommendations to learn how to improve scores for this device. Learn more about battery health.

Battery health score ⚠ Needs attention

Score
45

Estimated runtime trends (30 days)

Battery health details

Battery count	1
Cycle count	616
Max capacity	64%
Estimated device runtime	2 hrs, 8 mins

Estimated runtime
2 hr

Model performance comparison

This device model	Battery health score
HP ProBook 440 G8 Notebook PC	45

▲ = The average battery health score for this model in your organization

Top interactive apps consuming battery

Application	Battery usage over 14 days	
Microsoft Teams		16 %
Microsoft Edge		10 %
Microsoft Outlook		4 %
Microsoft Office		2 %

Better Handling of Mobile Devices

Better mobile device control features in Microsoft Intune now make it easier for businesses to manage a wide variety of devices. Applying security policies, configuring device preferences, and managing devices straight from a central location with the most recent features is simple. Microsoft Intune allows you to manage all of your devices, including PCs, tablets, and phones. This guarantees the security and functionality of your gadgets. Additionally, a variety of tracking and feedback capabilities are available with Microsoft Intune's enhanced mobile device management features. With these more sophisticated features, you can identify potential security threats, gain a lot of knowledge about how devices are used, and be prepared for any issues that may arise.

Usage of Devices

By monitoring how devices are used, you can gain insight into how they are used inside your organization. This information can assist you in identifying potential problems or areas where device allocation and use might be improved. By keeping an eye on how a device is used, you can also uncover any unusual or unlawful activity and take immediate action to reduce security threats. You can create comprehensive reports on how well devices and policies are being followed with Microsoft Intune's reporting capabilities. These reports, which provide a comprehensive overview of the overall security condition of your devices, can be used to identify any devices that are out-of-date or not compliant with the regulations of your organization. This enables you to ensure that all devices are always safe and up to date and to swiftly resolve any issues arising from breaking the rules.

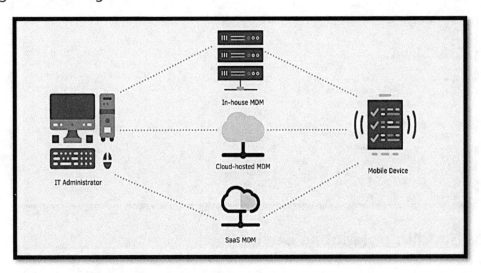

Enhanced Handling of Applications

The enhanced application management capabilities of Microsoft Intune allow you to fundamentally alter the way your company manages its apps. By streamlining the release and download processes, you can guarantee that your users can quickly get the appropriate apps at the appropriate time. This is so that you may save time and money by easily distributing and updating programs thanks to Microsoft Intune. The enhanced application management capabilities of Microsoft Intune provide you with a comprehensive toolkit to enhance the functionality and user experience of your apps. If you have more control over application policies and permissions, you can determine who can use specific apps and establish limits depending on user jobs. You may tailor the application environment to your company's unique needs and specifications with this fine-grained degree of control, making sure that only authorized user have access to secret apps and data. Additionally, Microsoft Intune can be used to provide stringent data protection measures that safeguard confidential company information. Safe access controls, data loss prevention policies, and encryption techniques can all be used to prevent data breaches and unauthorized access. It gives you peace of mind to know that your apps and data are protected from any threats thanks to these robust security features.

Extraordinary Security Elements

Security is the first priority for every business, and Microsoft Intune offers cutting-edge security features to protect your data and devices. Strong security features like multi-factor authentication, restricted access regulations, and data protection with the most recent upgrades are all available for usage. You may have a complete security system to safeguard the assets of your business when you integrate Microsoft Intune with other Microsoft 365 security products. Advanced security capabilities in Microsoft Intune enable the detection and mitigation of threats in advance. Machine learning can be used to detect suspicious activity, locate malware, and halt data breaches. With Microsoft Intune, you can provide the highest degree of protection for your devices and data while staying one step ahead of any threats.

Enrollment Process Streamlined

Enrolling in devices can be a complex and time-consuming process. However, the streamlined features of Microsoft Intune simplify the registration procedure, which speeds up and simplifies the addition of devices to your business' management system. The user-friendly interface of Microsoft Intune facilitates a quick and simple registration process, regardless of whether the devices are owned by the individual or the company. Microsoft Intune helps reduce time during the training process for both administrators and users. Businesses may ensure that everything happens promptly and without hiccups for everyone by eliminating the need for manual device joining. Managers and consumers alike benefit from Microsoft Intune's simplified registration process. Users can connect their gadgets and start working right away.

Option for Self-Service

Let people do things on their own is one of the best things about Microsoft Intune's streamlined registration procedure. Without professional assistance, users may connect their devices, download the required apps, and access corporate resources. This self-service approach reduces reliance on IT assistance while simultaneously increasing user output by enabling users to manage their own devices. Through self-enrollment, Microsoft Intune eliminates the hassle and waiting period associated with manually enrolling devices. Without waiting for IT assistance, users can register their devices whenever it is most convenient for them. Users can be more productive and autonomous since they can easily set up their devices and start using the resources and apps they require without experiencing any technical issues.

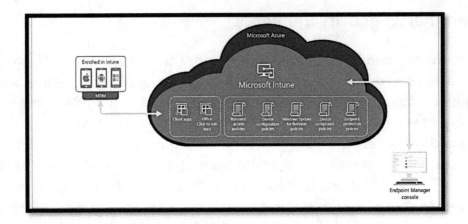

Integration with Microsoft 365 that is seamless

Microsoft Intune seamlessly integrates with Microsoft 365, providing a unified platform for device management and productivity. With ring security and compliance upheld, the interface enables you to leverage Microsoft 365 services such as Microsoft Teams, SharePoint, and OneDrive to their fullest potential. With Microsoft Intune, you can provide users with a seamless experience across all devices and apps. Additionally, the integration with Microsoft 365 facilitates collaboration and task completion. Sharing documents, collaborating in real time, and accessing files from any location can all be done with ease while maintaining data security and compliance. Thanks to Microsoft Intune, which combines productivity tools and device control, your business can easily accomplish more.

Microsoft Intune requirements

Licensing requirements

To utilize Microsoft Intune, you must be granted an Intune account. In order to test the service and ensure it functions, you may also obtain a trial ticket that is valid for 30 days. To use Microsoft Intune as a service, you do not require an Azure account. If you have Windows 365 + Entra ID Join, you can skip creating an Azure account. On the other hand, in order to use the service with Hybrid Entra ID join, you must first build up an Azure virtual network, which requires the use of an Azure account.

To utilize Microsoft Intune, you need one of the following licensing types:

- Intune-only license
- Microsoft 365 E3
- Microsoft E5
- **Enterprise Mobility + Security (EMS) E5**

It's likely that your business already has access to Microsoft Intune through one of these licenses. To create a free account, follow these simple steps. Simply navigate to https://admin.microsoft.com, select Billing, and then click on Purchase Services. Find one of the aforementioned titles to purchase the trial (for free). To complete this, you don't need a credit card or any other type of payment information.

OSes that are supported

- **For Microsoft:**
    - Windows 11 (Enterprise single- and multi-session versions)
    - Windows 10 (Enterprise single- and multi-session versions)
    - Windows 10 Pro Education
    - Windows 10 Enterprise 2019/2021 LTSC
    - Windows 10 IoT Enterprise (x86, x64)
    - Windows 10 Teams – Surface Hub
    - Windows Holographic for Business
- **Supported mobile OSes:**
    - **Apple:**
        - Apple iOS 15.0 and later
        - Apple iPadOS 15.0 and later
        - macOS X 11.0 and later
    - **Google:**
        - Android 8.0 and later (including Samsung Knox Standard 3.0 and higher)
        - Android Enterprise
        - Android open-source project device

Let's now examine the web browser versions that are compatible with Microsoft Intune.

Minimum versions of web browsers required

You may use one of the following admin portals, depending on the particular IT admin responsibilities you perform:

- Microsoft Intune admin portal
- Microsoft 365 admin portal
- Entra admin center

These portals work with the following browsers:

- Microsoft Edge (latest version)
- Safari (latest version – Mac only)
- Chrome (latest version)
- Firefox (latest version)

Let's look at the hardware requirements for Windows 11 now that we are aware of the OS and browser requirements.

Hardware requirements for Windows 11

Three releases of Windows 11 have been released since GA (General Availability). **Nonetheless, we would want to clarify certain significant modifications to the hardware specifications for Windows 11 in contrast to Windows 10:**

- **Processor:** A dual-core, 64-bit processor running at a speed of 1 GHz or above that can be integrated into a System on a Chip (SoC).
- **RAM:** 4 GB of RAM at the very least.
- **Storage:** To install Windows 11, you must have at least 64 GB of free storage space. Certain features and updates could require more storage.
- **Graphics card:** A WDDM 2.0 driver and compatibility with DirectX 12 or later are requirements for the graphics card.

- **System firmware:** Secure Boot-capable UEFI firmware.
- Version 2.0 of the Trusted Platform Module (TPM) is necessary.
- **Monitor:** A minimum 9-inch high-definition (720p) monitor that supports 8 bits per color channel.
- **Internet connection:** Some functions and updates require an active internet connection.

*Once upgrades and certain OS features are enabled, there may be more requirements in the future.

The following prerequisites must be met, or else you may encounter issues when trying to upgrade to Windows 11:

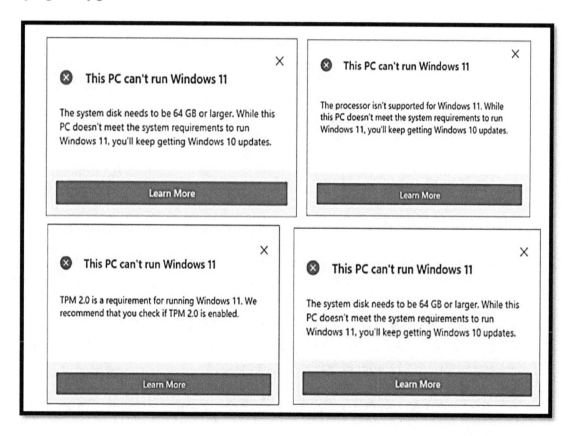

Screenshots of errors displayed during Windows 11 installation are seen in the image above. Prior to initiating the in-place upgrading procedure, it verifies which tools are required. Additionally, you should be aware of the following differences between Windows 10 and 11 before you upgrade.

Here's where you may locate them:

- **The Start menu in Windows 11 has the following major deprecations and changes:**

  > - Live tiles
  > - Dynamic previews
  > - Named groups and folders of apps

- After you upgrade from Windows 10, pinned websites and apps won't move.
- Updated and new Windows logos.
- A new version of the Windows Store app allows installation of Win32 programs.
- A new tool that enables you to snap apps next to each other and use multiple windows.
- Live tiles are no longer available for use. See the newly added widgets feature for content that is easily viewed and dynamic.
- The tablet mode has been removed and new capabilities for attaching and removing the keyboard have been included.
- **The following features of the taskbar have been modified:**
  - The taskbar no longer shows people.
  - Some elements that were configured in the past for newer devices may no longer be visible in the system tray (systray).
  - The bottom of the screen is the only alignment option.
  - Apps can no longer modify specific areas of the taskbar.
  - The timeline has been removed. Some elements of Microsoft Edge are comparable.
  - Internet Explorer is no longer available. The superior option is Edge, which also has an Internet Explorer mode that may be useful at times.
  - The Math Input Panel is no longer there.
  - The Snipping Tool is still functional, but its appearance and features have changed in Windows 10. Rather, those from the app formerly known as Snip & Sketch are now present.
  - Align the desktop in the center.

The upcoming picture illustrates the appearance and functionality of the new Windows 11 desktop:

Administrator licensing in tune

By default, a Microsoft Intune license is required for all Intune administrators. Admins can be granted access to Microsoft Intune without requiring an Intune account by modifying this at a later time in the Microsoft Intune admin center (https://intune.microsoft.com).

To obtain an administrator license, take the following actions:

- Select Administrator Licensing, then Roles, then Tenant Admin.
- **Select Permit unlicensed administrators to access:**

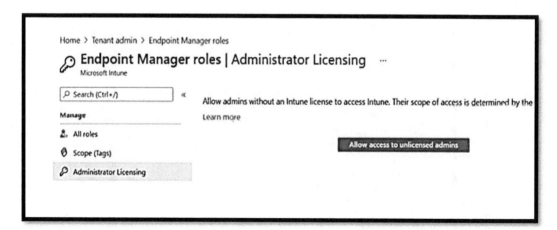

Please Note: There is no way to modify this setting once it has been created.

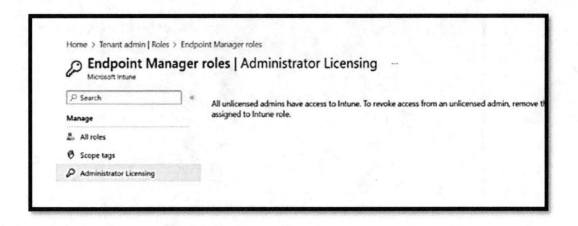

Navigate to the Microsoft 365 admin center at https://admin.microsoft.com. If you are a worldwide administrator, you can assign your Intune license to another person.

It includes EMS E3, Microsoft 365 F1/F3 for Firstline Workers, and Microsoft 365 E3/E5. Moreover, Microsoft Intune can be used independently. There are numerous licenses available for Microsoft Intune. Make sure you have the appropriate license for the job by speaking with your license partner at all times. A license is also required for the person in your client to add their device to Intune.

Practice Exercises

1. What do you understand by Microsoft Intune?
2. What are the Microsoft Intune features?
3. What are the Microsoft Intune requirements?

CHAPTER TWO

THE STEP-BY-STEP GUIDE TO BEGINNING YOUR MICROSOFT INTUNE EXPERIENCE

Configuring Microsoft Intune

Follow the step-by-step instructions, paying particular attention to setting up an Azure Portal account, opening the Microsoft Intune portal, defining Intune rules, enrolling devices, and handling apps and software updates, in order to successfully set up Microsoft Intune. Every subsection offers a resolution to address a particular facet of the configuration procedure.

Establishing an Account on Azure Portal

To begin using Microsoft Intune, create an account on the Azure Portal. This is necessary to protect the devices, apps, and information used by your firm. **How to carry it out:**

- Visit the Azure Portal page.
- Click "Create a Free Account".
- Fill in the information asked for.
- Use a code sent to your phone or email to verify who you are.

Right now, take control of your device management! Make the most of Intune's features to increase the security and productivity of your company.

The Microsoft Intune Portal's accessibility

- Sign up to your Microsoft Office 365 account.
- Go to the **Admin Center.**
- Click "**Intune**" on the "**Admin centers**" tab.

These procedures will send you to the Microsoft Intune Portal. It provides extensive feature and setting management over devices and apps. Security policy implementation, device and app management, and more! When Microsoft Intune was originally released in 2011, it was known as "Windows Intune." Over time, it evolved into a cloud-based device and app control tool.

Setting up Intune Policies

You have some options when you visit the Policy Configuration page. You may personalize them for compliance settings, device enrollment, app control, and more. Every method aims to handle devices and protection in a particular way. For instance, you may restrict the installation of apps or guarantee that access to company resources is restricted to devices under your control. To set up a policy, simply select the feature you wish to modify and adhere to the on-screen instructions. You may choose which websites and apps to access, how security is handled, and how lengthy your password must be. Assess the requirements of your organization before establishing Intune policies. Consider the gadgets that your employees own and how they may access personal data. Make use of these resources to assist you in crafting user-friendly and safe policies. Additionally, review and modify Intune's regulations frequently. Stay up to date with industry best practices and the most recent Microsoft Intune technologies. This will provide consumers with a positive experience and keep devices safe.

Device Enrollment in Intune

Setting up Microsoft Intune on your devices is a fairly simple and quick process. It enables you to manage and safeguard every device from one location. By doing these things and adhering to the policies established by your workplace, you can ensure the security of your devices.

- **Prepare your devices:** Before adding them to Intune, confirm that they match the requirements. Verifying that they are running a supported OS version and have an open internet connection are two ways to accomplish this.
- **Enroll your devices: To add a device to Intune, follow these steps:**
  - ➢ Turn on the smartphone, and then select Settings.
  - ➢ After choosing "Access work or school," click "Add an account."
  - ➢ Enter the email address connected to your Intune account here. Observe the directions displayed on screen.

- **Configure device policies:** After joining, configure device policies to ensure security and compliance. Setting restrictions on apps, enabling encryption, and establishing guidelines for passwords are a few examples of these policies. Adjust these options to suit your company's requirements.

It's crucial to understand that adding devices to Intune not only provides you more control over their security but also facilitates administrative tasks and boosts productivity for both IT managers and end users. Don't pass up the opportunity to manage your devices more easily with Microsoft Intune. Enrolling your devices as soon as possible will help you adhere to your company's policies and receive better protection. It's time to take control of your road towards gadget control!

Handling Software Updates and Applications

Determine Software/App Update Requirements

- Compile a list of all the tools and applications that require updates.
- List the requirements for every upgrade, such as repairing problems and enhancing system security.

Make Deployment Rings for Updates

- Arrange devices into deployment rings according to factors such as device type or user roles.
- Sort the program and app updates for every ring according to priority.

Set Up Fine-Tune Update Rules

- Navigate to the Admin Center for Microsoft Endpoint Manager.
- To establish guidelines for software and app upgrades, select "Devices" > "Update policies."
- Adjust rules to suit your organization's requirements by scheduling maintenance windows or allowing automatic installations to occur.

Special Thoughts

- You can schedule phased deployments with Intune.
- This entails distributing changes to various groups inside a deployment ring gradually.

⤶ This aids in identifying any issues before they have a widespread impact.

Real-Life history

It used to be difficult to manage a large number of apps and programs across numerous devices. Maintaining the most recent versions of all systems required a lot of labor and time. However, Microsoft Intune gave you a single platform to manage software and app upgrades. It made using IT more straightforward. Businesses still have control over their app environment and get the best protection and utility from it.

Resolving Typical Problems during Configuration

Address device enrollment issues, permissions issues, and authentication concerns to resolve common issues that arise during Microsoft Intune setup. These sections contain instructions on how to ensure a seamless Microsoft Intune setup.

Problems with Authentication and Permissions

Permissions and authentication are crucial during setup. They ensure that an application or system is only used by authorized individuals. However, issues related to authorization and authorization may arise. Check the login credentials once more if you're experiencing problems authenticating. Check to make sure the letter forms, username, and password are correct. Verify the account's permissions and whether two-factor authentication is enabled. Permission issues may also contribute to settings taking longer. Modify or examine the access levels. Give individuals and organizations the freedom to accomplish their goals so there won't be any problems. This contributes to environmental protection. There may be difficulties in unusual situations. In order to diagnose the issue, you should examine whether the components are compatible, the configuration of the network, and any firewall settings that might prevent access or rights. Don't put off starting the setup procedure for a lengthy period. Immediately resolve any permissions and login difficulties by taking the appropriate actions. You can contact customer service, read the instructions, or do an online search for assistance. To swiftly fix problems, users can make advantage of the capabilities and functions of the system or app. Permissions and authentication shouldn't impede the setup process. Utilize your new tools to the fullest and solve any difficulties you encounter!

Issues with Device Enrollment

Making a mistake when configuring your equipment can be very inconvenient. But persevere! **With this 3-step instruction, you can rapidly activate your device and solve these issues.**

- Verify the connection to the Internet. Ensure that it remains in place. If the connection is shaky or unstable, errors may occur. Altering the Wi-Fi router's settings or attempting a different network is two options.
- Check your qualifications. Please confirm that the password and login are correct.
- Inaccuracies in details can lead to authentication errors. Please double-check; there can be typos or additional spaces.

Update the software on your device. Older software is also susceptible to errors. Before attempting to join again, locate and install any available updates. These are the measures to take in order to solve the problem. Every error may have characteristics specific to the user or the kind of gadget. You should read the manufacturer's documentation or call the appropriate support lines for your device to get assistance. This information is taken from public materials released by major tech corporations such as Apple, Microsoft, and Google, as well as a few support groups. And that's it! You now understand how to correct errors that arise when devices are being set up.

Registering for Intune

Take advantage of a free trial of Microsoft Intune

You may test Intune out for free for thirty days. Using an existing account from work or school, sign in and add Intune to your contract. If you would want to utilize Intune for your business, you can create a new account. You cannot link your new account to an existing work or school account after creating one.

Simply do these actions to get a free trial of Microsoft Intune:

- Navigate to the website where you can create your Intune account.
- After entering your email address, press "Next."

You can use an existing account or establish a new one if you have one set up with another Microsoft service when you join up for the Intune trial. Here are the instructions for creating a new account.

+ Click set up account to create a new account.

Input your name, contact number, company name in its whole, company size, and area. After reviewing the final few details, click Next.

+ Click Send verification code to ensure the phone number you added is correct.

+ Enter the verification code on your mobile device and select "Verify."

Create a free account by providing a username and domain name that corresponds with your company or organization. Your name will have ".onmicrosoft.com" following it. Click "Save." To continue, click Next. To check if it's available. If you would like, you can subsequently change this domain name to your name.

Once you register, you will see your user name. You will log into Intune using this name. Additionally, a message containing your account details is sent to the email address you provided during the sign-up process. We would like to inform you that your account has been activated.

Remark: Selecting "Get Started" will direct you to the Microsoft 365 admin center homepage. If you select manage your membership, it will take you to Your Goods where you can view details about your Microsoft Intune Trial subscription. Open the Microsoft Intune admin center and log in to Intune.

If you haven't previously, sign in to the admin area by following these steps:

- In the address bar of a new browser tab, type https://intune.microsoft.com.
- Use the login ID you were given in the previous step to log in. This is how your user ID will appear on Microsoft.com: yourID@yourdomain.

When you sign up for a trial, you will also receive an email with your account details and the email address you provided during the sign-up process. This email indicates that your trial is now active. As a helpful hint, using a computer in normal mode rather than private mode may help you get better results with Microsoft Intune.

Getting to know the Intune dashboard

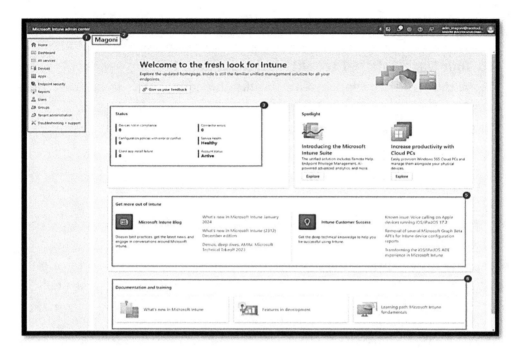

- **The Sidebar**
    - ➤ **Home:** The homepage is located here.
    - ➤ **Dashboard:** A customizable status page
    - ➤ **All Services:** An inventory of all services, including customizable favorites
    - ➤ **Devices:** This is a connection to the device panel, which contains every feature on your device.
    - ➤ **Apps:** Every app that is utilized with Intune
    - ➤ **Endpoint Security:** For your devices, Intune contains Endpoint Security-specific options.
    - ➤ **Reports:** These display a variety of information, including failed policies, Windows updates, and configuration status.
    - ➤ **Users:** Entra ID provides direct access to every user.
    - ➤ **Groups:** All groups in Entra ID are instantly accessible.
    - ➤ **Tenant Management:** Click this link to adjust pertinent tenant settings.
- The Name of tenant

- Synced Status
- Options for accounts and notifications
- Accurate News and Client Achievement
- Records and Instruction

First Actions

- **To your Microsoft 365 tenant, add a domain.**
  - ➢ Without this step, Intune could function, but it would only use Tenantname.onmicrosoft.com as the backup domain.
- Distribute licenses utilizing Entra ID groups that are dynamic or static.
- Create an Entra ID and Intune company logo
  - ➢ This is crucial for the Company Portal and the setup screens on Autopilot devices.

Knowing the terms and ideas of Intune

One comprehensive cloud-based service is Microsoft Intune. It's a component of the Microsoft Endpoint Management package. In the modern, mobile-first environment, it centers on managing and safeguarding gadgets, applications, and information.

Let's examine some of Intune's most crucial components before delving into its concepts and vocabulary:

- The process of adding a device to Intune's control range is called enrollment. This might be a computer, tablet, or phone. With Android Enterprise for Android devices, Windows Autopilot for Windows devices, or Device Enrollment Programs (DEP) for Apple devices, users can enroll devices automatically or directly.
- **Profiles:** After a device has been enrolled, Intune configures its settings and policies on it. These profiles can contain compliance policies (which ensure that devices adhere to security requirements), device setup profiles (which control settings like email, VPN, and Wi-Fi), and app protection policies (which safeguard company data within apps).
- **Apps:** Bring your own device (BYOD) and company-owned apps are handled by Intune. Web apps, Microsoft Store apps, and line-of-business (LOB) apps tailored to your organization can all be configured and managed by it.

- **Conditional Access:** This feature ensures that company resources like email or SharePoint Online may only be accessed by devices that are authorized and have the proper security settings (such as updated software and encryption switched on). The Conditional Access policies in Intune are a crucial component of its security features.

- **Compliance:** Intune assists companies in ensuring that devices abide by applicable laws. This entails checking for items like the operating system version, device security, and PIN requirement. Devices that break the guidelines are not allowed to access company data until they fulfill the requirements.

- **Security Baselines:** These are preconfigured security settings that are already configured to keep devices safe according to Microsoft's recommendations. By using Intune to deploy these baselines, you can enhance device security rapidly.

- **Inventory:** With Intune, you may get comprehensive details about the devices you manage. This contains details on the installed apps, hardware, compliance level, and other things. This information is needed to monitor the safety and health of devices.

- **Roles and Permissions:** To manage who can do what, Intune employs role-based access control, or RBAC. Individuals with varying occupations, such Global Administrator, Intune Administrator, and Help Desk Operator, have varying levels of access to distinct Intune capabilities and functionalities.

- Intune generates reports on a variety of topics, including device compliance, app usage, security vulnerabilities, and more. You can learn more about the general safety and health of the area around your device from these reports.

- **.Integration:** Microsoft Intune is well-integrated with other Microsoft services, including Azure Active Directory (AD), Microsoft Endpoint Configuration Manager (previously SCCM), Azure Information Protection, and Microsoft Defender for Endpoint. This allows you to manage gadgets, safeguard them, and maintain identity tracking all at once.

Practice Exercises

1. How do you establish an Account on Azure Portal?
2. Mention the steps in taking advantage of a free trial of Microsoft Intune
3. Explain the Intune dashboard navigational toolbars
4. Explain the terms and ideas of Intune

CHAPTER THREE
SETTING UP WINDOWS ENROLLMENT

How Update Rings Are Made

You don't want users to update themselves without your control over what and when they receive updates when you give them fully managed machines. Additionally, users shouldn't decide to install secret builds for themselves. If you would prefer to manage the updates manually or if you do not have the Windows Enterprise license to use Autopatch, you will need to set up some update rings. By configuring update rings, you can instruct Windows as a Service on when and how to update your Windows 10 or 11 devices with quality and feature upgrades.

All of the previous releases' new features and quality enhancements are included when you upgrade to Windows 10 or 11. If you have the most recent fix loaded, you can be certain that your Windows devices are up to date. Unlike with previous Windows versions, you must now install the entire update rather than just a portion of it. On devices that are compatible with Windows 10, update rings can also be used to install Windows 11. To achieve this, during the policy development process, use the setting named Upgrade Windows 10 devices to Latest Windows 11 update by choosing it as Yes. When you use update rings to switch to Windows 11, the device runs the most recent version of the operating system. If you later change the setting back to No, devices that have not yet started the update will not start it again, but those that are in the process will continue.

Previously upgraded devices will remain running Windows 11.

- ✦ To update Rings for Windows 10 and later, choose Devices, then Windows.
- ✦ Select "Create profile" from the Update Rings for Windows 10 and Later page.
- ✦ Provide useful values for the Name and Description. This is crucial in this case so you can distinguish them right away.

+ Adjust the settings under "Update ring settings" to suit your company's requirements. After adjusting the Update and User Experience settings, click Next. It's time to configure our settings. Since many of these will change based on your surroundings, we'll examine each of these and the best setting for each ring:

UI HINT

After you configure the options, they turn purple from blue at first. Your modifications won't make them any less purple.

> **Microsoft Product Updates:** These updates allow Windows Update to function. It is necessary to turn this on.

> **Windows drivers:** This enables the computer's Windows Update to find and install drivers. Block here if you would rather utilize the seller's applications for this.

> **Quality update deferral period:** By adjusting the quality update delay time, you may determine the number of days that the Patch Tuesday quality updates will be implemented.

> **Feature update deferral period:** In order to employ the feature update approach, this value for the feature update delay time should be set to 0. Intune won't take notice of the additional policy if the value is not 0.

- ➢ **Update Windows 10 devices to the most recent version of Windows 11:** Since Windows 10 support will expire in October 2025, doing this is the recommended course of action. To be precise, though, it depends on your level of readiness to get better.
- ➢ **Define the uninstall time for feature updates:** How many days after the update is installed will users be able to roll back the changes? This is the number of days following the deferral period for delayed installs.
- ➢ **Turn on pre-release builds;** these are required for your Pilot and Preview rings.
- ➢ **Automatic update behavior:** Here, you may control the download and installation schedule for updates as well as the hours that they are live. Should you select "Reset to default," the computer will detect peak hours and adjust its installation automatically. Choose a time slot that suits your company, such as "7 a.m. to 7 p.m." for most office workers.
- ➢ **Restart Checks:** These check if the computer is not in presentation mode, full-screen mode, the middle of a phone call, a game, or anything else, and if the battery is more than 40% charged. They also check if someone is at the computer.
- ➢ The ability to suspend Windows updates is available from a single location. This happens at the user level.
- ➢ **Windows update check option:** Users may choose to check for updates or may choose not to.
- ➢ **Apply deadline settings:** This necessitates updates, allows you to complete them in time, and enables automatic updates. It's advisable to leave this on most of the time so that you can force end-user devices to reboot and prevent people from repeatedly turning it off, which could endanger the devices.
- ✦ Select + Select Scope tags under Scope tags if you wish to use the tags on the update ring. Select Tags will open as a result. Choose one or more tags and click Select to add them to the update ring and go back to the Scope tags page. Click Next to go on to Assignments when you're ready.

Footnote: When adding or modifying certain types of Intune policies, the Scope Tags configuration page may not appear if the tenant does not have any custom configured scope tags. Make sure that at least one tag has been put up in addition to the default one if you are unable to view the Scope Tag option.

- Choose the groups you want to include by selecting + under Assignments, and then give them the update ring. Use the + Select groups to exclude to fine-tune the assignment. Click "Next" to continue.

We recommend delivering update rings to groups of devices most of the time. Device groups eliminate the need for a user to check in to a device before the policy takes effect, which is consistent with our recommendations for deploying feature upgrades.

- Select Review + Create and review the configuration options. Click Create when you're prepared to save your Windows update ring. It appears as your new update ring in the list of update rings.

Developing updates for features

Now that the update rings are set at 0 days, we must monitor the feature updates. If **we don't, on the next Patch Tuesday, every PC will automatically update to Windows 11 or any other new edition that comes out every six months:**

- In the Intune interface, select Devices | Windows | Feature Updates for Windows 10 and later. To create a profile, click Create.

Generally speaking, you want every device in your estate to be running the same version. You can make many profiles here and select which devices to include or exclude, though, if you have specific needs. In this example, we will set devices to the latest version of Windows 11, 22H2. This policy will bring all devices up to Windows 11 22H2 and keep them there until we change the settings. When 23H2 is released, the devices will continue to run on 22H2 until this policy is modified to reflect that:

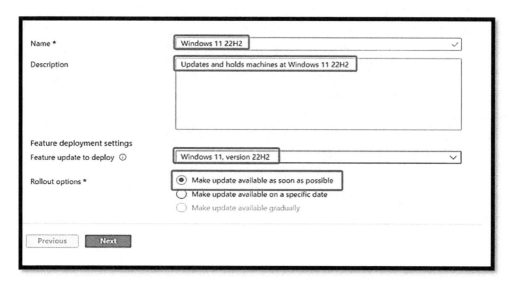

Note that only supported operating system versions are included in the list of feature upgrades. This implies that your computers will automatically update to the version you select here if they are running anything less than Windows 10 21H1. In order to release more than one area at once, you can also select which rollout techniques to employ. You can additionally specialize your assignment groups and establish distinct policies with deadlines if you'd want greater control. Click next once you've adjusted these settings. Give Autopilot Devices access to the policies so they may document every aspect of the estate. This will bring everything into alignment. Click Next after that. Review your policy once again, and then select Create.

Personalized driver updates

To have more exact control over driver updates for your devices, you can also use Intune. This gives you the option of deploying them automatically or requiring permission beforehand. This will enable you to verify whether the drivers are malfunctioning prior to a complete release. As soon as possible, Intune will examine your estate and add the required drivers. If you have chosen not to share data with Microsoft, you will have to do so once more in order for driver updates to appear.

- To start, select Devices, Windows 10, and then any updates.
- Choose Driver updates for Windows 10 and later to create a new profile.
- After entering your profile's name and description, click "Next."

This is the point at which you determine whether updates should be approved instantaneously or manually. You will need to remove the existing profile and establish a new one since once you select this option, you cannot change it. In this instance, we will manage drivers manually for improved control. Once finished, select Next.

- You will be prompted to select the number of days that drivers must wait before being accepted if you select Automatic.
- Click Next since there are no scope tags to be set at this time.

Giving to Device groups is the greatest option for the time being because most assignment policies are based on devices. We are going to provide Autopilot gadgets in this instance.

- Verify everything is in order, then select "Create."

We were able to construct a driver update mechanism in the user interface. We can now examine our automation processes.

How to use Microsoft Intune to distribute Windows Autopatch

Windows Autopatch is a Microsoft service that handles feature updates as well as quality updates for Windows, Microsoft Teams, Microsoft Edge, Microsoft 365 programs for Enterprise, and Office programs. Once the device is successfully added and the service is enabled for your user, you don't need to bother about updates for approved goods. Microsoft will take care of it.

Minimum requirements for Windows Autopatch

- Windows 10/11 Enterprise E3 or higher licenses
- Azure AD P1 or higher licenses
- Microsoft Intune licenses
- Windows build 1809 or higher
- Users must exist in Azure AD (synced or cloud-only)
- Devices must be controlled by Microsoft Intune or Configuration Manager Co-managed by Microsoft

✦ Make Windows Autopatch active.

For the following steps, visit the Microsoft Intune admin center.

> ➤ To begin, select Tenant Administration > Tenant Enrollment. After checking the box, click "Agree."

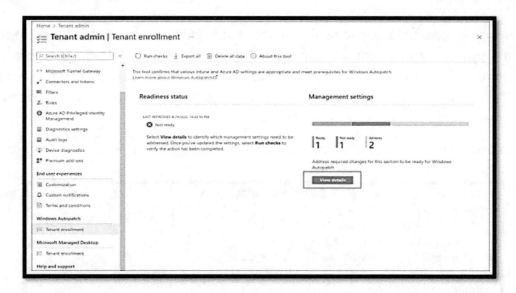

To ensure we meet all requirements and can begin the service, we must first use the Readiness assessment tool. Regarding the test findings, one of these scenarios may hold true.

- ✓ "Ready to go" denotes that no action is required.
- ✓ **Recommendation:** This is merely a recommendation for how to get the most of the service once it is operational. It's not a problem because it's not necessary.
- ✓ **Not ready:** Something that halts the performance and requires attention before continuing.
- ✓ **Error:** Insufficient privileges prevent this task from being completed.

As for me, I have a few recommendations that aren't quite ready. Let's discuss them in ascending order of importance. Select "View details."

The issue of unlicensed admin comes first. I haven't switched it on yet, but I need this for the service. The necessary actions are displayed on the right when you click on the setting on the left.

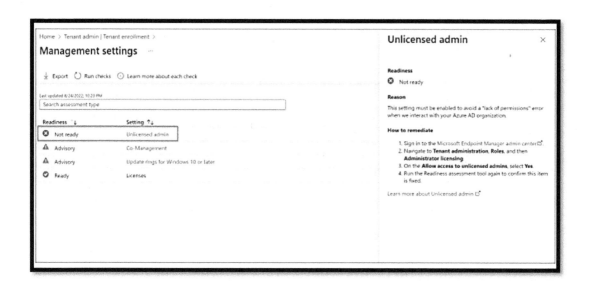

The issue of unlicensed admin comes first. I haven't switched it on yet, but I need this for the service. The necessary actions are displayed on the right when you click on the setting on the left.

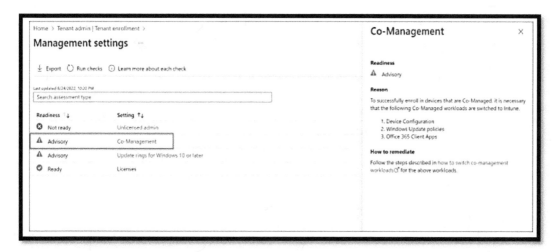

The second piece of advice is establishing co-management. I'll disregard this since co-management isn't configured in my workspace.

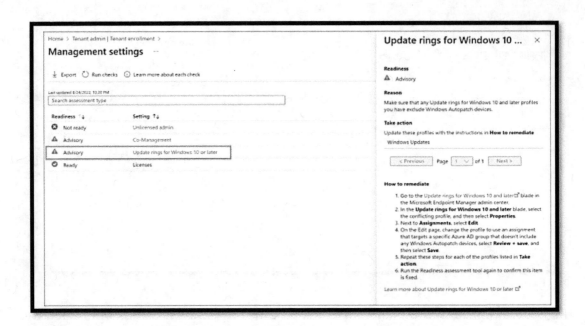

The next point is crucial. I configure Update policies for Windows 10 and later devices. There may be conflicts between these settings and Windows Autopatch. Devices that utilize Autopatch should not be subject to the present Windows Update ring policies. Verify that this isn't the situation. See the steps on the right for additional information in the picture.

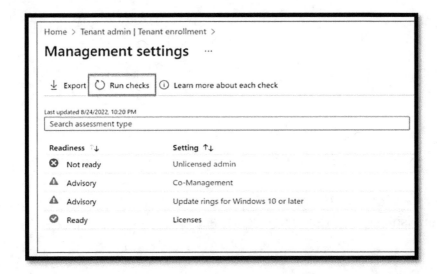

Click Run check once the settings have been adjusted as necessary.

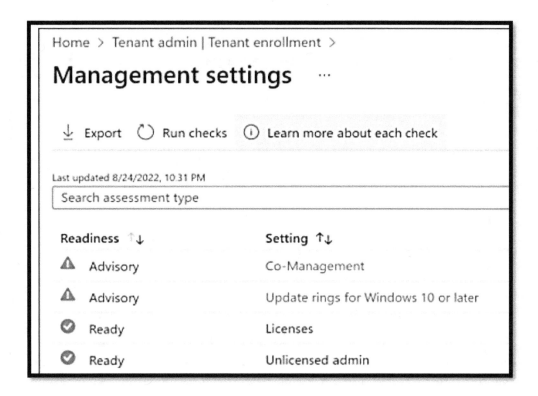

We can now proceed.

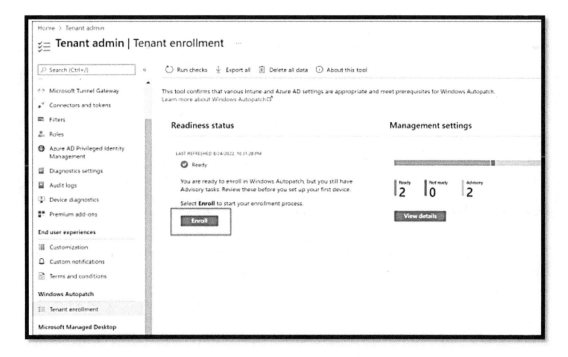

Press Enroll.

CHOOSE If you do, I grant Microsoft permission to administer my Azure AD organization on my behalf. Click "Agree." After entering the primary administrator's contact details, select "Next."

Click "Continue." The tools will now be configured in the background; including security groups in Azure AD and policies in Microsoft Intune.

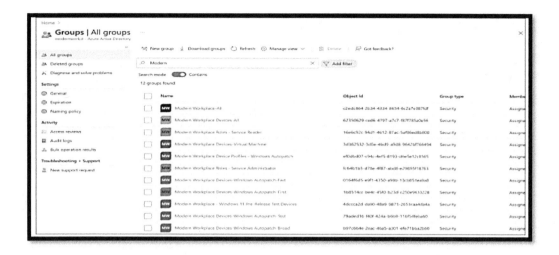

When you install the Windows AutoPatch ring in Azure AD, the groups seen in the above image are created.

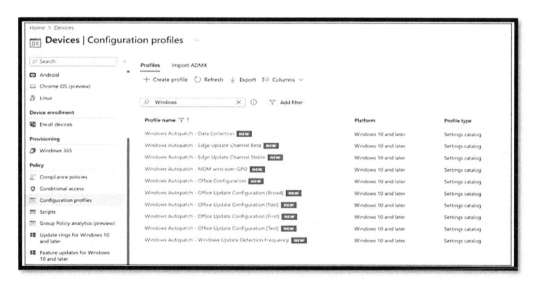

Windows device configuration profiles are created during Windows AutoPatch deployment. Update rings and feature updates for Windows 10 and later are also released in addition to these policies.

♦ Integrate hardware with Windows Autopatch

Devices must be a part of the Windows Autopatch Device Registration security group in order to be added to Windows Autopatch.

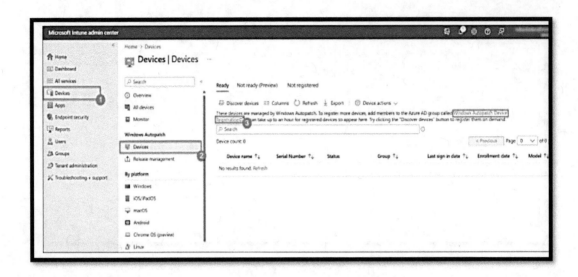

Navigate to the Microsoft Intune admin center's Devices > Windows Autopatch Devices section. To register a Windows Autopatch device, click.

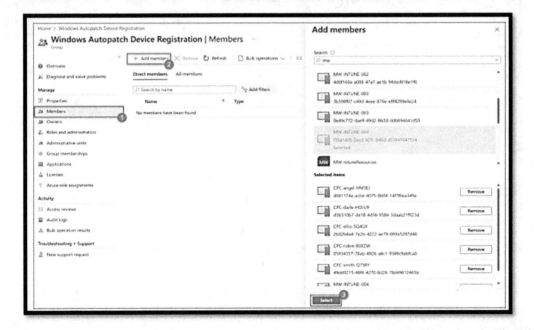

Clicking that link will launch the Windows Autopatch Device Registration security group in a new tab. make sure the Members page is open before clicking "Add members" to add the computer accounts. Return to the Microsoft Intune admin center and select Devices from the menu. You can see which ring the device is assigned when you connect it to the Windows Autopatch service.

This could be any of the subsequent rings.

❖ **Test**—**Deployment** ring for testing updates before they are rolled out to production.
❖ **First**-Early users
❖ **Fast**—Quick rollout and use
❖ **Broad**—The last ring for the broad rollout

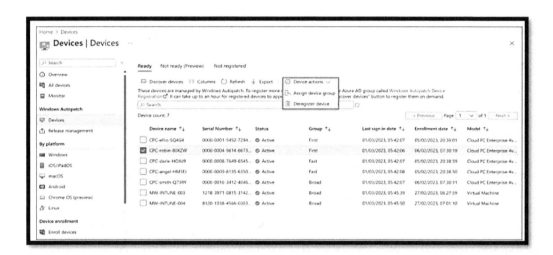

After choosing a device, navigate to Device actions > Assign device group to modify the update ring.

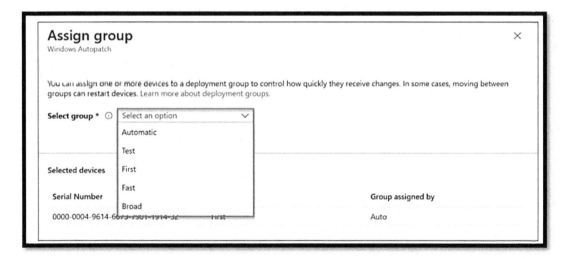

⊥ Handling Autopatch on Windows

I'll quickly go over how to manage Windows AutoPatch in the Microsoft Intune admin center.

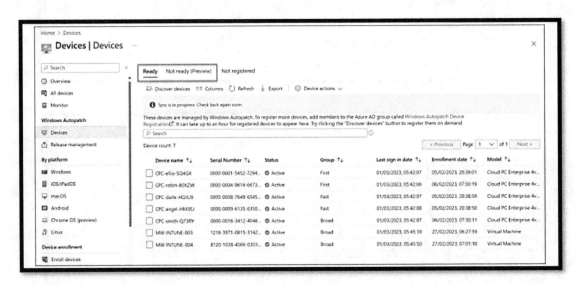

After registration, I updated the devices list with a Windows Autopatch section. On the Devices tab, a list of Ready (onboarded) and Not Ready devices is visible. Unfinished business could be the cause of a device's unavailability.

On the Release Management page, updates for each ring can be stopped and started. You can also view the changes that have been made available to the public on the Release Announcements tab. In the Release settings page, you have the option to apply the Microsoft 365 app updates (which are enabled by default) and/or the Accelerated quality updates.

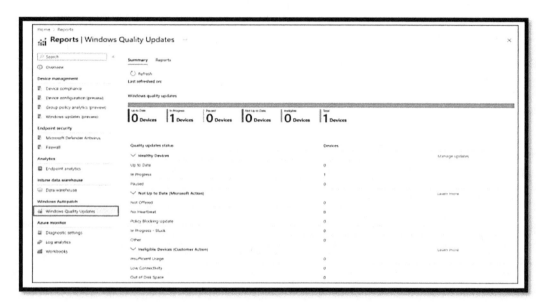

Windows Quality Updates is a new area about Windows AutoPatch under Reports in the Microsoft Intune admin portal. Here is a list of all the device states that are visible. It can take a few hours for this report to be updated.

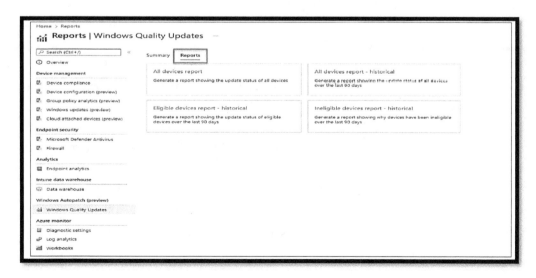

Reports can also let you see how the environment has evolved over time.

How to Set Up Windows Hello for Work

For multi-factor authentication (MFA) on Windows devices, Windows Hello for Business (WHfB) enables you to utilize a PIN, biometrics (such as a fingerprint or face), or a FIDO2 security key. You can configure this at the tenant level or at a finer level using the Device Enrollment menu or the Settings library. Here, we shall discuss both approaches. We start at the tenant level, which is required to remain at "Not Configured" in order for the Settings store to function.

Make a Windows Hello policy for business use.

- ⬇ Visit and log in to the Microsoft Intune admin center.
- ⬇ Choose Devices, followed by Windows Enrollment, Device Enrollment, and Windows Hello for Business. Windows Hello for Business pane displays.

- ⬇ **Choose one of the following options under Configure Windows Hello for Business:**
  - ➢ **Enabled:** Choose this option to configure Windows Hello for Business settings. Upon selecting "Enabled," further Windows Hello device options become visible and modifiable.
  - ➢ **Disabled:** Select this option if you wish to disable Windows Hello for Business during device enrollment. When Windows Hello for Business is disabled, users are unable to configure it. When this policy is set to Disabled,

Windows Hello for Business won't activate, but you may still make it function by adjusting the parameters below.

➤ **Not set up:** Choose this option if you don't want Intune to control the Windows Hello for Business configuration. On 10/11 devices, any pre-existing Windows Hello for Business settings remain unchanged. None of the other settings on the pane are modifiable.

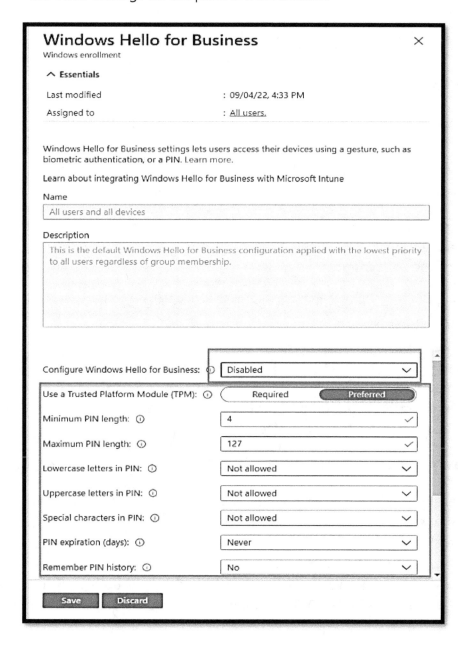

- If you selected "Enabled" in the previous step, configure the required parameters that will be used on all registered Windows 10/11 devices. After adjusting these parameters, select "Save."
  - **Employ a Trusted Platform Module, or TPM:**

Data security is further enhanced by a TPM chip. Select a number from the list below:

- **Essential (by default).** The only devices on which Windows Hello for Business can be configured are those with an accessible TPM.
- **Suggested.** First, the devices attempt to employ a TPM. If they are unable to select this option, they can utilize software encryption.
- **Minimum and maximum lengths of PINs:** helps ensure that sign-in is secure by configuring devices to use the minimum and maximum PINs you choose. Even though the standard PIN is six characters long, you can ensure that it is at least four. A PIN cannot be longer than 127 characters.

PIN characters that are lowercase, uppercase, and special: Adding capital, lowercase, and unusual characters to the PIN can make it more difficult. **Select one for each of the following:**

- **Permitted.** Although it's not required, users are free to utilize the character type in their PIN.
- **Essential.** Users are required to utilize at least one of the character types in their PIN. For example, you usually need one special character and one capital letter.
- **Not permitted (by default).** These characters are not appropriate for use in PINs. (This is also the result of leaving the setting unset.)

Here are a few unique characters: @ [\] ^ _'{ | } ^ # $% &'() * +, -. /: ; ^ = >?

- **Day-by-day PIN expiration:** Encouraging customers to update their PIN after a predetermined period of time (41 days by default) is a wonderful idea.
- **Recall your past PIN:** restricts the use of previously used PINs; in most cases, the latest five PINs are not reusable.
- **Permit biometric verification:** Users must still set up a backup PIN in case biometric security fails. This option allows you to utilize a biometric login

technique, such as a fingerprint or facial recognition, in place of a PIN for Windows Hello for Business. **Choose from:**

  ➢ Windows Hello for Business supports biometric authentication.
  ➢ No, not all account types are able to use Windows Hello for Business biometric authentication.

+ **Where possible, make use of strengthened anti-spoofing:** Sets whether Windows Hello anti-spoofing technologies are utilized on compatible devices. This includes the ability to identify fake faces by looking for pictures of faces. When anti-spoofing for facial features is enabled and set to Yes, Windows forces all users to use it.

+ **Permit phone check-in:** If this option is enabled, users will be able to log in to their desktop computer using a remote passport as a portable device. The desktop computer must be connected to Microsoft Entra, and the other device must be configured with a Windows Hello for Business PIN.

+ **Enable stronger security for sign-in:** Configure Windows Hello Enhanced Sign-in Security on compatible hardware-equipped devices.

  ➢ **Default:** On systems with compatible hardware, enhanced sign-in security will be enabled.
  ➢ Third-party accessories cannot be used by device users to log in to their device using Windows Hello.
  ➢ All systems will have enhanced sign-in security disabled. Users of the device can use other Windows Hello-compatible devices to log in to their device.

+ **To log in, use security keys:** When this setting is set to "Enable," you can remotely turn Windows Hello Security Keys on and off for every machine in a customer's place of business.

Setting up a group configuration

As you can see from the above, nobody can be left out as these options are made instantly available to all users. **Alternatively, if this isn't working for your system, you can set the general setup to "Not configured," which is the default setting if it hasn't been configured yet:**

+ Go to Devices, Windows, Configuration profiles, click +Create, and select +New policy to accomplish this.
+ After deciding on Windows 10 and later, click Create in the Settings Catalog.
+ After entering the data for Name and Description, click the Next button.

- The first is to Click "Add settings." And secondly Scroll down to "Windows Hello for Business."

This group contains both user and device settings, so select the ones that apply to your situation. You can select the same settings as you did at the tenant level, along with some additional features that are only available here, such as enhanced security against face feature spoofing. You can also use the majority of the tenant level settings and expand upon them with a settings catalog policy. The key here is to avoid making too many changes at once.

- After configuring your settings, select Next
- On the Scope Tags page, click Next.
- Assign as necessary for your setting. Remember that you can copy Settings catalog policies to quickly construct very similar rules. Click Next.
- Examine it, and then select "Create."

Configuring Enrollment Profiles for Windows Autopilot

Now that we have our policies in place to handle them, we can start setting the policies so that we can ring enroll and supply devices. It instructs the device on what actions to take when it encounters the Autopilot service during the Out of Box Experience (OOBE). The first of these is the Windows Autopilot Enrollment Profile. Generally speaking, you can assign multiple names to a distinct Entra ID group using the Group Tag feature. When you add devices to Autopilot, you can use group tags to place them in the appropriate Autopilot profile. This allows you to add devices to Dynamic Entra ID groups.

The following are some reasons why you might want more than one profile:

- **Kiosk devices (using self-deploying mode):** When a kiosk device is in self-deploying mode, its profiles are automatically configured and require no user assistance during setup. This means that a device account on the local device can be configured to automatically log users in, and policies can be configured to run the device in a single app mode, usually a web browser.
- **International organizations:** You can utilize group tags to assign a separate identity according on the language required. The operating system language is selected during Autopilot setup for international firms.

How to proceed...

We will demonstrate this by putting up a typical user-driven deployment.

To configure and adjust as necessary for your environment, utilize these steps:

- Select Windows, then Devices, Enrollment, and finally click on Deployment profiles.
- Select Windows PC after clicking on Create profile.
- Name the page, provide a description, and select all the devices you want to put on autopilot. When you apply this profile to an Entra ID group that contains devices that aren't registered or supplied through Autopilot, the devices is added to the service right away, and any subsequent restarts during OOBE will also be handled by Autopilot.
- It's still safe to set it to Yes in this scenario, even though we are only interested in Autopilot devices. Click Next after that.
- The basic OOBE settings, including language and what users see when configuring their devices, can be adjusted on the following screen.
- As a result, your deployment mode must be user-driven (i.e., the user signs in during OOBE and configures items as needed); self-driven deployment is reserved for kiosks and other devices without a fixed customer.
- Assign "Microsoft Entra joined" as the value for "Join to Microsoft Entra ID as." You can use hybrid join, but it is not compatible with Autopilot, so it is best to avoid it. Since we are building up a whole new tenant and workspace, it is best to avoid bringing any technical debt with you.
- It is always advisable to set the User account type to Standard. You can use Windows LAPS, Endpoint Privilege Management, or the Entra ID role in place of granting administrative rights.

Pre-provisioned deployment (previously known as "White Glove") allows an IT administrator to set up all policies and device-specific apps by simply pressing the Windows key five times during OOBE; users only need to go through the user registration process. This can be useful in large rollouts or for users on slow lines, but it's important to consider how quickly your environment changes as well; if your apps get updates frequently, users may receive devices with outdated apps if the devices were pre-provisioned too far in advance. The serial number of the device (or%SERIAL%) is also configured in a ring template for device names, though this is not as important with Intune as it once was.

+ After adjusting the settings to suit your region, click the Next button.
+ At this point, we would want to include this in the group of Autopilot devices. After creating the group, click Next. This group is configured to include devices as soon as they register for the Autopilot service, so they can pick them up sooner.
+ The final step is to click Create after reviewing your settings.

Configuring an Enterprise State Roaming system (ESP)

This page, which users see after entering their credentials during OOBE, shows them how their device is being set up and how they are moving with onboarding. Configuring our ESP is the final step before we can utilize Autopilot to deploy a Windows device.

The actions to take are as follows:

+ First, navigate to Devices, and then click Enrollment. From the Windows menu, choose Enrollment Status Page.

The ESP is used to prevent a device from being used until a certain set of applications has been installed; you may need more than one if different departments, areas, or groups need to install critical applications before they can log in and use the computers. As you can edit the Default page, we will create a new one; we have added the Microsoft To-Do store application to show setting an ESP since we haven't deployed any apps into this system yet.

+ Select "Create" from the menu.
+ Click Next after entering numbers for the Name and Description fields.
+ Now that we have instructed Intune to display an ESP, adjust the Show app and profile configuration progress setting to "Yes."

The following extra settings will appear if you do this:

> Display an error when the installation takes longer than the allotted minutes: The apps that are being deployed and the fastest internet connection that your users may be using should be taken into consideration

when deploying this setting. If you set this too high and an app or script goes awry, the ESP will remain on the screen until the timeout is satisfied, even though nothing will happen until the error is fixed. This is not a good way to engage with users. Conversely, if you set this too low and your application is extremely large or complex, the ESP may time out before the setup is completed as intended. Generally, 60 to 120 minutes is sufficient.

➤ Display custom message when time limit or error occurs: Enter a helpline or specific phone number that users should contact when configuring a new device here, along with some instructions. This will display a customized message when the time limit or error occurs. This is the message that will be displayed in the event that Autopilot malfunctions or runs out of time.

➤ Enable end user log collection and diagnostics page: This will assist you in troubleshooting. In the event of a machine failure, users will have access to logs directly from the device through a button that they may press.

➤ Only show page to devices provisioned by out-of-box experience (OOBE): You should set this to "No" if you want to limit the page to only those devices that were configured by out-of-box experience (OOBE)." If you set this to "Yes," the first time someone logs in to an account other than the primary user after the machine has been provisioned, it will display the ESP. Your IT staff won't appreciate that you turned this off when they need to log into a machine to fix something.

➤ Block device use until all apps and profiles are installed: If you set this to "No," you won't be able to block till apps are launched. This option also toggles the next three settings on and off.

➤ Allow users to reset the device in the event that installation fails: In the event that Autopilot fails, you have three options: either reset the device, allow users to continue using it, or take no action at all. Resetting the device will result in the display of a "Reset" button, which you may click to attempt provisioning once more.

➤ Permit users to continue using a device in the event of an installation error: This is the second option. If you select Yes, a "Continue" button will appear, and if users select it, it will direct them to their screen. If you select "No," both options will be ignored.

➤ Block device use until required apps are installed if they are assigned to the user/device: If you set this to All, users won't be able to log in until all required apps are installed on the devices of all users or devices in any groups that the user or group is a part of. If you set this to "Selected," you'll be able to select from the apps that have already been launched. As previously mentioned, we'll be using Microsoft To-Do for this scenario.

➤ An additional option is to restrict the blocking of applications to those that malfunction during the technical process. This option is related to pre-provisioning and ensures that the apps of your choosing are loaded on a device at the time of user enrollment; however, pre-provisioning downloads all necessary apps.

⦁ Click Next once the parameters have been adjusted.

➤ In this example, we will deploy to our Intune users group; if at any point you decide to add more than one ESP setup for multiple user groups, you will have more options. One ESP can be distributed to all users or devices if that's all you ever require.

⦁ After selecting your deployment group, click Next.

⦁ To move on to the Scope Tags page, click Next.

⦁ Finally, click Create after making sure everything is in order.

How to Sign Up for a Windows Device

IT administrators can use this communication to deploy policies, manage Intune, and perform general management tasks on devices such as Windows PCs. The initial step in managing devices with Microsoft Intune is always the same: enrolling the device. As part of the enrollment process, Intune must install a mobile device management (MDM) certificate on the device.

Which alternatives are available for Windows device enrollment?

There are a number of ways that IT departments can integrate Windows devices with Intune; the primary distinction between these options is typically the ownership of the device. There are many methods for integrating individually owned and corporately owned devices.

This ensures that gadgets owned by corporations remain corporate and those owned by individuals remain personal.

- Windows Autopilot is the most widely used option for business-owned devices. It is a service that combines several technologies to simplify the setup and deployment of new devices; in the process, the device will be automatically registered for Microsoft Intune and linked to Microsoft Entra ID, making it ready for management and use.
- When IT managers are unable to use Windows Autopilot, they can configure company-owned devices to enroll in Microsoft Intune automatically. During the out-of-box experience (OOBE), they can select to connect the device to Microsoft Entra ID and provide a work or school account. During that process, registration will occur in the same manner as it did with Windows Autopilot. The disadvantage of this method is that it gives you less control over the device's entire lifespan.
- **Bulk enrollment with a provisioning package:** This option can be quicker than Autopilot when IT needs to enroll a large number of company-owned devices. Administrators can install a setup package during the OOBE to ensure that the device is immediately linked to Microsoft Entra ID and signed up for Microsoft Intune.
- **Intune Company Portal app:** This is the most widely used option for personally owned devices. To add a device to Microsoft Intune, users download the app from the Microsoft Store, follow the instructions, and the device is registered as a personal device, providing IT with limited control and information.
- **Connecting a work or school account:** You can also add a work or school account on your own devices by following the instructions in the Settings app. This will give you a similar experience to the Intune Company Portal app, but with less detailed information about the device's condition and a less intuitive view of all the apps that are available.

Which situation applies to Windows devices owned by corporations the most frequently?

The majority of sellers and OEMs allow enrollment when buying new devices; in most cases, this means that the seller gets access to the tenant's devices so that they can easily send the necessary data; if the seller only gives it to them, the IT administrator must upload the CSV file with the device details to the Windows Autopilot service. Most of the time, Windows devices are added to Microsoft Intune by using Windows Autopilot to join devices that belong to a business. In this case, those devices must be linked to the Windows Autopilot service. Planning that during the purchase of those devices will accomplish this in the most straightforward manner.

What prerequisites must be met in order to use Windows Autopilot?

There are a few requirements that must be fulfilled before an IT administrator may use Windows Autopilot.

These include ensuring that the following settings and rights are set up:

- Users must have received from IT at least a Microsoft Entra ID P1 license for expedited enrollment and a Microsoft Intune P1 license for Intune management.
- Assigning Microsoft Intune MDM authority and establishing a basic Intune tenant.
- Devices that run Windows 10 or 11 Pro, Windows 10 or 11 Enterprise, or Windows 10 or 11 Education at least with the appropriate version activated.
- An administrator Microsoft account assigned at least the roles of Intune Service Administrator or Global Administrator.

How to use Intune to set up Windows Autopilot for automatic enrollment

Before administrators can use Windows Autopilot to automatically add devices to Microsoft Intune, there are a few things they must perform.

Set up auto-enrollment

The first step is to enable automatic enrollment, which will ensure that the device automatically enrolls in Microsoft Intune as soon as it joins Microsoft Entra ID.

- Open the Microsoft Intune admin center interface and navigate to Devices > Windows > Windows enrollment > General > Automatic enrollment.
- To configure the MDM user scope, select one of the options listed below on the Configure page (Image below).
  - ➤ None. MDM's automatic enrollment is disabled.
  - ➤ Some. The automatic enrollment feature of MDM is exclusive to the selected group.

> Every user has the option to enable MDM automatic enrollment.

+ Click Save to save the modifications after leaving the MDM terms of use URL, MDM compliance URL, and MDM discovery URL unchanged.

Set up the gadgets for Windows Autopilot

The addition of devices to Windows Autopilot is the second phase. Only in the event that the vendor hasn't previously uploaded the devices is this step necessary. This will make use of data from a CSV file.

+ Open the Microsoft Intune admin center portal and navigate to Devices > Windows > Windows enrollment > Windows Autopilot Deployment Program > Devices.

+ To view the Windows Autopilot devices page, click the image below. Click Import on that page. Once the CSV file has been selected, click Import again.

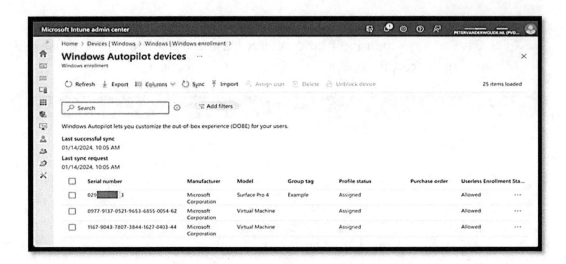

The Windows Autopilot admin interface allows IT managers to sort and group devices and provides views with important data. The most crucial of them is the Group tag, which IT may modify with ease.

To establish an Entra device group based on that tag, use the sample code that follows:

```
device.devicePhysicalIds -any (_ -eq "[OrderID]:Example"))
```

Construct a deployment profile for Windows Autopilot

The third stage involves adjusting the user's OOBE, setting the device deployment mode, and creating a Windows Autopilot deployment profile.

The steps below will walk you through creating that profile:

- Go to Devices > Windows > Windows enrollment > Windows Autopilot Deployment Program in the Microsoft Intune admin center interface to locate Deployment Profiles.
- Click Create profile and select Windows PC once you reach the Windows Autopilot deployment profiles screen.
- On the Basics screen, give the user a name and select Next.
- Click Next after configuring the first two settings at the very least on the Out-of-box experience (OOBE) screen (see the image below).

- ➢ **Mode of deployment.** For a typical Windows Autopilot deployment, choose User-Driven. Users provide their passwords upon enrollment, and the gadget is then handed to them.
- ➢ **Register for a Microsoft Entra ID.** Choose Microsoft Entra joined to access the Microsoft recommended place for joining new devices.
- ➢ Select the options that are applicable to the remaining ones based on internal policies. Select the type of account, select the language, select the default name, and choose which pages to display.
- ✦ To move on to the Scope Tags page, click Next.
- ✦ On the Assignments tab, configure the user's assignment according to an Entra device group. Consider using a group that is constructed using a Group tag.
- ✦ Review the options on the Review + Create screen, then press the Create button.

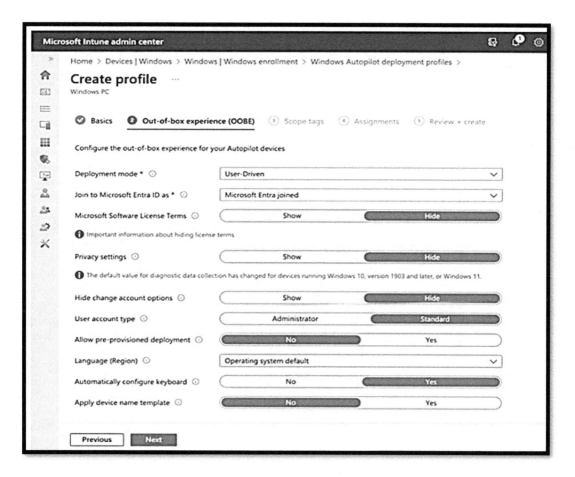

Once these settings are complete and set up, IT managers can utilize Windows Autopilot to deploy company-owned devices. Additionally, administrators ought to configure an Enrollment Status Page that prevents the device from being used until all required configurations and applications have been installed. Remember to modify the programs that need to be started and the configuration options that will be used.

Practice Exercises

1. Explain the process of making an Update Rings
2. What are some actions to be taken in configuring an Enterprise State Roaming system (ESP)?
3. Which alternatives are available for Windows device enrollment?
4. Which situation applies to Windows devices owned by corporations the most frequently?
5. What prerequisites must be met in order to use Windows Autopilot?
6. Explain the process of setting up the gadgets for Windows Autopilot

CHAPTER FOUR
PROTECTION FOR WINDOWS DEVICES

To assist safeguard your group and Windows devices, you can configure and distribute various Microsoft Intune security baseline profiles to various groups of Windows Intune and users. A set of pre-configured parameters that represent the security posture recommended by the product's security team is called a baseline for each product. You can deploy an unaltered basic baseline or edit your profiles to configure devices with the parameters required by your organization.

Establishing a baseline for security

A summary of security baselines

Intune allows you to construct a template with numerous device configuration parameters when you create a security baseline profile. When there are numerous copies of a security baseline accessible, only the most recent version can be used to make a new copy of that baseline. You are free to use previously created baseline versions and modify which groups they are assigned to. Nevertheless, previous iterations do not permit you to modify their configuration settings. If you need to add new setting combinations, update older baselines to the latest version or create new baselines using the most recent baseline version.

You should update prior basic versions to the latest version as soon as possible.

- It is possible to add new settings that were not available in previous versions.
- Discard previous configurations if they are no longer required.
- Verify that the initial configuration complies with the most recent security recommendations for the relevant product.

When working with security baselines, frequent tasks include:

- Creating a new profile instance, configuring desired settings, and assigning the baseline to groups.
- Replace an outdated baseline version with the latest version. Have a character alter the currently-used baseline version.

- Remove an assignment from the baseline. Examine the consequences of ceasing to use a security baseline for setting management.

Fundamental Requirement

- To implement security baselines using Intune, a Microsoft Intune Plan 1 subscription is required.

A helpful hint is that while Intune makes it simple to build up and implement security baselines, it doesn't actually establish or define them. Other than Intune, there exist alternative technologies for deploying security baselines.

- A subscription to the active controlled product is required in order to use baselines through Intune. You are not automatically able to use Microsoft Defender just because you are using the Microsoft Defender for Endpoint standard. Rather, the standard provides you with an interface to configure and manage settings on devices licensed to and managed by Microsoft Defender for Endpoint.
- You must have the Policy and Profile Manager Job integrated with your account in order to manage baselines in Intune.

Establish a security baseline profile

- Visit and log in to the Microsoft Intune admin center.
- To view the list of available baselines, select Endpoint security > Security baselines.

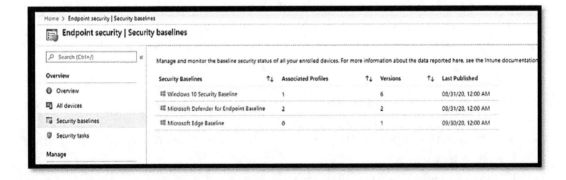

- Click Create Profile after choosing the baseline you wish to utilize.
- **On the Basics tab, adjust the following parameters:**

- ➤ **Name:** Assign a name to your security baseline identity. Enter the Defender for Endpoint Standard profile, for instance.
- ➤ **Description:** Fill in the description area with some text explaining the purpose of this baseline. Anything you wish to write can be included in the description. Although it's not required, it's advised.
- ➤ Click Next to advance to the next tab. You can return to a tab you've previously seen by clicking on the tab name when you're in a new tab.

✦ Examine the groups of settings that are accessible in the selected standard on the Configuration settings tab. You may view a group's settings and the default values associated with those settings by clicking on the group. **You can use the following to find specific settings:**

- ➤ Choose a group to view every setting inside that group. The icon of a lightbulb has information next to it. By providing knowledge about what other organizations have accomplished effectively, setting specifics fosters trust in setups. For certain settings, but not all of them, you can obtain insights.
- ➤ Enter terms in the search bar to make the view only display the groups that match your criteria.

Every baseline version has a default configuration for every setting. To make the settings more effective for your company, adjust them. The same parameter may be present in multiple baselines, each with a different beginning value, depending on the baseline's intended use.

- After selecting the Scope Tags tab, click Select Scope Tags. By doing this, the Select tags pane will open, allowing you to add scope tags to the profile.
- Giving the baseline to one or more groups comes next. Go to the Assignments tab and select "Select groups to include." To ensure that the assignment is perfect, feel free to use Select groups to omit.

It's crucial to keep in mind that, depending on the settings in place, security baselines must be assigned to either user groups or device groups. This implies that you may require more than one standard when allocating settings for individuals and devices.

When you're ready to implement the standard, navigate to the Review + create tab and review its specifics. Click Create to save and launch the profile. Upon creating a profile, Intune immediately forwards it to the designated group for usage.

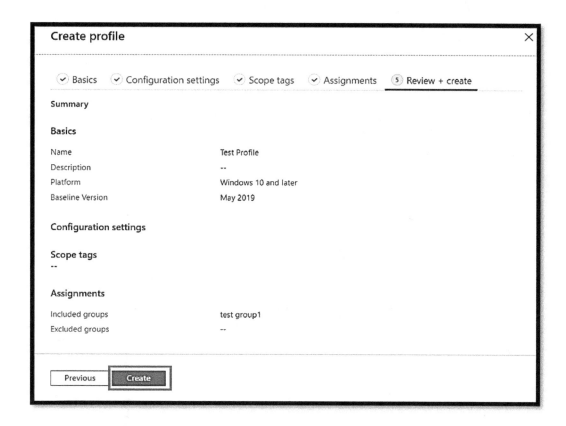

- Once a profile is created, it can be modified by selecting Profiles from the list of options under Endpoint security > Security baselines, after selecting the baseline type you set up. After choosing your desired name from the list, select Properties. Any of the setup tabs allows you to modify the parameters. To preserve your edits, choose Review + Save.

Modify a profile's baseline version

Test any changes on a duplicate of the profile before making them to the version that is distributed to a group. **In this manner, you may ensure that a test set of devices is able to operate with the updated baseline values.**

- Log in at the Microsoft Intune admin center.
- To modify a profile, select Endpoint security > Security baselines and click on the tile corresponding to the desired baseline type.
- Navigate to Profiles and select the desired profile by checking the box next to it. Next, select Change Version.

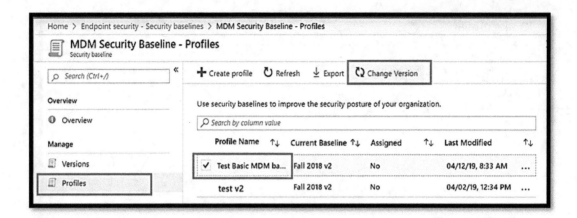

To select the version instance you wish to use, utilize the dropdown menu next to "Select a security baseline to update to" in the Change Version box.

To obtain a CSV file displaying the differences between the selected version and the current version of the profile instance, select Review Update. Examine this file once more to determine what options have been added or removed, as well as the default values for each in the updated profile.

> As soon as you're ready, proceed to the next stage.

- ᛌ **Choose one of the following two options when choosing how to update the profile:**
  - ➢ Accept baseline adjustments but preserve my current settings customizations: This option updates the baseline profile to reflect the modifications you made to it.
  - ➢ Accept baseline adjustments and remove current personalization options to completely erase your initial profile. The new profile has all of its settings set to their default settings.
- ᛌ Click "Submit." As soon as the change is complete, the baseline is deployed to the designated group and the profile is updated to the selected baseline version.

Eliminate an assignment for a security baseline

The settings on a device might not return to a pre-managed condition if the security baseline's settings are set to "Not configured" or if a baseline's setting no longer applies to that device. The security baseline's parameters determine this. The configurations are based on CSPs, and each CSP has a different method for reducing change. Additional procedures that could later modify device settings include creating a new or different security baseline, a device configuration profile, Group Policy configurations, or a direct edit of the device's settings.

Make a copy of the security baseline

It is possible to make more copies of your security baselines. Creating a duplicate of the baseline can be useful when you want to provide a comparable but distinct baseline for a collection of devices. If you create a clone, you won't need to manually recreate the entire baseline. Alternatively, you might create a replica of any baseline you currently have and then only make the adjustments the new instance requires. It's possible that you can only adjust one parameter and the group to which the standard is assigned. When you make a replica, give it a new name. The duplicate lacks assignments but has the same scope tags and setting sets as the original. You must adjust the new standard if you want to add assignments. Every security baseline supports the creation of duplicates. After copying a baseline, you can modify its parameters by going back and making changes to the new copy.

To reproduce a baseline
- Log in at the Microsoft Intune admin center.
- To duplicate a baseline, navigate to Endpoint security > Security baselines and select the desired baseline type. Click on Profiles after that.
- You can either click on the ellipsis "..." symbol to the right of the baseline and select "Duplicate," or you can right-click on the profile you wish to copy and select "Duplicate."
- After renaming the baseline, select "Save."

Following a Refresh, the admin center displays the updated default profile.

To modify a baseline
- Click Properties after first selecting the baseline.
- **From this view, you may select Edit for the following lists to modify the description:**

> o Basics
> o Assignments
> o Scope tags
> o Configuration settings

Only when a profile is using the most recent version of that security baseline can you edit its configuration. For profiles that use previous versions, you can view the profile's settings by opening Settings, but you are unable to modify them. Once a profile has been updated to the most recent baseline version, you can modify its parameters.

- Click "Save" to save your changes when you're finished. Before making changes to other categories, you must save changes to one category.

Setting up a virus-fighting policy

- Use the dropdown option to select Microsoft Defender Antivirus as the policy type.
- Give the policy a heading and an explanation.
- Adjust the settings to suit your surroundings. For further information, click on the small letter (i) in a circle next to each field if you're unsure about any of them. Click Next after your settings are in place.
- Click Next on the Scope Tags page.

- After completing your setup, assign the policy to your Autopilot Devices group.
- To view all of your settings, click the arrow next to Defender, then select Create.

You've now established your policy.

How to Adjust Windows Security Preferences

Now let's configure the Windows Security Experience policy to alter the way users see Windows' security settings:

- To create a new policy, choose Windows Security Experience from the Endpoint Security Antivirus menu.
- Enter the policy's name and description, then select "Next."
- You have the most control over most of these, but be sure to activate Tamper Protection at the very bottom. Since this is a corporate system, turn off Family UI. After that, adjust whatever that needs to be adjusted in your environment.
- Click on the "Next" button.
- Designate Autopilot Devices for the policy.
- Examine it, and then select "Create."

How to set up the preferences in BitLocker

- Choose disk encryption and develop an endpoint security plan.
- After naming and describing the insurance, click the Next button.
- **Modify the Base Settings to correspond with the image displayed below:**

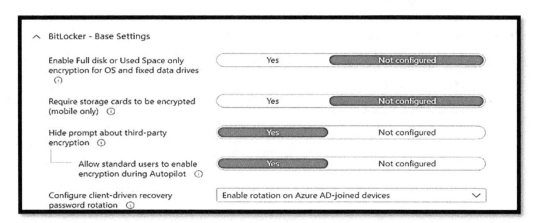

- **Adjust the Fixed Drive Configuration according to the following image:**

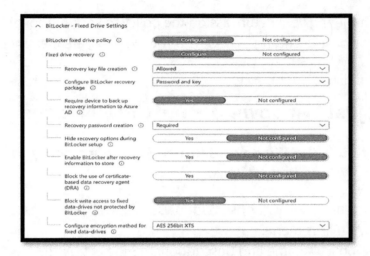

The encryption technique is the only setting under OS Drive Settings that needs to **be altered, however if you wish to comply with CIS regulations, you may also want to set Startup authentication required to Yes:**

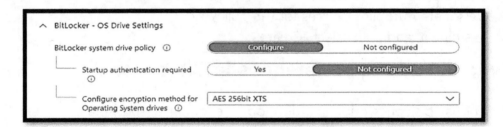

The USB sticks belong to the Removable Drive Settings. This setting becomes less significant when you block fully, but you should still do it for safety's sake. **In certain situations, CBC encryption is used in place of XTS encryption:**

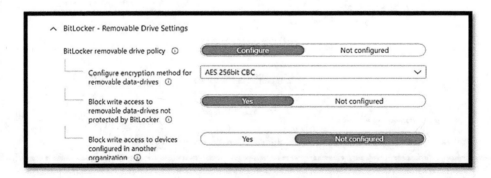

➕ Click on the "Next" button.

- After setting it to Autopilot Devices, click Next.
- After taking one final look at the settings, click Create.

Customizing the Windows Firewall

When we examine Windows Firewall, the Reusable settings option will be displayed. Multiple firewall policies for different user and group groups are often present in an environment to permit the usage of a piece of software or to further restrict the devices that can be used. You may create your own firewall rules once and use them across policies with Reusable Settings, saving you the trouble of adding new ones each time. **To give you an example, all Google domains would be blocked by this rule:**

Auto Resolve ⓘ	Keyword ⓘ	Configure settings
True	*.google.com	+ Edit instance

Once you've learned about Removable Drive Settings, you may configure the Microsoft Defender firewall default policy by following these steps:

- Log in at the Microsoft Intune admin center.
- To create a policy for Windows 10, Windows 11, and Windows Server, select Endpoint Security > Firewall > Windows Firewall > Create.
- Enter a name and a description if desired > Next
- **Set the following configuration parameters (Domain, Private, and Public) for each kind of network site:**

> ○ **Log file path**
> ○ **Enable log dropped packets**
> ○ **Enable log success connections**
> ○ **Log max file size**

- Choose Next > Next.
- Add the policy to a group that contains the users or devices you wish to add as members, then select Next > Create.

Putting ASR regulations into practice

The more well-known and well-documented vulnerabilities in a typical machine design are frequently targeted by bad actors. Java Script, Office Macros, and Adobe Acrobat Reader are a few examples. Fortunately, there are pre-installed ASR rules that can be enabled to prevent problems. If you are concerned about the potential impact they may have on your application, you can also choose to enable them in Audit mode.

- To configure these, navigate to the Endpoint security blade, select Create a new policy after clicking Attack surface reduction.
- Choose Attack surface decrease from the drop-down menu.

Once more, you'll see that we have reusable settings; you may adjust the device IDs for the printer and USB here. These are unrelated to ASR regulations, but they are related to other policies that can be configured in this blade.

The following procedures will walk you through creating a new ASR policy:

- Click Next after naming and describing your policy.
- Examine each policy on the Settings screen and consider the potential effects on your environment. Set it to Audit mode initially if you're not sure or suspect it might be. It's better to be safe than sorry.
- After that, check the reports, and if there are no issues, turn it on. Although having it enabled is safer, users and apps still need to be able to use the tools.
- Since this is a lab setting and there are no legacy apps to be concerned about, we're setting everything to Block in this instance.
- When you adjust a configuration, ASR Only per Rule Exclusions will become visible. This may result in the policy setting not being applicable to a certain program (enter the executable for the application).
- Selecting the letter "i" within a circle, just like with other policies, will reveal the purpose of the policy. Use Audit or Warn if you're still unsure.
- After configuring your policy parameters, click Next.
- On the Scope Tags page, click Next once more.
- Based on the appearance of your user profiles, decide which devices or users to assign to on the Assignment screen. If your financial department, for example, makes use of an Office add-in, you may wish to create a slightly looser

policy just for them. It is not necessary to loosen it for every employee in the organization.

+ Next, proceed as usual, check your policy and click Create to give it official status.

Registering for Endpoint Defender

+ Select Settings.
+ Afterwards, select Endpoints.
+ Go to the bottom of the page now. A setting named Microsoft Intune Connection ought to be visible to you. Turn that slide to On.
+ Click Save Preferences after that to return to the Intune portal.
+ Create a new policy by selecting Endpoint Security, Endpoint detection and response, and Windows 10, Windows 11, and Windows Server.
+ Decide on a title and an explanation for the policy.
+ After turning on the Intune Connector in Security Center, we may select the Microsoft Defender for Endpoint client configuration package type by selecting "Auto from connector" from the dropdown menu. If it isn't there, confirm that the Intune Connector was correctly saved and switched on during the previous Security Portal procedures.
+ After configuring your sample sharing, click Next.
+ To go to the Scope Tags page, click Next.

Defender for Endpoint is device-only, thus you must either grant access to all of the devices or only a subset of them. This may be the one occasion where All Devices comes in handy.

+ Lastly, select "Create."
+ To confirm that everything is connected, we can now select the Microsoft Defender for Endpoint link from the menu.

Additional settings for iOS and Android devices not managed by Intune can also be found here. Examine them to make sure they fulfill your requirements, and then turn them on as necessary.

Configure the Application Control

Application Control is a new Intune utility that facilitates quicker deployment while enhancing the capabilities of Windows Defender Application Control (WDAC). Application Control can be deployed in two ways: either via an XML file designed specifically for WDAC or via a GUI with checkboxes. Instead of utilizing the GUI that we will be using in this instance, you can create the file with greater precision by using the Microsoft WDAC wizard. The Managed Installer needs to be enabled before we can generate our policy. This makes it possible for the Intune Management extension to load apps without issue.

Follow these steps to put it up in your environment:

- Go to App Control for Business under Endpoint Security.
- Click Add after selecting the Managed Installer tab at the top.
- In the fly-out menu, select Add.
- Confirm that you wish to add the managed installer by pressing "Yes".
- Now that this has been enabled, we may draft our policy. Choose App Control for Business to start creating a policy.
- Everything will appear normal going forward since this makes use of the standard Unified Settings catalog.
- Enter the policy's name and description, then select Next.
- The following screen will make use of the GUI. Thus, for the format of the configuration settings, select Use built-in controls.
- **This will modify the display of various options (again, this will resemble the Settings catalog):**
  - Enable app control policy to trust Windows components and Store apps; the only options available are Enforce and Audit. If you select Audit, it will log events without halting any running programs.
  - **Choose extra app trust guidelines to follow:**
    - ✓ Apps with a solid reputation can be trusted, enabling Microsoft Intelligent Security Graph to do so.
    - ✓ AppLocker is able to allow some installers to function, such as Configuration Manager, when it trusts software from managed installers.
- Since we will only be using Intune in this instance, the two additional rules should be left empty. Click Next after your environment's settings are ready.

⁺ We don't need scope tags in this instance, so click Next.

Generally speaking, we want to configure every security policy at the device level. This is an anomaly, though. If we apply this to every device, then every app—including the one-time installs or debugging versions—will need to be installed via Intune. We're going to give at the user level to prevent that from happening and enable us to make exceptions for IT support professionals as needed. As necessary, complete the blanks in the groups, then select "Next."

⁺ After making sure everything is correct, click the Create button.

Practice Exercises

1. Establish a baseline for window device security
2. How will you Adjust Windows Security Preferences?
3. Mention the steps in Registering for Endpoint Defender
4. Mention the steps in Configuring the Application Control

CHAPTER FIVE
INTUNE: MANAGING IOS DEVICES

In order to protect your user-owned bring-your-own-device (BYOD), this chapter looks at implementing device policies to handle company-owned and controlled devices as well as app security policies. For our business devices, we'll use Apple Business Manager (ABM), sometimes known as Apple Education. We will also cover how to use the Volume Purchase Program (VPP) to install apps and configure Intune to function with ABM. Finally, we will register a managed device as well as a bring-your-own device (BYOD).

Important information

You must remember to jot down your Apple device's certificate renewal dates and keep an eye on when they're due. Another option is to utilize Azure Automation to set up the alerts to run automatically. The MDM push certificate allows your devices to establish a connection with the Intune MDM service. If this one does expire, you can renew it by giving Apple a call within thirty days after the expiration date. The only thing left to do is wiping and re-enrolls all of your devices if they are unable to or if 30 days have passed. Yes, all of the data has been completely erased. You need a registration code in order to connect your devices for the first time. If this enrollment page fills up, create a new one and move your devices to it. It may not be as awful as a wipe, but in the Intune portal, it can make the devices appear less pristine. The Apple VPP certificate is used to deploy apps to devices. After that one expires, users won't be able to download or install any further apps. Though you might waste time trying to figure out why an app won't run and miss this as the issue, it's not a major deal and they're simple to alter. To get the best protection without sacrificing the user experience, you should customize the settings for your device limits and settings catalog policy. Blocking the App Store, iCloud, and other services is a good idea from the start.

Setting up an Apple and Intune connection

Before adding or modifying devices, a connection must be made to link Intune to ABM or Apple Education. Before you begin, log into your ABM account and navigate to your account settings. From now on, we can add an MDM server. It is important keeping

Intune open in a separate tab because we will be switching between the two while configuring the certifications.

The actions to take are as follows:

- Navigate to iOS under Devices in the Intune interface.
- Click on iOS/iPadOS Enrollment after that.
- As you can see, there is only one option available on this screen: Apple MDM Push certificate. Press that button.
- Download the CSR certificate and check the box in the pop-up window. Afterwards, select the "Create your MDM push Certificate" link. You can access the Apple portal by doing this.
- Click "Create a certificate."
- After checking the box, click Accept.
- Post the CSR we obtained from the Intune site on the internet.
- Click Download after noting the expiration date or placing a note someplace so you can remember it.

- Submit your Managed Apple ID (don't use your own Apple ID), select the certificate to upload, and click "Upload." In the same panel, you should now see a success message.

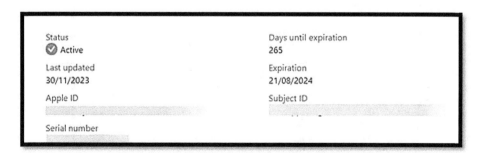

As you can see in the graphic above, Intune is now connected to ABM, and the state ought to change to "Active." The process of deploying devices starts with this.

How to set up an Apple VPP token

We must configure our VPP token now that our settings are connected in order to launch an app.

Starting off

Open one tab for Apple Business Manager and the other tab for Intune. As for certificates, we'll flip between them once more.

How to proceed...

- Open Apple Business Manager's settings and select Payments and Billing.
- Locate the content token at the page's bottom.
- Return to Intune at this point, select Tenant Administration, and then select Connectors and Tokens.
- Press the Apple VPP Tokens button.
- Click Create at the very top.
- After entering your name and Apple ID, upload the previously stored certificate, and select Next.
- Since this is the only MDM server we have, we may leave the top option set to "No".
- Unless you're setting for a school, choose the area, account type (often Business), and whether you want to allow automatic app updates. After accepting the terms, click Next in the end:

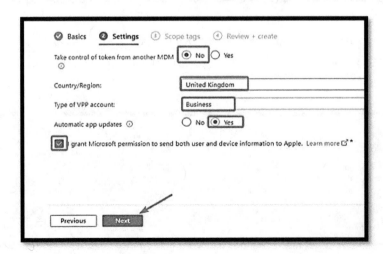

- Click Next after you've reached the Scope tags tab.
- Verify all the details, and then select "Create."

Tokens for enrollment profiles are added

Enrolling devices requires only the final step of setting up an enrollment profile token. Next, we configure ABM to use this token for device deployments.

- Click on iOS/iPadOS after selecting Devices.
- Afterwards, select "Enroll in iOS or iPadOS."
- Click on the "Enrollment program tokens."
- Hover over "Add."
- Select "Agree" and download the public key that Apple Business Manager requires.
- **To access Apple Business Manager, click this link:**

- Click on "Add" next to "Your MDM Servers" in Apple Business Manager under your profile.
- Enter the name, attach the certificate, and hit "Save."

- Select the Token to download.
- Return to the Intune site, sign in with your Apple ID, choose the newly downloaded certificate, and click Next.

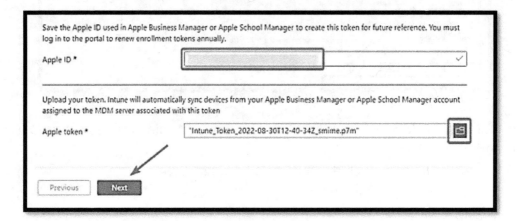

- Lastly, confirm everything is correct and press "Create."
- There are now two enrollment steps to complete.
- Click MDM Server Assignment on the Apple Business Manager site to get started.
- Select Edit.
- Choose your MDM server for each category of compatible hardware and click Save.
- **Return to the Intune website now, and select the program token associated with your fresh enrollment:**

Token name		Status	Program type		Apple ID		Devices synced
Intune		⊘ Active	Apple Business Manager				1

- Click on the profiles.
- Go to "Create profile" and select "iOS/iPadOS."
- Complete the form and press "Next."

You have a choice of these options on the following screen:

- **User affinity:** Here, you may select whether devices are shared (enroll with Microsoft Entra shared mode) or tied to a single person (enroll with person affinity). Alternatively, you can enroll without user affinity if the device is a kisok. Since we are using a regular user device, the option to enroll with User Affinity is available.

This will present you with a few further options. The method of authentication should be the first consideration. To verify users, you can install and use the Company Portal or use Setup Assistant with the current security.

- We'll utilize Setup Assistant with contemporary authentication in this instance because it has a higher chance of working with the present security. Furthermore, this enables you to see the device's home screen before logging in with your Entra ID credentials during the out-of-box experience (OOBE). To register for Just in Time, it is also required.

We wish to leverage the VPP, so users do not require an Apple ID in order to use the app.

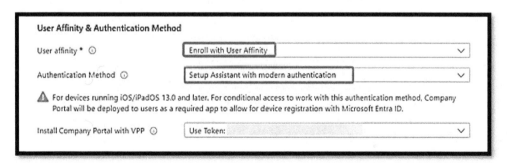

Irrespective of the login method selected, ensure that Supervised is set to "Yes." This will enable you to configure an uncontrolled device in additional ways. While enrollment is locked, users are unable to remove their name off the device. Unless you are using Apple Configurator, you should set Sync with computers to Deny All:

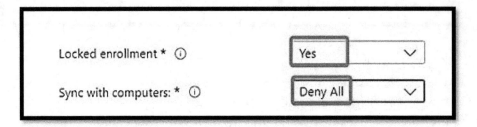

- Lastly, the Device Name Template can be configured. Any plain text or the variables {{SERIAL}} and {{DEVICETYPE}} can be used for this.
- Any eSIM devices that have the option should turn on cellular data; if you select "Yes," you will want the server URL of your carrier. Click "Next."
- In the upcoming screen, you can select the options available for setup and provide IT with your contact details in case there are any issues.
- Your users will benefit from a quicker setup time and safer devices thanks to this.
- You want to hide as many setup screens as possible.
- Password protection and support for Touch ID and Face ID ought to be sufficient.
- Click Next once the parameters have been adjusted.
- Check the options one more, and then select Create.
- Click Set default profile to complete the process.
- After choosing the newly created profile, click OK. Any devices that have been added to Apple Business Manager will be added to Intune and configured with the created enrollment profile code as soon as all of these settings have been created.
- You can assign a profile to a device directly if necessary by selecting the device, clicking the Assign profile button, and choosing Devices in the token.

iOS policy configuration with the settings catalog

ABM and Intune are now fully connected. If we so desired, we could enroll devices immediately; however, as we haven't done so yet, we must first put up any policies or apps. Policies can be established using the device limits feature or the settings catalog. They both configured the same parameters. Using the settings catalog is more up to date, but either approach will function. In this area, we will use the settings catalog; in the following section, we will employ device restrictions.

How to proceed...

- Navigate to the Devices section of the Intune console. Next, select iOS/iPadOS.
- Select Configuration Profiles, followed by New Policy.
- Click Create after selecting the Settings catalog from the drop-down menu.
- As usual, click Next after giving it a name and a description.

The configuration picker that we discussed earlier while creating your Windows profile is now visible to you. Here, you can select the parameters that suit your environment the best. This list will continue to grow as additional settings are added, thus the items that are now on it might get longer as more are added. We'll put up a few device constraints to meet the strategy we'll set up in the next part, using this as an example.

- **After making the necessary changes, select Next:**

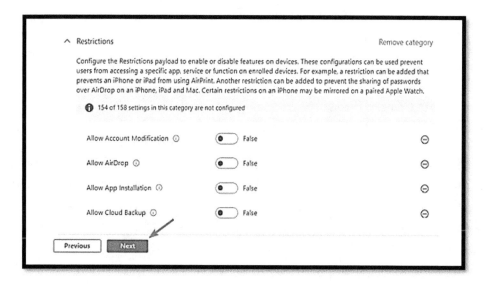

- Click Next since scope tags are not required.

We are able to provide this based on our selection. For device limits, you have two options: either use a simple user or device-based group, or choose all devices and establish a dynamic group. These kinds of configurations are typically the same throughout the estate. By using filters or a dynamic group, you may handle the groups more quickly and reduce the likelihood that a device will be distributed without the limits in place. Using enrollmentProfileName = xxx, where xxx is the profile name we previously set up, or deviceOSType equals iOS are two methods to use a dynamic group. Additionally, you have the option to filter just devices running iOS or the App Store by using the name of the registration profile.

- Click Next after Assignment.
- Lastly, check that everything is in order, and then select Create.

Setting up iOS policies with device limitations

You can also utilize a device restrictions policy to build a new profile for your iOS devices, as demonstrated in the preceding steps using the new settings catalog. Here is where we will walk you through setting up and automating your strategy using the device restrictions profile type.

How to proceed...

- Select Devices from the Intune console as previously. Select iOS/iPadOS after that.
- Select Configuration Profiles, followed by New Policy.
- Choose Device limitations this time, rather than Settings Catalog, after selecting Templates. Click "Create."
- Complete the general information as usual and click Next.

This is where all of the device restrictions are gathered, however unlike the settings catalog, there is no search function for them. To disable AirDrop, the App Store, and iCloud backups, we'll make the same three settings as before. These settings are accessible through the App Store, Cloud and Storage, and Connected devices, in that order. **Next, click this:**

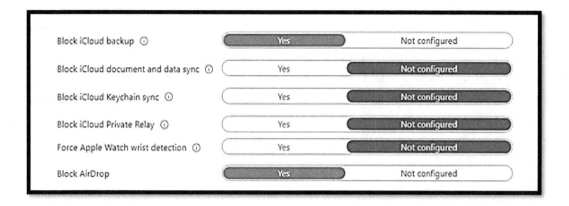

Since a device restrictions policy does not allow you to create a scope tag, we are led directly to the assignments page. It's the same as the previous method. Here, filtering is another option. Once you've completed the task, click Next.

- Lastly, confirm everything is correct and press "Create."

Using Apple VPP to deploy applications

Our users will be disappointed if they are unable to access the App Store and there are no centrally located apps, but we have set our limitations and are now confident that the devices are safe. This section will mostly cover Apple VPP applications because they are the ideal for delivering apps in a business environment.

It's crucial to go over the other application options in order to understand what's available:

- Apps that are just connected to the App Store are added by the iOS store app. Users must create an Apple ID, and you should configure your restriction policy to prevent the store from being prohibited. It follows that consumers are free to install anything they choose.
- **iOS/iPadOS web clip:** This adds a link to a web application on the device's home screen.
- **Web link:** This gives devices' home screens a web link.
- **Built-in app:** You can use these carefully selected and authorized apps without using the App Store. They've already been configured to safeguard apps.
- **Line-of-business apps:** Follow these instructions to install personalized iPad apps (up to 2 GB) on the devices under your control.

Starting off

Make sure all of your information is accurate by first logging into your Apple Business Manager account. If you wish to add any premium apps, this includes establishing a payment mechanism. Click on Apps and Books after that. Proceed with the section after you reach this screen.

How to proceed...

- Start by finding your application. To ensure that our users are configured for MFA (multi-factor authentication), we will utilize Microsoft Authenticator. Next, take these actions:
- Select the application from the results pane.
- Look up at the top and notice that it reads "Device Assignable." It is vital to keep this in mind during application assignments.
- Choose your MDM server from the drop-down box, enter the number of licenses you require, and click "Get."
- Should you possess fewer than 5,000 licenses, the application ought to appear in the Intune interface nearly instantaneously. Orders ranging from 5,000 to 19,999 are handled daily at 13:00 (PST). Over 20,000 orders are handled by 16:00 (PST).
- To be safe, we will expedite this by syncing the VPP.
- Go to Tenant management in the Intune console to access connectors and tokens.
- Press the Apple VPP Tokens button.
- To locate the three dots to the right of the token, you might need to scroll down.
- **After clicking them, select Sync:**

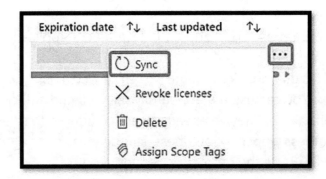

- Select iOS/iPadOS after selecting Apps.
- Although it hasn't been assigned yet, your app ought to be on the list. Click on the app to select it.
- Click Properties.
- Press the Edit button next to Assignments.

The reason for this is that, in contrast to Android, you do not have the option to select "Available for unenrolled devices." This is due to the licenses we previously discussed. You have the option of selecting Forced Uninstall, Available (self-service), or Required (forced installation). In this instance, we will force installation on all devices because we want every user to receive the software immediately.

- **Following the addition of the assignment, the options below will appear:**

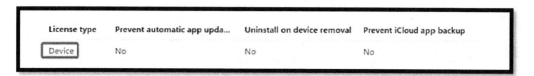

Here, the kind of license is the most crucial factor. We made it so that users no longer require an Apple ID. Therefore, we must ensure that device licensing is used. Any of the blue text links will open in a pop-up menu with further options when you click on it. These configurations are modifiable as needed. Unless the device becomes unmanageable, we do not wish to remove the app in this particular situation. Additionally, because it stores passwords, we do not want it to be saved. When you're finished configuring your needs, click OK.

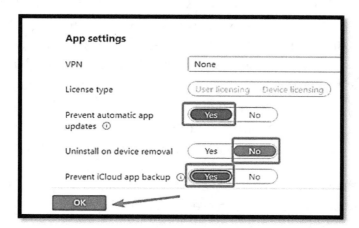

- Tap Review to save it now.
- Verify that everything appears correct, then select "Save."

Since we're only making adjustments to an application assignment rather than creating something entirely new, we don't use Create.

Setting up the iOS update settings

Similar to how we manage feature updates for our Windows devices, we may likewise wish to manage software updates for our iOS and iPadOS devices. This can mean keeping them updated all the time, restricting devices to a specific version, or providing guidance on when to perform updates. We accomplish this by using an update policy. Users can still search for and download updates on their own; however, you can provide them a 90-day grace period by establishing device limits (either through the settings catalog or a device restrictions policy).

How to proceed...

- To create the new policy, select iOS/iPadOS from the Devices menu.
- Click on Create profile after selecting Update policies for iOS and iPadOS.
- As always, click Next after giving it a name and a description.

On the screen that follows, we set the policy. From the first option, you can select the OS version that will operate on your devices. The most recent version that is compatible with your device will be installed if you leave it set to Latest update. If necessary, you can limit this to earlier iterations for a particular software. You may also create a plan that includes all of the apps or just a few, or you can tell Intune to adjust preferences when the device checks in again. You might schedule your hectic hours to begin at 8 a.m., just like any other workday. Until 8 p.m., at which point you may opt that you want updates to only run sometimes, like at night. Set to Update outside of scheduled time in this instance. In the event that they are on-call gadgets, you should configure them during the working day so they are prepared for use when the office closes. In this instance, select Update during the allotted period. We will install the most recent set of changes at our next check-in.

- After finishing the environment setup, click Next.
- Click Next on the following screen since this is not the appropriate place to utilize scope tags.

When thinking about your assignments, carefully evaluate your estate and user base. A one-size-fits-all approach might not be effective for you due to the possibility of having distinct change policies. If every device is configured and utilized consistently, you can use All Users or All Devices here, but creating groups would be a better idea. Employees who work shifts or are on call may require a different plan than office workers who use the device only throughout the workday for the same reason. Remember to utilize Exclusions as well. All Users could have a catch-all role, but you should make sure that there are exceptions for users that require slightly different configurations. On the other hand, you should never combine device and user assignments. Remember to give your leaders and anybody else who might require the device during or after work considerable consideration. Prior to implementing any significant modifications or policies, it is best to check, particularly when installing new systems like Intune. It might be challenging to win over individuals to your setup as much as it is to make it function.

- In this instance, we are providing configurations to the Intune-Users group.
- Click Next after that. Finally, make sure all the options are correct by giving them one last look before clicking Create.

Setting up a strategy for app protection

Device limits do not apply to our bring-your-own-device (BYOD) devices; they are only effective on fully registered company devices. To ensure that user-owned devices retain data securely, we want to put up app security policies, much like we do with Android devices. Unlike Android, iOS lacks numerous profiles. Thus, the data is not as segregated on the device even though it is protected.

Starting off

Both iOS and Android devices were compatible with the Conditional access policy that was configured in the Android app protection policy. Instead of following the instructions in this section, if you haven't previously, read the Android section and properly set up the policy. This allows you to control which devices will join the network exclusively in cases when the app is policy-managed.

How to proceed...

- We must first navigate to Apps and select App Protection Policies.

- After selecting iOS/iPadOS from the list that displays, click Create Policy.
- As usual, identify and describe your policy. The selection made in the drop-down box has already determined the platform. Click Next after that.

Here, we may choose which apps to safeguard. To protect certain apps, click the box that says +Select custom apps or +Select public apps. If not, adjust the drop-down menus to suit your requirements.

- In this instance, we will select All Microsoft Apps and click Next.
- We configure the security settings for the data contained in these applications on the next screen. These can be configured according to your business's requirements. **These settings are usually a good place to start:**
  - Back up organization data to iCloud and iTunes backups: Select Block. You won't need to consider another hack in this approach.
  - Transfer organizational data to other applications: Since we don't want data to leave the device for work, this should be set to policy-managed apps. Here is where you can add exceptions if necessary.
  - Save copies of organization data: Select SharePoint and OneDrive from the list of options, and set this to Block. We don't want any data on this unsecured device, but if it's acceptable to you in your settings, you can select Box.
  - Transfer communication data to: Ideally, this is set to "None," but it's important to think about since consumers may become upset if they are unable to copy and paste a phone number.
  - Recieve data from other apps: Either Policy Managed Apps or All Apps with Incoming org Data should be selected.
  - Limit copying, cutting, and pasting between other apps: This needs to be adjusted to paste in policy-managed apps (restrict within the bubble).
  - Verify that the encryption of organization data is set to "Require."
  - Sync policy managed app data with add-ins or native apps: Block this setting. Use caution while utilizing this setting as it prevents Outlook from adding contacts to the built-in contacts app.
  - Printing organization data: If someone wants to print organization data, they should set this to "Block." There's no need to be stringent if they can print it themselves.

> Limit the sharing of web material with other applications; Microsoft Edge is the best option for this. It's easier to maintain one browser across numerous devices, but that's up to you.

+ Click Next once the parameters have been adjusted.

You can adjust the admission requirements for the apps directly on the following screen. While the app can request a PIN on its own, the device cannot be made to request one. Adapt these to your needs; if they meet the company's device PIN requirements, it's usually the simplest to explain to end customers. Here, you should pay attention to the "Work or school account credentials for access" setting. If you set this to require and require fingerprints, users will ask for these.

+ Select "Required" and press "Next." Further parameters that you can specify to view the program are available on the following page:

> The maximum number of times a PIN can be input incorrectly is known as the max PIN attempts. The PIN can be altered or the data deleted.

> Offline grace period: This is how long you allow users to access the data again after you halt access for a predetermined number of minutes or days.

> **Disabled account:** You can allow users to access it or keep it closed.

> **Minimum app version:** The most basic version that is functional. You have the option to warn, wipe data, or block access.

> **Min SDK version:** Has three settings: Wipe data, Block access, and warn.

Limits like the ones listed below can also be set on the device itself:

+ Jailbroken or "rooted" devices: You can erase data or disable access.

+ If you have specified an OS version minimum or maximum, you should either prohibit access, remove data, or issue a warning. If you decide to set this, be sure to monitor it.

+ The minimum patch version is either delete data, block access, or warn.

+ Device model(s): Nothing should get past you; either block or remove it. Be cautious while adding to it because it's an allow list rather than a block list.

+ **Maximum threat level (Secured, Low, Medium, or High) for an approved device:**

+ Remove or block data. A Defender for Endpoint connection is required for this. Principal MTD service: Select Mobile Threat Defense (non-Microsoft) or Defender for Endpoint as your primary MTD service. This is the antivirus for your device. Click Next once the parameters have been adjusted.

Below are the configurations that were employed in this instance:

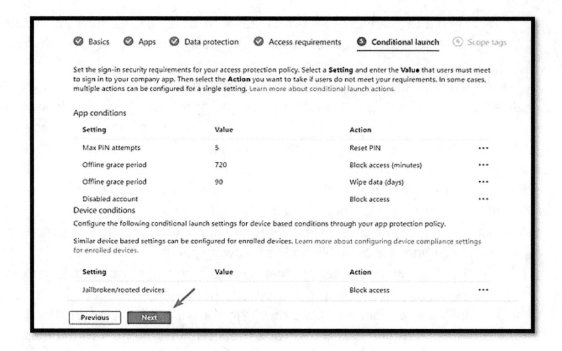

- Select Next from the Scope Tags page.
- The All Users and All Devices virtual groups cannot have this policy applied to them, as the following page will indicate. This policy is also focused on the individual because we don't know anything about the gadgets themselves. Transfer it to the group of Intune Users. Click Next after that.
- Finally, confirm that everything appears well. It will include important links to the policy that it can independently include and exclude. Click Create after that.

It's possible that you've seen more settings under "App protection policies" in the menu. To assist you understand better, let's go over those immediately.

Examining the policies for app configuration

If an app supports it, settings unique to the app can be configured using app configuration policies at the device or application level. Configuring line-of-business apps or the Outlook application are two examples. The program will determine if you can enter the raw text (which might be S/MIME/XML, JSON, or another format) or utilize a setup creator. The setup builder contains all the necessary settings for some apps (like Outlook), but it merely contains text boxes for other apps. Verify what you are putting in them. **Let's take a look at Outlook as an example to get you thinking:**

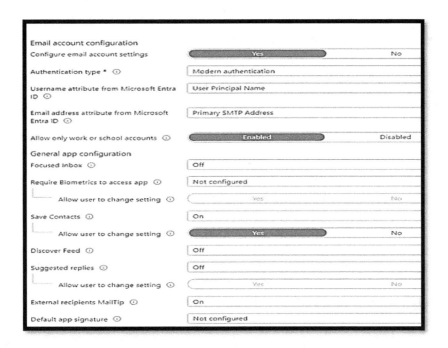

For instance, you must manually enter the Microsoft Word settings:

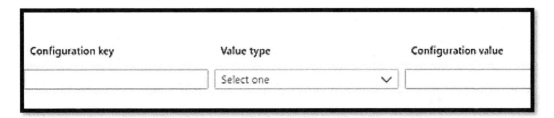

When you choose the settings in Outlook, the following values will be automatically filled in:

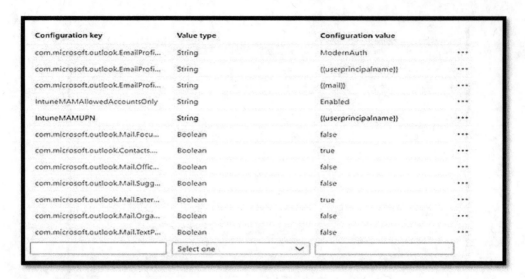

Configuration key	Value type	Configuration value	
com.microsoft.outlook.EmailProfi...	String	ModernAuth	...
com.microsoft.outlook.EmailProfi...	String	{{userprincipalname}}	...
com.microsoft.outlook.EmailProfi...	String	{{mail}}	...
IntuneMAMAllowedAccountsOnly	String	Enabled	...
IntuneMAMUPN	String	{{userprincipalname}}	...
com.microsoft.outlook.Mail.Focu...	Boolean	false	...
com.microsoft.outlook.Contacts....	Boolean	true	...
com.microsoft.outlook.Mail.Offic...	Boolean	false	...
com.microsoft.outlook.Mail.Sugg...	Boolean	false	...
com.microsoft.outlook.Mail.Exter...	Boolean	true	...
com.microsoft.outlook.Mail.Orga...	Boolean	false	...
com.microsoft.outlook.Mail.TextP...	Boolean	false	...
	Select one		

Activating your gadget – business

We can now start registering our devices, starting with those that are owned and managed by the company, now that our configuration is complete.

Starting off

Initially, confirm that you are logged in to either Apple Education Manager or (ABM) of a completely reset iOS or iPadOS device.

Observe these guidelines:

- First, confirm that the language and region are configured on your device.
- Select the manual setup option from the Quick Start screen.
- Use your phone's data plan or connect to your Wi-Fi network if necessary.
- After that, the remote management screen will appear. Click "Next."
- After logging in with your credentials, click Next.
- If your policy requires one, you will be prompted to create and verify a PIN after logging in.
- Ultimately, your home screen containing all of your deployed apps will appear after a few minutes.

There is additional

Just in time enrollment has recently been added to Intune for iOS and iPadOS. Using the single sign-on (SSO) plugin, you can complete registration and a security check by logging in to any app that is compatible.

Registering your gadget (BYOD)

Enabling personal devices to register is ineffective due to the differences between Android and iOS, such as Google Play, VPP, and no work profile. It is preferable to use app security policies instead. As a result, in this section we will solely demonstrate how to connect utilizing app security.

Starting off

You must set up and use an Apple ID to log in to an iOS or iPadOS device in order to access Microsoft Store apps.

How to proceed...

- Get an app by opening the App Store. In this instance, Microsoft Word will be used. When you're done installing, click Open.
- Click Current Users of Microsoft 365? Log in.
- After entering your email address, press "Next."
- After entering your password, select "Sign In."
- After logging in, the message below will appear. Click OK to restart the application:

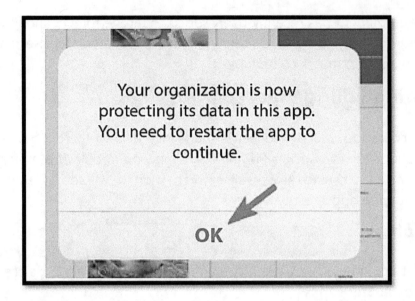

- Every time you access or create a document in the app, you will be prompted to enter a PIN. Any PIN restrictions that are a part of the security settings for your app will also be disclosed to you.
- Apply the same strategies to any further organizational apps.

Practice Exercises

1. What are the processes of setting up an Apple and Intune connection?
2. Discus how you can set up an Apple VPP token
3. Explain the process of setting up the iOS update settings
4. Explain the process of setting up a strategy for app protection
5. Explain the process of examining the policies for app configuration
6. Explain the process of Activating your gadget – business
7. Explain how you will register your gadget (BYOD)

CHAPTER SIX

HOW TO USE INTUNE TO MANAGE ANDROID DEVICES

Configuring a controlled Google Play account

Before we configure any Android policies or settings, we must link Intune to a controlled Google Play account. After that, we'll use this to send out apps and connect gadgets. To accomplish this, you don't need a Google account; we can create one for you while you're at it. If it was an Android Enterprise account, that would be ideal. Using a shared or general account rather than one associated with a particular employee is another smart move.

Take these actions:

+ First, we must click Devices under the Intune tab.
+ Click Enrollment after that. On the outdated website, select Enroll Devices.
+ Click now on Android.
+ Press the Managed Google Play button.
+ Select the "Agree" checkbox and click the "Launch Google to connect now" button.
+ Select a Sign In button from the pop-up window.
+ Select Create Account rather than Sign in.
+ Choose the option "For work or my business."

Here, you can make a new Gmail account or configure it to utilize one associated with your name (a personal account should not be used). If you want to use a personalized email, you will have to provide proof that you are the account owner. Since using a Gmail account is simple in this situation that is all we will do. Once you have entered all the necessary data, select Next.

+ Yes, for security purposes, you will require a phone number verification. After entering a number, select "Next." It's not necessary for this to be a phone.
+ After entering the verification code you received, click "Next."
+ After entering your recovery details, press "Next."
+ On the screen that reads "Get more from your number," click Skip.

The choices for advertising preferences are as follows. Since this account will only be used for maintaining Intune, Express should function just fine. However, if necessary, you can set it up with more precision. After making your selection, click "Next." Press the "I agree" button to accept the rules.

- To avoid creating a company profile at this time, select "Not Now."
- Click "Get Started."
- Enter your company's details and press Next.
- Complete the form by providing your contact details (if desired), and then hit "Confirm" to accept the guidelines.
- Click "Complete Registration" to finish the process.

The window will now dismiss, and you'll return to Intune, where you may verify that the provided link is active:

You've now connected your renter to Google Play successfully. This is now what we can use to configure our devices and install apps.

Setting up profiles for enrolling

Now that our Google Play account is connected, we can create a profile that allows devices to register. This will provide us with a QR code and a text code that we can use when configuring a new device.

Before we create a profile, let's first understand what each option on the Android device enrollment screen means:

- **Zero-touch enrollment:** This eliminates the need for you to set up any steps during device setup and enrollment and allows you to add several devices to your profile simultaneously. It functions similarly to Apple Business Manager's Automated Device Enrollment (ADE) and Apple iOS. It requires specific gadgets, and the dealer or service provider must register the device for the service. Samsung Knox is a well-known example that is free to set up and utilize. Android Zero Touch is also compatible with non-Samsung devices.
- **Individually owned devices with work profile:** This button only displays an unchangeable information page for personally owned devices with a work profile. The apps will be added to a separate profile on the device to safeguard the data they contain when a user enrolls a personal device through the Company Portal.
- Normally, it is activated.
- **Corporately owned dedicated devices:** These are devices in the form of kiosks that are not assigned a specific user.
- **Fully managed user devices owned by the company:** These are the most common accounts for regular users who receive fully managed business phones. We will set up this character ring in this section.
- **Firm-owned devices with work profile:** This refers to a device that the firm owns but that is also utilized for personal purposes. To protect the data on this kind of device, the apps are kept in a work profile.
- **AOSP Corporate-owned, user-associated devices:** These are Android devices that run AOSP rather than Google Play, but they are still fully managed user devices. You will be informed by your gear supplier if you own these devices. Most of the time, like the ones created by Zebra, they are made for specific purposes.
- **Corporately owned userless devices by AOSP:** This is for AOSP-owned kiosk devices that do not run Google Play services.
- **Android Supervisor Devices owned by individuals and businesses that have device administrator rights:** This method is limited to outdated devices and those owned by the company with device administrator privileges. Using it on new devices is not advised.

We will create a profile in this area for fully managed, company-owned individual devices given that we are aware of what each component does:

- Select user devices that are fully handled and owned by the company first.
- Click on "Create profile."

Creating a profile is a pretty simple process. It just needs a name and a description; there are no further configurations or tasks to complete.

- Click Next after entering your Name and, if desired, a Description value. It's still a good idea to peek over here even though there isn't much to see. Click the Create button after that.
- At this point, your profile will appear in the list. You will have to create a new token after the 90-day expiration period. Naturally, you can use the automation steps to have an Azure Runbook or anything similar performs this task for you automatically.
- Select the recently created page.
- Click on Token now.

Here is where you can get your token and QR code, which you may offer to people so they can enroll their devices. If necessary, you can also revoke a token and export it in JSON format.

Including a Google Play app

Since we will need apps in the tenancy for both OEM regulations and device restrictions, it is appropriate to discuss application deployment first. This section will primarily focus on managed Google Play apps, as they represent the most effective solution for integrating apps into a business environment. It's critical to discuss the alternative program options so that we are aware of what is available: Apps that are simply linked to the Play Store are added by the Android Store app. You'll need to restrict what users can do with their Google account if you want them to be able to leave the store open. After that, users are free to include anything.

- **Google Play app management:** This adds a smoothly functioning app that does not require a Google Play account. Access to the store is restricted to authorized apps only.
- **Web link:** Displays a web link on the device's home screen.

- **"Built-in app":** This term describes manually selected and pre-approved apps that don't require the Play Store to be used. Additionally, these are the apps that already have App Protection configured.
- **Line-of-business app:** Android device administrators utilized this method to send customized APK links to their devices. You ought to add it to the hidden Google Play Store while using Enterprise. The software package name must be distinct, not simply within your settings. It must be distinct throughout Google Play.
- The Android Enterprise system app is utilized for installing pre-installed apps, often those from the manufacturer. The entire application name, such as com. Microsoft.word, must be added.

Now that we have an understanding of the various kinds of apps, we can go and add our first managed Google Play app.

- To get started, select Apps.

FOOTNOTE: Intune adds the apps you need to enter a device right away as you sign up for the managed Google Play Store. Microsoft Managed Home Screen, Microsoft Authenticator, Microsoft Intune, and Microsoft Intune are among them.

- Afterwards, select Android.
- Hover over "Add."
- Select the Managed Google Play app by selecting it from the list.
- This will open the Intune app's Play Store.
- Locate the application you wish to use. Because Microsoft Outlook is widely used, it will be used. Click the app that appears in the search results.
- Click "Approve" to confirm.
- Please confirm that you accept the rights before clicking "Approve."
- You will now be asked what happens automatically in the event that those rights are changed. After choosing the option that best suits your needs (remove permission when the app requests it or leave it enabled when the app requests it), click "Done."
- App approval is imminent. However, you can still adjust the settings you already selected or turn it down:

- Ultimately, we must click the Sync icon at the top in order to add the app to Intune.
- The app will not appear in Intune for a few minutes. One thing to bear in mind is that we must click Microsoft Outlook because it hasn't been given yet.
- Select Properties.
- Select Edit by selecting Assignments.

You have the following options:

- **Essential:** This will cause all managed and enrolled devices to load the app instantly. The virtual group All Users/All Devices or groups of users or devices can get it.
- **Available for enrolled devices:** This displays the application on enrolled devices in the Company Portal. The app can only be directed towards consumers because it is already available.
- **Available with or without enrollment:** If the device isn't enrolled in Intune, it still displays the apps in the Company Portal (much like a BYOD with MAM). It can only be directed towards users, and only those with active Intune licenses.
- **Uninstall:** This removes the application without prompting you. It might be directed toward the subject or the object.

We want to launch both with and without enrolling our Intune customers in the Entra ID group since we want to demonstrate both corporate and BYOD. Click Included or Default under Update Priority to select whether the assignment is included or not and to modify the update priority. Once you have finished configuring everything, click Review + Save. When you are certain that everything on the review screen is correct, click Save.

Setting up a policy for device restrictions

Now that we can connect a device, it will function just like any other off-the-shelf gadget and won't require any setup. In order to provide them with a comprehensive business experience, we must establish a plan to manage them. We will put up a device limitations policy with some basic settings to get you started because Android policies have not yet been transferred to the Settings store. There will be further configuration in the PowerShell script and the accompanying JSON file.

How to proceed...

- Click Devices on the Intune page to get started.
- Afterwards, select Android.
- Select Configuration Profiles now.
- Lastly, to add a profile, select +Create | +New policy.
- Choose Android Enterprise and then Device Restrictions under Fully Managed, Dedicated, and Corporate-Owned Work-Profile. Click Create after that.
- After naming and characterizing your insurance, click Create.

A list of every setting that an Android device can have appears on the following screen. Take note of the headers, as many settings are device-specific (e.g., kiosk settings only function with specific devices).

- **Some recommended settings for our fully managed, user-assigned devices are as follows:**
    - Configure the Wi-Fi access point in block mode.
    - Block access to hotspots and tethering.
    - Block USB files transfer.
    - Block is the external media.
    - Factory reset protection emails: This lets you limit factory reset to admins who have been approved.
    - Block is the factory reset.
    - Turn off the notification windows.
    - **Device location:** Permit.
    - **App threat scan:** Mandatory.

- **Fully managed enrollment profile type:** This loads extra configuration information for the device using Microsoft Launcher. Verify that Microsoft Launcher is a necessary program.
- **Password:** Choose a password that works for your setting. Disabling everything from the lock screen is always advised.
- Block and add new users.
- **Remove user:** Block.
- **Individual Google accounts:** Disable.
- **Lock screen message:** As an additional security measure, set this to something for misplaced devices.

- After adjusting your parameters, press the "Next" button.
- Select All Users/All Devices or your Intune users group, and then click Next.
- Verify everything is in order, then select "Create."

Setting up an OEM policy

Along with allowing you to customize settings specific to your device, the majority of major Android manufacturers also provide an OEM policy and a Google Play app. Subsequently, device filters can be used to ensure that these policies and applications are only executed on the appropriate devices. Deploy the Microsoft Surface OEM tool in your settings and give it to someone; we're going to utilize the Surface Duo OEM configuration for this example.

Once the application has been approved and allocated, go to the next stages to configure the policy.

- Go to Devices first, and then click on Android.
- Click Configuration Profiles after that.
- Click +Create | +New policy to get started.
- Finally, select OEMConfig and Android Enterprise, then click Create. As usual, give it a description and a name. Click the "Select an OEM Config app" blue text to select the OEM Config app you have already deployed.
- After selecting the app, click "Select."
- Click Next once you've configured.
- Either modify the JSON on the following screen, or utilize a graphical user interface (GUI) to set up the parameters.

The setup builder will remain our choice because all of Microsoft's options are user-friendly. But you should always make sure the option you choose is the best fit for your maker. In this instance, we shall disable Bluetooth and NFC for added security. After adjusting the settings for your environment, select Next:

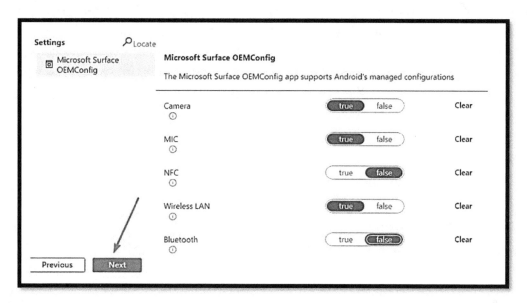

Click next to bypass the Scope tags page. Select the assignment that best fits the requirements. **To narrow the selection to only your Surface devices, first select All Devices. A Surface filter looks like this:**

For the time being, we will only click Next and give to All Devices. Once everything appears to be in order, click "Create."

Setting up a Wi-Fi policy

You want a secure Wi-Fi network that users can't connect to themselves and shouldn't connect to in an office or commercial setting. Either a certificate-based link or a secret, staff-only secure code can be used for this. To do this, a Wi-Fi strategy needs to be implemented for our mobile devices. But remember, unless you're utilizing a zero-touch enrollment solution like Samsung Knox, the devices won't be aware of this new approach until after enrollment. Thus, the first time you log in and setup any new devices, you will need to establish an internet connection. This might be an enrollment-only network with strict security guidelines, a guest network, or a 4G or 5G connectivity. Only a basic WPA2 network configuration will be demonstrated in this example, as an Enterprise setup requires the issuance of certificates.

Starting off

You will need the WPA key and a secure Wi-Fi network in order for this to function. If you wish to use an Enterprise Wi-Fi network, you will have to configure the certificate policies beforehand.

- To establish our policy, navigate to Configuration profiles under Devices and then Android.
- Click +Create | +New policy after that.
- Choose the Wi-Fi profile type of Android Enterprise and click "Create."
- After naming and characterizing it, select "Next."
- Choose the Wi-Fi model from the inventory. You can select Basic for WEP/WPA key-based authentication. You can select Enterprise for EAP/PEAP certificate-based authentication. In this instance, a Basic network is being put up.
- Once the correct information has been entered, click "Next."
- Give the policy to the appropriate location now. If the estate has only one network, then All Devices or All Users will function. Use group-based assignments if your networks are diverse so that IT has a less constrained network. Click Next once you've configured.
- Examine the parameters, and then select Create.

Including a policy for app protection

What about user-owned devices that they wish to use to access other company apps and email? To keep our corporate-owned devices secure and under control, we have recently established policies for them. Most people don't think it's a good idea to buy and manage so many more work devices if we completely prevent this. Alternatively, you might take no action and let them to add the apps without monitoring. You won't be able to govern the data of your business, thus this is not a smart option for data security. Instead of using Mobile Device Management (MDM), we may accomplish this by enrolling devices in Mobile Application Management (MAM) and using app security policies. Both can be utilized to increase security, but this is uncommon since it requires users to take additional actions on their devices, and we can presume that a device that is under control is secure at the device layer. It makes sense to ban certain devices since we don't want consumers to fully integrate their own devices into the Intune tenant. We will also want to link this to an Entra restricted access policy to ensure that unauthorized apps cannot access any data. Only the managed apps will be erased from these devices upon receiving a remote wipe; the device's overall contents will remain intact. App protection standards are applicable to all relevant apps, including core apps, Microsoft apps, and customized apps.

How to proceed...

We shall discuss the application protection policy first. We'll discuss restricted access next. We will safeguard every Microsoft software to demonstrate this. What if there's another alternative that suits you better?

It's as simple as selecting again after putting the menu down:

- We must first click on Apps to get started.
- After that, we must select App Protection Policies.
- Click Create Policy after that.
- Choose Android from the list.
- After entering your name and a brief description, click "Next." You will see that the platform is already configured for you.
- On the following page, we can select which apps to safeguard. To secure certain apps, you must select +Select Custom Apps or +Select Public Apps. If not, adjust the options to suit your requirements.
- In this instance, we will select All Microsoft Apps and click Next.
- We must adjust the settings for safeguarding the data kept in these applications on the next screen. These can be configured according to your business's requirements.

These settings are usually a good place to start:

- **Store organizational data on Android backup services:** Block (one less security breach to contemplate)
- **Transfer organization data to external apps:** Managed policies (we don't want information on the device to leave our business premises)
- **Save copies of organization data:** Since we don't want data on unprotected devices, OneDrive and SharePoint will be blocked. If Box is appropriate for your setup, select it.
- **Transfer communication data to:** Any dialer application that is regulated by policies (remember, stay in control).
- **Open data into organizational documents:** Select SharePoint and OneDrive for Business in the block. It can be loosened if necessary; however this is for inserting into documents.
- **Limit cut, copy, and paste between other apps:** Write in (limit inside the bubble) with policy-managed apps.
- **Snapshots and Google Assistant:** Disable
- **Encrypt organization data:** Need
- **Encrypt organization data on connected devices:** Need
- **Sync policy-managed app data with native applications or add-ins:** Block (take caution when adjusting this setting as it prevents Outlook from adding contacts to the local contacts list).
- **Printing organization data:** Block (if they can print it, why is this necessary?)
- Microsoft Edge can limit the sharing of web material with other apps. Although it's a personal preference, using a single browser for all devices is more convenient.

Click Next once the parameters have been adjusted. You can adjust the entrance requirements for the apps themselves on the "Access requirements" screen that appears next. You may make the app request a PIN even when you are unable to make the device ask for one. Make these your top choices. Matching the PIN requirements for company devices is the greatest way to make things easier to grasp for end users. The following page, titled "Conditional launch," allows you to specify more guidelines for opening the application, like the ones listed below:

- **Maximum PIN tries:** The maximum number of times an erroneous PIN can be input. You can then choose to either erase all the data or modify the PIN.

- **Offline grace period:** How long after access is blocked do you allow users to use the data? How many days do you remove the information after?
- **Disabled account:** Grant access or block.
- The minimum app version is the most recent version that is still functional.

Additionally, you may ensure that the gadget doesn't do the following:

- **Devices that are jailbroken or rooted:** Remove or disable information.
- **OS version, minimum or maximum:** Block, erase, or warn data. If you are setting this one, you should watch it closely.
- **Minimum patch version:** Block, wipe, or warn about data.
- **Device manufacturer(s):** Disable or remove any unnecessary content. When adding to this list, exercise caution as it is a "allow" list rather than a "block" list.
- **SafetyNet device attestation:** A security API verifies the authenticity of the operating system and app before deleting, blocking, or alerting users.
- Scan apps for threats and either block or alert them.
- Hardware-backed safety net examination is required.
- **Device lock required (low, medium, or high complexity):** Data can be wiped, blocked, or warned.
- **Minimum Company Portal version or Maximum Company Portal age:** In order to alert, halt, or remove data, it's critical to monitor the Minimum Company Portal version and Maximum Company Portal age. Your minimum will soon become obsolete nevertheless if it is out of current.
- Maximum permitted device threat level (secured, low, medium, or high): You must establish a connection with Defender for Endpoint in order to remove or block data.
- **Main MTD Service:** The primary MTD service on your device should be Defender for Endpoint or Mobile Threat Defense (if it's not from Microsoft). Its antivirus is this.

Click Next once the parameters have been adjusted. The following picture shows the configurations that were applied in this instance:

- We don't know anything about the devices themselves, thus this strategy is likewise focused on the user. You will notice on the following screen that we can't add this to the virtual groups "All Users" or "All Devices." We'll give it to the group of Intune Users. Click Next after that.
- The final step is to click Create and double-check your options.

Formulating the policy for conditional access

We currently have our app protection policy in place, complete with beautiful Block Access settings. But Intune is powerless to prevent customers from using Microsoft 365 apps on their own. Conditional access is required in order for that to occur. In this instance, we will draft the policy ourselves so you can comprehend the configurations. For most purposes, fresh policy examples are available. When configuring conditional access restrictions, it's crucial to keep in mind to put up a break-glass account that is unaffected by any policies. If you unintentionally set a policy that prevents anyone from entering, you can utilize this to enter the area and address the issue. A non-user account with an extremely strong password that is kept on paper in a secure location—ideally a fireproof safe—should be designated as a break-glass account. If possible, link it to an additional FIDO2 key that is stored in a separate safe. Remember that this account needs to be appropriately sealed off because it has full access to your environment and none of your conditional access controls are in effect. **The steps to access conditional access policies are as follows:**

- You have two options: click Conditional Access in Endpoint Security or use the Entra portal.
- Step 2: Click "Policies" and then "+New policy."
- After giving your policy a name, select "0 users and groups."
- Click Include, choose All Users, and then click Exclude to remove your break-glass account.
- Click on No cloud apps, actions, or authentication contexts selected in the following step.
- Choose every Cloud app. This setting should be all-inclusive.
- Select 0 conditions to proceed.
- Click Device Platforms Not Configured after that.
- Configure is set to Yes. We must limit the application of this method to Windows, iOS, and Android as app security is only compatible with those three operating systems.
- After choosing between iOS and Android, click "Done":

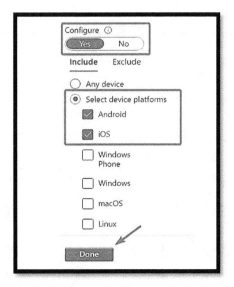

- Select the 0 controls located beneath Grant.
- Click Choose after selecting Require app protection policy.

- Session controls allow you to adjust various session-based parameters, such as how frequently you wish to check in. These are not required in this instance.
- At the bottom of the page, you can set the policy to Report -Only, Off, or On. The best method to observe what occurs with most policies is to set it to Report-Only. But since we don't want users to be able to access insecure apps, we can just set this security policy to On. Click Create after that.

Adding a controlled Android device to the enrollment

We can start registering our devices now that all of our policies are in place, starting with corporate accounts that are completely monitored. To accomplish this, we'll need an Android smartphone that can be completely erased. As soon as your Android smartphone reaches the page asking for your Gmail account, make sure your previously created QR code is ready.

How to proceed...

Depending on how old the device is, you have two options on the screen where you enter your credentials. On earlier devices, you will need to input afw#setup. **Continue tapping the same screen on modern devices:**

- Select Accept and Proceed from the "Let's set up your work device" prompt.
- Click Accept & Continue after you have scanned or manually entered your QR code.
- Click Next on the privacy screen.
- Select "Accept and Continue" from the Chrome screen.
- To log in, enter your email address and password.
- Configure the screen lock.
- Modify the notification settings, and then click "Next." Since we have it configured via policy, the settings are irrelevant in this case.
- Click "Install" when the "Install work apps" screen appears.
- After verifying the necessary applications (which vary based on each configuration), select "Done."
- Click "Set up" on the "Register your device" screen.
- Click the Sign In button on the Intune screen.
- Click "Done" to finish.

Your device's home screen will show up. You've finished! You've enrolled your Android device now.

Bringing Your Own Device (BYOD) to enroll

The section pertaining to corporate-owned devices came before this one. However, if you own a device, you can't restart and enroll it without a lot of objections. We will install our deployed apps in the secure work profile using the Company Portal app because these are work devices. Recall that individually owned devices associated with a work identity are turned on by default. You can either allow personal devices to register with a work profile or prevent them from doing so, depending on how your system is configured. Each has a somewhat different registration process, which we shall cover in this article for each.

Starting off

To see this, you'll need a current Android device that can connect to the Play Store and has a signed-in account.

How to proceed...

Let's first observe the results of your acceptance of personal enrollment in your tenancy.

Personal enrollment is permitted for enrollment.

Take these actions:

- Search the Google Play Store for the Intune Company Portal app, then select "Install."
- After finishing, select "Open."
- Upon loading, select Sign In.
- You will need to configure and register your work page after entering your login details. Click "Begin."
- Verify the permissions settings and press the Proceed button.
- After that, you have one more set of terms to agree to and proceed.
- The phone will now configure the work profile. A few minutes may pass during this process. You should click Next on the screen that appears after that.

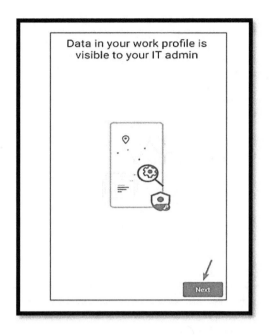

Data in your work profile is
visible to your IT admin

Next

- This will activate the system and return you to the Company Portal. You will be returned to the initial screen when logging in once more, but this time you will be allowed to access the work page. Click "Continue."
- After about a minute, you will be brought back to the screen where everything should be configured. Click "Done."
- I'll now give you a quick rundown of how a work profile works. Click "Got It."
- To view the available apps, click the Open button in the bottom notification. You can also click on the Play Store symbol that has a bag next to it:

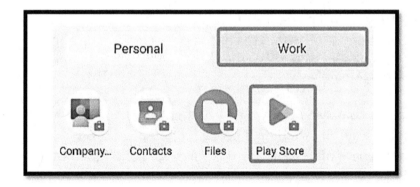

As you can see, we made Outlook an open application, and it now appears here. If we install it, it will be added to the work profile, over which we have control over the data.

Every app with a work profile has a bag-like symbol. Let's now examine the consequences of having your personal enrollment banned.

Blocking enrollment by personal enrollment

This procedure still makes use of the Company Portal to ensure adherence to our app protection guidelines. **The program serves as an intermediary and does nothing else; you cannot add apps from within it.**

- Locate and install Microsoft Outlook (or Word, Excel, or any other program).
- Once installed, select "Open."
- **Following your login, you will see the following screen. Select "GO TO STORE":**

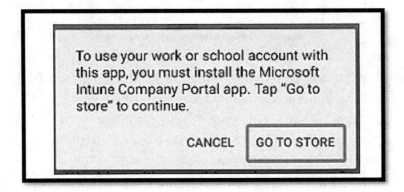

- You can access the Company Portal by clicking this link. Select Install. Once installed, select "Open."
- Afterwards, you will be redirected to Outlook, where you can carry on normally. All of the information within the app is protected by the app security policy.

Practice Exercises

1. Configure a controlled Google Play account
2. Explain the ways of including a policy for app protection
3. Explain the ways of formulating the policy for conditional access

CHAPTER SEVEN
USING INTUNE TO MANAGE MACOS DEVICES

We'll look at how to deploy and set up a business device. For this, it will be configured for Apple Education or Business Manager. You can enroll and configure your macOS devices by following these instructions. We will also cover configuring Intune to operate with Apple Business Manager and deploy apps via the Volume Purchase Program.

Setting up a policy for the macOS Settings catalog

After reviewing the many policy kinds available, it is evident that the settings catalog offers the greatest flexibility. This is the greatest approach to acquire settings on your macOS device because it is updated with new ones all the time. The fact that you can now export and import the settings catalog directly from the user interface is another feature that sets this policy option apart from others.

To discover how to configure your devices, read this section.

Using the settings catalog, we will configure our first macOS policy:

- First, select macOS from the Devices menu.

- After that, select New Policy from the Create menu under Configuration Profiles.
- After choosing the Settings catalog, press the Create button.
- Click Next after giving it a name and a description, if desired.

As with our iOS and Windows devices, we must add settings. Here, you can select the parameters that suit your environment the best. Apply the same "less is more" mentality that Windows did. Numerous minor policies are preferable to a few large, difficult-to-manage policies. In order to accomplish this, we will protect the device, apply a few basic restrictions, and enable OneDrive Known Folder Move (KFM) and Files On-Demand. Again, for basic security, the CIS and NCSC baselines (additional information available by clicking the link in the "Important Notes" section) can be of use. Remember that most of the macOS settings we utilize are often set to "allow" rather than "block." Use caution while choosing your phrases so as not to create a system that let through everything you intended to restrict.

Click Next as soon as the settings are correct:

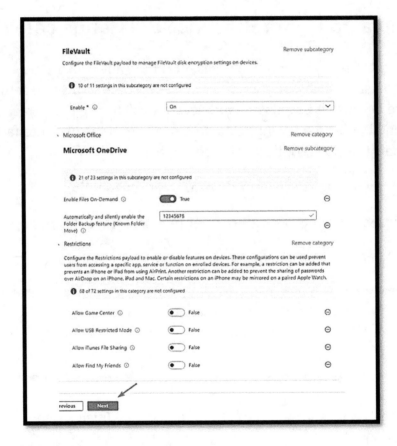

➢ Click Next on the Scope Tags page.

We selected settings that will apply to all devices because this is a device-restricting policy, allowing us to use the "All Devices" assignment. We could even go so far as to restrict the application of the filter to macOS devices alone. It's preferable to omit any options that might need to be configured differently for various user groups when creating basic policies. This holds true for every other policy as well. In this manner, you may establish a single standard for the entire estate and handle on/off scenarios that aren't covered by the standard using the smaller, more straightforward rules. When you have finished configuring your task, click Next. Make sure everything appears good in the final step before clicking Create.

Shell script deployment on macOS

Using PowerShell scripts, you may do operations on Windows devices, such as using a custom OMA-URI or the settings catalog, that are not possible with any other tool. On macOS-powered computers, shell scripts can be utilized in their place. These can be configured to operate at the user or system level. Owing to its foundation in UNIX, macOS has the ability to configure nearly any device.

Starting off

We'll start by going over the requirements and considerations for using shell scripts:

Required conditions

Before you can accomplish this, you must be running at least macOS 11.0. There must be a direct internet connection available to your devices—proxy servers are not allowed. Scripts must begin with #!

Taking into Account

- Shell scripts execute concurrently, meaning that many scripts deployed will execute simultaneously.
- Scripts that are deployed under the signed-in user's account will execute on all signed-in accounts on the device at that moment.
- User-level scripts require the user to be logged in in order to function.
- Higher command-level user-level scripts must be executed by root.
- While you can control the frequency of a script's execution, it may run more frequently if the device undergoes any changes (cache clearing, device restarts, etc.).
- Shell scripts are limited to 200 KB in size.
- If a script runs for longer than an hour, it will time out, stop, and be recorded as failed.

When these are completed, we may start writing our first shell script. You will not learn how to write shell scripts from this article. Rather, it will cover how to set them up on your devices. Before you begin, a shell script in a.sh file is required. You will also learn how to deploy a custom profile with these procedures, which is necessary for your script to function on devices.

How to proceed...

The shell script needs to be deployed first. Following that, we may organize the deployment plan.

How to Use a Shell Script

Follow these steps to insert a shell script into Intune:

- First, we must select Devices, then macOS.
- Select Shell scripts from the macOS policies menu, then click Add. After giving it a name and a description, select Next:
- Click the folder button to select your script.
- **The read-only editor will display the contents of the script beneath the script path on the screen. If you need to make changes, you will have to upload the file again:**

```
# Define variables
usebingwallpaper=true # Set to true to have script fetch wallpaper from Bing
wallpaperurl="https://numberwang.blob.core.windows.net/numberwang/macOSWallpaper.jpg"
wallpaperdir="/Library/Desktop"
wallpaperfile="Wallpaper.jpg"
log="/var/log/fetchdesktopwallpaper.log"

# start logging

exec 1>> $log 2>&1
```

The details are displayed beneath the script name. Run script as signed-in user is set to No because, as the figure above illustrates, we want the script to run as an administrator. Don't send any alerts to us, please. Daily execution of the script is required in order to alter the backdrop.

+ **After configuring the parameters for your script, click Next:**

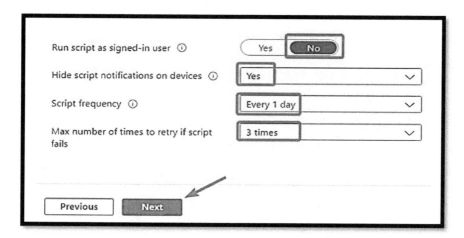

Click Next as we are not currently establishing any scope tags. Assign as required. In order to have distinct images for every user group, we'll use Intune users; however, if the corporate background is pre-set, all devices with a filter will also function as intended. After completing your assignments, click Next. Finally, confirm that everything is correct before clicking "Add."

Setting up an individual profile

Our script is ready to download the wallpaper image to the device; all we need to do now is instruct it to use it.

How will we accomplish by deploying a customized profile?

+ Navigate to Configuration Profiles to get started. Click Create after that, and then select New policy.
+ Choose Templates | Custom from the drop-down menu. Click Create after that.
+ Choose a heading and summary for your new page.
+ Choose whether the option is effective for the user or the device and give it a name. Rebuilding the profile is your sole choice if you make a mistake in this selection as it cannot be altered once the profile has been created.
+ Your file can only be read when it appears in the window below after you upload it. In this instance, the file must run in the device context. After making any necessary adjustments, click Next: to proceed.

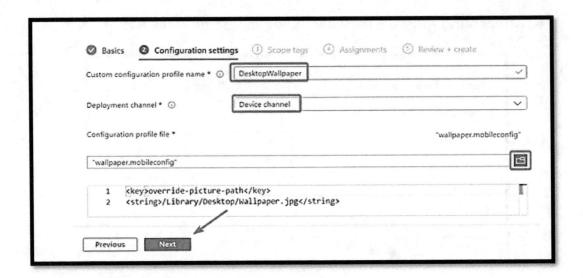

- Again, scope tags are not needed in this instance, so click Next.
- Click Next after making sure that this assignment matches the custom script that was started earlier.
- Verify that everything appears correct, and then select "Create."
- Going one step further, you can set Allow Wallpaper Modification to False in the settings menu to prevent users from changing the wallpaper.

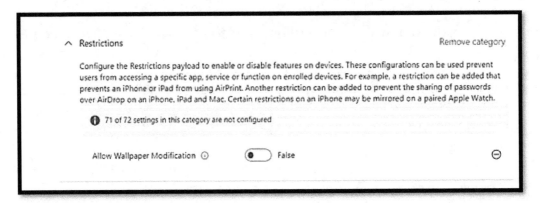

Setting up macOS update policies

Like our Windows and iOS devices, we want to make sure they're all running the most recent version of the operating system to keep the entire estate safer. You can build an update policy for macOS using the Software Updates group in the Settings catalog, the Software Updates template in Profiles, or a specific menu item. In this instance, we will maintain consistency across all platforms by using the dedicated update policy page. You will constantly be aware of where to obtain your updates in this manner. Similar to Windows devices, it is recommended to employ deployment rings for a large macOS area in order to test upgrades before to their distribution to all users.

How to proceed...

+ Select macOS after going to Devices.
+ After that, select Update Policies for macOS.
+ Choose "Create profile."
+ As usual, we'll begin by giving it a name and a description before clicking Next.
+ You have the option to select what to do with Firmware updates, Configuration file updates, critical updates, and all additional upgrades.
+ **Here are the options available to you:**
  ➢ **Unconfigured:** Take no action.
  ➢ **Download and install:** Depending on the situation, either download or install.
  ➢ **Download only:** Just download; don't install.
  ➢ **Install right away:** Download and wait for a notification to restart (this works best for devices without users).
  ➢ **Notify only:** Install the updates and enable notifications in system preferences.
  ➢ **Install later:** Download and put off installing (not for significant operating system upgrades). When this option is used, the maximum number of user deferrals prior to installation as well as the priority (low or high) for all additional updates will be displayed.

Similar to iOS, you can also create a plan that includes or excludes devices. For instance, you can program a schedule to only install upon the device's subsequent Intune check-in. To align with the regular workday, the active hours could be adjusted to 8:00 AM to 18:00 PM. If you only want updates made when it's not active, you may also set it to update when they're not scheduled to happen. However, in order to ensure that updates are installed, you must require them to occur throughout the workday as your users might turn off their devices at the end of the day. In this instance, select Update during the scheduled time. We'll install the most recent updates during our next check-in.

⬇ **Click Next once your environment has been configured.**

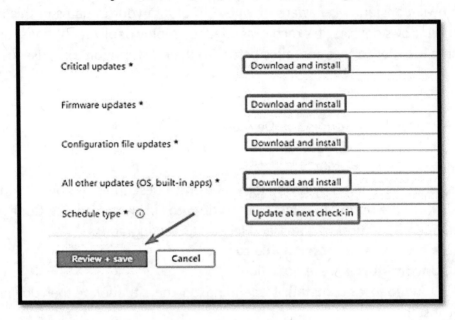

⬇ Select Next again; scope tags are not needed.

Review your assignments now with the modifications you made to the policy. You might want to think about establishing many rules for various user groups or device kinds, each with a separate set of settings. Here, we'll limit our designation to Intune users, giving us the freedom to leave out other groups as needed. iOS devices don't let you change the OS version, in contrast to Windows devices that let you choose between several deployment rings.

⬇ Choose Next once everything has been configured.
⬇ Make sure everything is in order before clicking "Create."

We may construct our update policy using the Intune UI.

Installing programs on macOS

The end users will still want some apps to be installed even after we have configured and secured our devices.

Among the options available in Intune are:

- Microsoft 365 Apps: A GUI to deploy M365 apps
- Microsoft Edge: To deploy Edge version 77 and later (Chromium)
- Microsoft Defender for Endpoint: To protect your devices
- Web link: Deploy a URL to the desktop
- Line-of-business app: Deploy a custom pkg application
- macOS app (DMG): Upload and deploy a DMG-based application
- App Store app: Similar to iOS, this deploys a VPP app from the App Store

Starting off

To deploy programs from the App Store, make sure you have a DMG file ready to go and that you can access Apple Education or ABM.

How to proceed...

The instructions for each of these can be found on the Intune website under Apps, followed by macOS apps.

The App Store

Take the action listed below:

- Visit ABM and select Books and Apps.
- **Find the desired software and confirm that it is a macOS app. In this instance, GarageBand will be used:**

After selecting the app, purchase permissions for your MDM, and then select Get:

- This app ought to appear in Intune very immediately.
- **Returning to the Intune website allows you to view the application that hasn't been distributed yet. Click on it to set up assignments:**

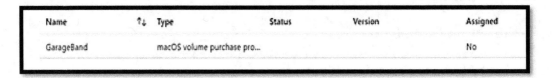

- **Navigate to Properties and select Assignments > Edit.**

Assign the application the necessary role. As is usually advised for programs such as this one, create install and uninstall groups specifically for this application. For a common app like M365 or Edge, the assignments may be more generic. Additionally, the application has the option to be forced to install (Required) or self-service (Available). One option for using license-free free apps is to require group members to install them (only those required for work), then allow others to install them as needed.

Following the addition of the assignment, the options listed below will appear:

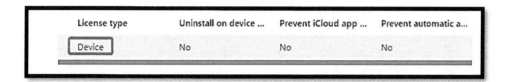

License type	Uninstall on device ...	Prevent iCloud app ...	Prevent automatic a...
Device	No	No	No

The most crucial decision in this case is the kind of license. We must be careful when selecting a Device license because we don't want our users to require an Apple ID in order to run apps. Any of the blue text links will open in a pop-up menu with further options when you click on it. You can adjust these settings to suit your requirements. Since the program saves passwords, we want to require updates and prevent it from being backed up until the device is removed from Intune management. When you're finished configuring your needs, click OK.

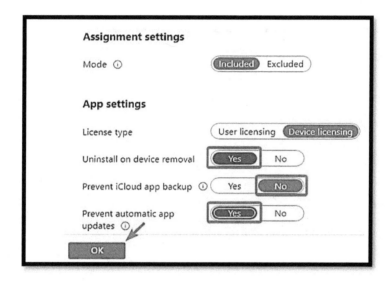

Click Review and Save once your settings and assignments are satisfactory. We are making adjustments to an existing app; therefore there isn't a Create or Add option. Once everything appears to be in order, click "Save."

DMG programs

Apps had to be packaged in the.intunemac format when Intune for macOS originally launched; this is comparable to how Windows Win32 apps are packaged in the intunewin format. We were fortunate that the ability to directly deploy.dmg files appeared in early 2022. You must install a DMG file on your devices in order to proceed with this part. We'll be using Adobe Acrobat Reader for this example (click More Options to select the macOS version if you're coming from Windows):

Now, carry out these actions:

- Go back to the Apps/macOS Intune page and click "Add."
- Choose macOS App (DMG) from the drop-down menu, and then click Select.
- Choose Select app bundle file.
- In the pop-up window, choose the DMG file you downloaded previously, and then click OK.
- Complete the remaining application fields. Giving end customers an image and topic will help them navigate the corporate website more easily if you allow them do this on their own. Once you've entered the necessary data, click Next:

- You can select the OS version that the program requires in order to run on the next screen. We'll go with the most recent OS version because the installer is compatible with all of them.

- You can use device filters to ensure that only the appropriate devices are installed when you grant them access to a mixed estate, even if you have multiple versions of the same software deployed.
- After you've selected a version, click Next.
- Now, we have to examine application detection. Examine or ignore the app version first. In order for the app to remain accessible after an update, you should leave the Ignore app version set to Yes if the app updates itself.
- If you select "No," the program will not be uninstalled until the app bundle ID and version match (when a person or device is added to the uninstall group). When this is set to "Yes," Intune ignores the version and simply examines the bundle ID.
- **Install the application on a test PC, then type the following command in Terminal (instead of using Adobe Acrobat Reader) to obtain the bundle ID:**

```
osascript -e 'id of app "Adobe Acrobat Reader"'
```

- The app list verifies the case, therefore pay special attention to the name.
- We need to enter the app version, however it won't be used because we have it set to Yes in the Ignore app version field. Click Next once you've configured.

- By selecting Next, we may bypass the Scope Tags page.
- As with the shop app, groups will be used for both needed and uninstall assignments. Applications that DMG deploys lack a self-service option. When you have finished adding your groups, click Next.
- Make sure everything is in order before clicking "Create."

Apps for Microsoft 365

After discussing the more complex programs, let's speak about the simpler, graphical user interface (GUI) versions of your most essential Microsoft applications. It is normally recommended to install Microsoft 365 apps as Win32 software that comes with the Office Deployment Tool (ODT) due to the way applications and policies are handled.

However, the GUI functions flawlessly and is free of the following issues on macOS:

+ In the macOS apps, create a new app, select macOS from the Microsoft 365 app list, and then click Select.
+ Fortunately, all of the standard application information is already filled in for you when you go to the following screen.
+ Although there are more options available here for Windows deployment, this is a straightforward macOS setup.
+ After making any necessary adjustments to your settings, click Next.
+ We don't currently require scope tags, so click Next once again.
+ Assign the application the necessary role. Although these apps are typically required by all users, you can alternatively use this dynamic rule to establish a dynamic group that consists only of users with licenses for Office desktop applications.

```
(user.assignedPlans -any (assignedPlan.servicePlanId -eq "43de0ff5-c92c-
492b-9116-175376d08c38"   -and   assignedPlan.capabilityStatus   -eq
"Enabled"))
```

+ The deployment options in this instance are either required or optional. Unlike a DMG program, you can utilize self-service with accessible assignments, but you cannot uninstall it.
+ Next, we'll click and utilize the Intune-Users group.
+ Verify everything one last time, and then click "Create."

Microsoft Edge

Installing Microsoft Edge on your macOS devices may also be a good idea if you want to maintain control, sync your work across platforms, and use Defender for Endpoint. Fortunately, this is just another easy GUI configuration. Make a new application. Select macOS from the menu this time, under Microsoft Edge, version 77. The update to the latest Edge Chromium version was version 77. Click Select after that. Remember that the data is pre-filled, just like with M365 apps, but you are unable to upload or edit the photo at this moment. This is because the image selection is dependent on the channel selected on the subsequent screen. Make any necessary adjustments, and then click the Next button. You can select the version of Edge to use from Dev, Beta, or Stable on the next screen. Like with OS updates, you should offer the Dev and Beta versions to test users in addition to making stable the default option for the majority of your consumers. This enables you to verify that, prior to applying the changes, all web-based applications function as intended. Additionally, it notifies you in advance of any UI changes that you might wish to communicate to your users.

In this instance, we will use the Stable version:

⊹ **Press Next as usual on the Scope tags screen.**

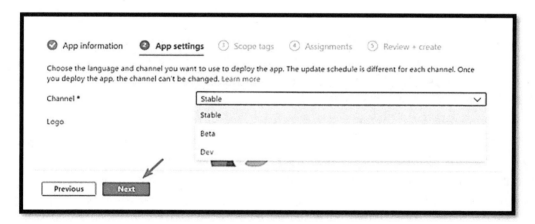

⊹ As previously discussed, you should have this app installed on all of your users' devices, but you might choose to use deployment rings instead for testing purposes.
⊹ Giving the application to a group offers you extra authority as a result.

- Remember that there is no "uninstall group" option; however, you can include it in a standard "Required" installation so that users can perform the removal themselves.
- In this instance, the Intune-Users group will be used.
- Making sure that everything appears excellent is the final stage. Click Create after that. Remember that the badge has already been added to match the channel you selected.

Microsoft Endpoint Defense

The last program we might want to install is Microsoft Defender for Endpoints. This can be used to prevent malware from getting in our system and, if we have a license, to use some of the additional functions, such as web filtering. NOTE: There are certain prerequisites that must be installed on your system before you can launch the software.

Follow these steps to configure Microsoft Defender for Endpoint on macOS:

- Like with other Microsoft products, the UI is straightforward. Create a new application and select macOS under Microsoft Defender for Endpoint this time. Click Select after that.
- Again, everything you need is already there, including the unchangeable picture. Once you've made any necessary adjustments, click "Next."
- We move directly to the Scope tags page for Defender for Endpoint because it lacks any settings or other configuration options. Click "Next."
- Again, we have the option to deploy whenever necessary or feasible, but we are unable to uninstall it. Since this is a security application, we want to make sure that it is installed on all of our devices; therefore we will choose All Devices.

To make things more organized, as we've already discussed, you might apply a filter to just include macOS devices. Click Next once you've entered your assignment.

- Make sure everything is in order before clicking "Create."

Setting up an enrollment profile for macOS

Before we can enroll our first macOS device, there is one more step to take: much like with iOS, we must create an enrollment profile.

Starting off

You must set up an enrollment token and connect your Intune instance to ABM in order to accomplish this.

Before proceeding, please complete the following sections if you haven't already:

- Setting up an Apple and Intune connection
- Tokens for enrollment profiles are added

Take the action listed below:

- Click Devices first. Click on macOS after that.
- To enroll in macOS, click.
- Go to Enrollment Program Tokens and click.
- **Press the token that you previously created:**

Token name	↑↓	Status	Program type	↑↓
Intune		⊘ Active	Apple Business Manager	

- Click on Profiles after that. This is where your iOS profile should be if you've already setup one.
- From the drop-down menu next to "Create profile," choose macOS.
- After entering a name and a description, click the Next button.
- Just like with our iOS profiles, there are a few things we need to configure.

User affinity: This indicates whether or not a person will be connected to the gadget. In order to enroll non-kiosk devices, you must select "Enroll with User Affinity." After selecting this, an additional option for Authentication Method will appear. Here, we should select Setup Assistant with contemporary authentication. If the page is locked, it indicates if the user can remove it. This should be set to "Yes" for corporate devices to prevent users from unenrolling their devices from the network.

- When you're finished, click Next.

- On the next configuration screen, you may select what to show and hide. You can simply set them all to Hidden as you don't need to use any of them. It is necessary to place the area's information at the top. Click Next after your settings are in place.
- Right now, we have to research and develop the profile. Verify everything, and then select "Create."
- We must set it as our default profile right now. It will be the default operating system on all new macOS devices sold by ABM.
- When you see the profiles screen again, select Default Profile.
- Choose the most recent profile created under the macOS Enrollment profile, and then click OK.

We have created our first macOS profile in Intune by using the UI.

Activating your work device

We may add our first device now that our system is configured to manage and control macOS devices. Since the majority of these are typically controlled by corporations, this section will solely address full ABM enrollment. It is advised to disable personal enrollment for macOS devices.

Starting off

You will need a smartphone that has been reset to factory settings and is already enrolled in ABM or Apple Education in order to complete this part. It needs to be accessible online as well.

How to proceed...

You will see a screen where you can select your language when you initially power on your device. After making the appropriate selection, click Proceed.

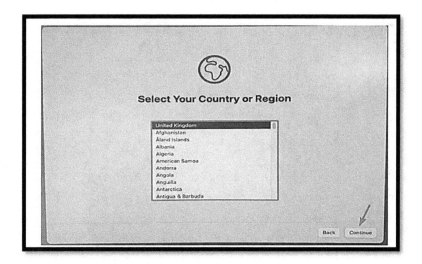

Now that you've selected a nation, macOS will automatically adjust the language settings; but, if necessary, you may click Customize Settings to make modifications.

+ Click Continue after that.

Depending on how your enrollment profile is configured, you may see additional screens here, such as the Accessibility settings.

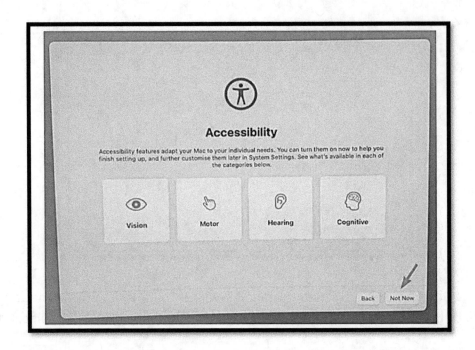

After adjusting any additional settings, you will be prompted to connect to a Wi-Fi network if the device is not already connected physically. After choosing your network and providing your password, click Proceed.

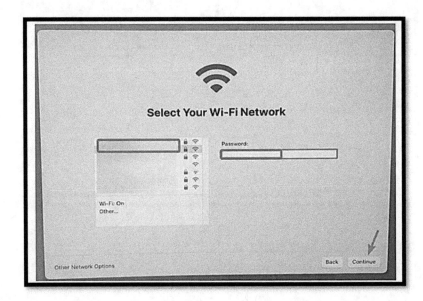

Unlike when you set up an unmanaged device, you will be prompted to accept remote management. Click "Continue."

Enter the details for your Microsoft account (password and username). If prompted, create a user account on the gadget, and then select Proceed. Enter the account details after that. Lastly, select your time zone and press the Proceed button: Fantastic work! For your very first macOS device, you have enrolled in Intune.

Practice Exercises

1. Set up a policy for the macOS Settings catalog
2. Explain Shell script deployment on macOS
3. Set up macOS update policies
4. Install programs on macOS
5. Set up an enrollment profile for macOS

CHAPTER EIGHT
SETTING UP YOUR PROTOCOLS FOR COMPLIANCE

Enrolled devices (Windows, macOS, iOS, and Android) can be guaranteed to be under control, up to date, and compliant with our requirements by using compliance policies. Devices need to adhere to a set of guidelines that we can establish with these in order to be deemed functional in the world. Subsequently, a conditional access policy can be implemented to ensure that devices that do not comply with the standards are unable to access company data. This not only makes you safer but also enables you to rapidly inspect your estate for any major issues. Along with demonstrating how to implement these policies, we will examine the requirements for each setting on the device. We will also discuss the more sophisticated bespoke compliance technique for Windows. Finally, we will examine how to restrict access from non-compliant workstations using conditional access. We must first put up one setting for the renter before we can set up our policies. This configuration instructs Intune on how to handle devices that aren't assigned any compliance policies. Navigate to Devices, then Compliance to accomplish this. Next, click on the Compliance policy settings.

The two settings we have are as follows:

- **Devices without a compliance policy should be noted as:** Without a policy, a device may not adhere to various settings, which could pose a security concern. The best option is always to set this to "non-compliant".
- **Validity term of compliance status (days):** You can select how long to accept an outdated status report here. For example, if a device hasn't checked into Intune, how many days should pass before it's flagged as noncompliant? To put it simply, consider Windows updates. You can presume that a machine missing at least one set of updates—which might include malware descriptions and updates—if you haven't seen it in thirty days or more.

We'll maintain the second setting at 30 days, and devices without a policy will be labeled as "Not Compliant." Once these are configured, click Save. What to deal with non-compliant devices is another setting that is used by all compliance policies.

Reactions to non-adherence

After choosing the compliance settings, we also need to tell Intune what to do if it discovers devices that don't comply with the requirements:

- **Note the non-compliant device:** It is up to you to decide how long a device must remain non-compliant before being labeled as such. Although, as we have previously stated, setting it to "immediately" might not be compatible with every verification rule, doing so increases the risk to security.
- **Email the final user:** The number of days that will elapse before the user receives an email informing them that the device is noncompliant can also be selected. You have the ability to modify the sent message and forward a copy to another party, such as your IT personnel. Here, you have the option to set up many forms that, before simply denying them access, issue various warnings to the offending party.
- **Add the following gadget to the retire list:** The device will be placed on a list to be retired when the number of days has been selected. Until the administrator retires the devices using Compliance Policies' Retire non-compliant devices menu, nothing will happen.

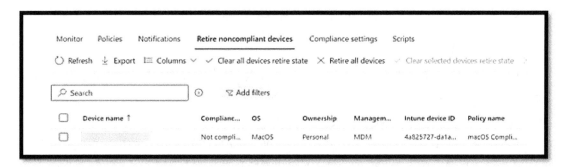

- Send an end-user push notification (available only on Android and iOS): This functions similarly to email except that the message is displayed on the screen and cannot be altered.
- **Lock the non-compliant device remotely (available only on iOS and Android): This option prevents the user from using the device:**

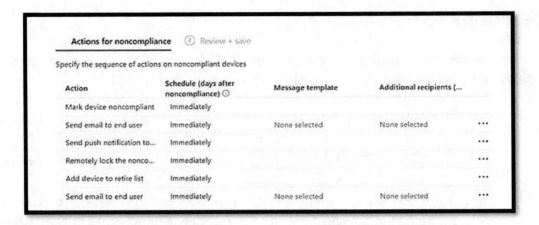

How to Personalize Templates for Notifications

When a system reaches its threshold, it can notify the end user via email (which it can also forward to other distribution lists) that their device isn't compliant. People can be informed of this in advance of the gadget becoming non-compliant.

Since these are cross-platform, the first portion will walk you through the process of creating your template.

- Go to Devices and then Compliance to get started.
- Click Notifications to create a new notification.
- First, you need to select the corporate appearance and name for the template. Tenant information is the source of the business data. Once finished, select Next.
- On the following screen, you can alter the language and message. If your business is international, you may receive more than one notice. You must set one as the default before you can click Next to proceed.
- To proceed past the scope tags, click Next.
- Once you're certain that everything is correct, click Create.

Putting a Windows Compliance Policy into Practice

There are two approaches to set up compliance policies for Windows devices. Although we will discuss both of them here, we will begin with the simpler, GUI-driven one.

Starting off

As previously stated, before drafting our policy, we should examine the settings and what they accomplish.

Configurations for Compliance

Let's start by talking about the current compliance settings that are available.

Adherence to customs

A customized PowerShell utility allows for the tracking of device modifications and their addition to a compliance policy.

Device Safety

The Device Health regulations make use of the Device Health Attestation service. It's crucial to understand that, among other things, they are checking the BIOS, thus they must restart the machine in order to report back. Therefore, wait before marking devices as non-compliant if you make changes to these settings.

Your new devices won't be able to access them if you do. Now let's review the settings located under Device Health:

- **Bitlocker:** This application determines whether a drive is BitLocker-encrypted.
- **Secure Boot:** This verify that UEFI has enabled Secure Boot.
- **Code integrity:** scans firmware and drivers for indications of corruption or malicious activities

Properties of the Device

The following options are available to us under the heading "Device Properties":

- The operating system version, expressed in the format major.minor.build.revision, is the minimum OS version. Assume for the moment that we desired Windows 11 22H2 May 2023. That would be 10.0.22621.1702 in the number.
- **Maximum OS version:** This is the same as Minimum OS version, but if you wish to restrict it to non-test builds, you may also choose a maximum version.

- For mobile devices, the minimum and maximum operating system versions are as follows: don't worry, this is for Windows Mobile.
- **Valid builds for operating systems:** This allows you to specify several minimum and maximum builds. Adding one entry for each of the Windows 10 and 11 versions, with the minimum set to the most recent Authorized Version, would be one example. Only supported versions would be compatible with this.

Compliance with Configuration Manager

- Set require device compliance from Configuration Manager if your environment and Configuration Manager cooperate.
- All of your devices must abide by the configuration manager's rules in order for Configuration Manager to be required.

Safety of System

These choices are found under "System Security": Make mobile devices require a password to unlock: This is a Windows option that deals with Windows Hello for Business PINs, not smartphone passwords.

- Easy passwords: Easy PINs, such as 0000 or 1234, will not be permitted.
- **The password type could be any of the following:**
  - ➢ **Device Default:** Numeric PIN, Password, or Numeric PIN with Letters
  - ➢ **Numerical:** Only utilize PINs or passwords composed entirely of numbers.
  - ➢ **Alphanumeric:** Only alphanumeric or a password

Selecting the alphanumeric option will add an additional layer of complexity.

- The amount of digits in the PIN (as long as it fits how you set up other PINs and is permitted by business policy) is the minimum password length.
- The maximum amount of time that can pass before a password is needed is one minute, eight hours, or even Not Configured. In order to strike a decent balance between security and user experience, it is advised that you wait fifteen minutes.
- **Password expiration:** Before a password expires (1–730 days), how many days do users have to change it?
- The number of past passwords that must be entered before a password can be used again in order to avoid its reuse.

- Password required when device returns from idle state: Only Holographic and Windows Mobile demand a password upon device return from idle mode.
- Instead of pressuring users to utilize the options, they will simply check to see if the gadget can handle them. In the event that no additional rules (Settings library, for example) were configured, the device would be flagged as non-compliant.

The use of encryption

Let's examine the configurations found under the Encryption section:

- Require device data storage to be encrypted: This security check doesn't require a computer restart, but it is less complicated than the "Require BitLocker" option.

Security of Devices

"Device Security," the next section, contains the following configurations:

- Windows Firewall needs to be activated in order to monitor traffic.
- **Trusted Platform Module (TPM):** Only Windows 10 computers can install Windows 11 since a TPM is necessary for the installation.
- **Antivirus:** There has to be antivirus software installed. As long as the Security Center has identified it and has access to it, this might be Windows Defender or something else entirely. If you're collaborating with a third party, a bespoke compliance policy might provide you with more choices.
- Similar to antivirus software, antispyware prevents spyware.

Defender

Within "Defender," the following configurations are available:

- Verifies that the Microsoft Defender antimalware service is operational and turned on.
- Microsoft Defender Antimalware minimum version: 4.11.0.0 is the bare minimum of anti-malware software.
- Current security intelligence for Microsoft Defender Antimalware: Verifies that the signatures have changed.

- Protection in real time: This check verifies that the protection in real time is activated and operational.

Microsoft Endpoint Defense

Remember that in order to utilize these options, you will require a Defender for Endpoint license. Make sure you own the appropriate licenses before turning this option on. **Limit the device to being at or below the machine risk score. There are a few choices for this:**

- **Not Configured:** No configuration will be used.
- **Unambiguous:** There cannot be any hazards to the gadget.
- **Low:** Only low-level threats are possible for the gadget.
- **Medium:** There may be low to medium dangers to the device.
- **High:** All danger levels are permitted.

How to proceed...

Now that we know what each setting does, we can create our policy. We'll keep things really basic for this example, but you can modify it to suit your needs:

- Go to Devices and then Compliance to get started.
- Select "Create Policy" from the Policies menu.
- Click Create after selecting Windows 10 and later using the drop-down option.
- As with any other policy or profile, we begin with the Name and Description values and click Next.
- We now need to adjust our settings using the information we discussed before. In this scenario, we will require the use of all Device Health settings in addition to Firewall, TPM, Antivirus, and Antimalware.
- Once its set, click Next.
- The noncompliance actions are up next. We'll change that to 0.5 days because we previously said that our device health guidelines require a restart. The machine will be removed from the list of machines that must be retired once it hasn't been spotted for 180 days. After configuring your environment, click Next.

FOOTNOTE: This is just for reporting purposes; adding a device to the retire list does not actually retire it.

- We don't want to set Scope tags, therefore click Next.

FOOTNOTE: Verify that the appropriate set of users is assigned the policy when reviewing assignments for user-based devices. The policy will check the user account and the system account for non-compliance if the device is a part of a device group. The device will not comply if one of them is discovered.

- Device-based assignments are best suited for unmanned tools such as kiosks.
- The group Intune-Users will be utilized by us. When you're finished, click Next.
- Make sure everything is in order before clicking "Create."

The user interface now has a Windows compliance policy set.

Putting in Place an Android Compliance Policy

It's time to examine our company Android devices now. BYOD devices are handled by the App Protection policy because we have no control over them. To enable restricted devices to access company data, we can ensure that they continue to comply. Here, we will only be examining devices that are under corporate ownership and control. As with the Windows policy, we will begin by examining the available options and their functions.

Configurations for compliance

We may go over the many various compliance settings on our Android smartphones.

Properties of the Device

The following parameters are modifiable in Device Properties:

- The minimum and maximum operating system versions are simple to comprehend. Remember that they are simply for compliance; they won't prevent individuals from joining or force them to use a certain version.
- Minimum security patch level: Android upgrades include larger operating system modifications and security improvements, just like Windows updates do. These are often released once a month, and a compliance policy may stipulate a minimum version requirement. If there are any zero-day vulnerabilities, this might be useful. It must be formatted as YYYY-MM-DD.

Safety of System

The System Security configuration is as follows:

- Demand a password to open mobile devices: Keep in mind that this won't force them to use one, and if you don't take any action regarding your non-compliant devices, they will be able to continue using them without one.
- **Type of password that is required: There are the following options:**
  - ➤ **Device default:** Since this cannot be used to verify compliance, it is not a good idea to set it.
  - ➤ **No restrictions, no password needed:** You are not allowed to impose any additional restrictions.
  - ➤ **Numeric:** Only numbers are acceptable. An additional option is to choose a minimum length (4–16).
  - ➤ **Numerical complex:** There can only be numbers in this kind of complex; no patterns are allowed. An additional option is to choose a minimum length (4–16).
  - ➤ **Alphabetic:** Only letters found in the alphabet can be utilized. An additional option is to choose a minimum length (4–16).
  - ➤ **Alphanumeric:** Limited to numerals, tiny and capital letters. An additional option is to choose a minimum length (4–16).
  - ➤ **Alphanumeric with symbols:** Alphanumeric with symbols consists of numbers, symbols, punctuation marks, and both uppercase and lowercase characters. This also displays the lengthiest password that can be between four and sixteen characters, the bare minimum of characters that must be used between one and sixteen, the bare minimum of alphanumeric characters that must be used between one and sixteen, the bare minimum of non-letter characters that must be used between one and sixteen, and the bare minimum of symbol characters that.
- **Maximum minutes of inactivity before requiring a password:** Strike a balance between usability and security here. Anything from a minute to eight hours is possible.
- **Days till password expire:** There's no need for this field. It displays how many days remain till the password expires. To turn it off, you can leave the dates blank or provide a number between 1 and 365 days.

- The number of passwords that must be entered before a user can reuse one is also optional and can be set to any value between 1 and 24 if necessary. Once more, consider both the security implications and potential user issues.

Security of Devices

Lastly, Device Security has just one setting:

- **Runtime integrity for Intune App:** This verifies that Intune App (formerly known as Company Portal) is signed correctly, has the default runtime environment installed, and is not in debug mode.

How to proceed...

We now know how the settings function, so we can put up the rules. This time, we'll establish a few crucial points:

- Go to Devices and select Android to get started.
- Select the Compliance policies option.
- Select "Create policy."
- Select Android Enterprise from the drop-down box, and then select the fully managed, corporate-owned work profile.
- Click Create once these selections have been made.
- After entering a Name and a Description, click the Next button.
- **After making any required adjustments to the parameters, click Next. In this example, the following has been put up:**
  - **Perform Integrity Verdict:** Verify the fundamental and hardware integrity
  - **Type of password required:** The password must be six characters long, alphanumeric with symbols, and contain at least one of the available selections.
  - Need Encryption

Setting the noncompliance actions is now necessary. Since this is a mobile device, we will activate these additional options. After they're configured, select Next.

- Since scope tags are not required in this instance, click Next.
- Decide on your tasks. It's recommended to configure non-kiosk workstations with user-based assignments, just like Windows. In this scenario, you might utilize an Android filter in place of Intune users, and use All Users. You may

145

want to have various guidelines for different items. Once your assignments are established, click "Next."

- Once you're satisfied with how everything appears, click Create.

We have finally configured our Android compliance policy in the UI.

Putting in Place an iOS Compliance Policy

- Go to Devices and then Compliance to get started.
- Select "Create Policy" from the Policies menu.
- Click Create after selecting iOS/iPadOS from the drop-down option.
- After entering the title and brief description of your insurance, click the Next button.
- As necessary, adjust your settings. In this instance, we are blocking devices that have been compromised and email accounts that the user has set up.
- We're also going to set the password. Click Next once your environment is configured.
- For devices that aren't compliant, set the steps. You have the same option to select between emails and push alerts as you have with Android.
- Click Next as we won't be setting any Scope tags in this instance.
- We are implementing a user-based assignment once again for a better experience. Here, we are utilizing the Intune-Users group that we created. Since iOS devices are typically used by senior users, you might need to implement various policies for each user category. Once you've adjusted everything to your liking, click Next.
- Once you're certain that everything is correct, click Create.

Putting a macOS Compliance Protocol in Place

- Click Devices first, and then click Compliance.
- Select "Create Policy" from the Policies menu.
- Select macOS using the drop-down option, then press "Create."
- After entering a Name and a Description, click the Next button.
- With the information above serving as a guide, make the required adjustments to the settings. Click Next once you've configured.
- Establish the noncompliance steps. Since this isn't an iOS or Android smartphone, we can still lock the device remotely, however we are unable to send push notifications.

- Click Next since, as usual, we're not establishing any Scope tags in this instance.
- We are distributing to our Intune-Users group in accordance with our previous discussion on how giving to users yields better results.
- Verify everything one last time, and then click Create.

Putting a Linux Compliance Protocol in Place

- Navigate first to Devices and then Compliance.
- Select "Create Policy" from the Policies menu.
- From the fly-out's drop-down menu, select Linux. The Settings catalog will then appear in the bottom drop-down menu. Click Create after that.
- Click Next after filling out the Name and Description sections as usual.
- Click "Add settings."
- As needed, add your parameters. To find out which versions are still supported, start by visiting the Ubuntu version URL. After that, discard the ones that aren't supported any more. This is the only place where we will set a password because encryption is required.
- If we select "non-compliance," our sole option is to email the offender. You cannot retire the devices because they are unmanaged, and Linux does not support push notifications. The rest will be handled by the restricted access policy. We'll just label it as non-compliant for the time being.
- Click Next since, as usual, we'll ignore the Scope tags in this instance.
- We're dispersing them at the user level, just as with other regulations. Linux devices pose less of a risk to compliance, but they may be used by coders and other IT professionals, so you may need to adjust your policies. In this instance, we are using our Intune-Users Entra group. Once you've selected your task, click Next.
- After making sure everything is correct, click Create.

How to set up and put into practice a custom compliance policy for Windows

Occasionally, you will find that the built-in settings do not match your compliance. For example, you may need to monitor products sold by third parties or prohibit machines running specific software. You might also restrict your setting to a specific maker, model, and RAM capacity for compliance. Anything may be found and used for compliance with PowerShell. Using Intune, you can quickly establish a JSON policy that compares the PowerShell output to the parameters and values we specified in the JSON after the script is configured. When a setting is consistent, it achieves the desired result. It is not compliant if it isn't. A single noncompliant setting can significantly reduce a device's functionality. Now that we understand how it operates, we can configure our scripts.

A PowerShell script

The first step is to write our PowerShell script and send it to Intune. To complete this, take these actions:

- Click Devices first. Click Compliance after that.
- Scripts is now open. Click "Add," then select "Windows 10 and later."
- Put your Name and a brief description here. Additionally, you have a Publisher field that you can edit to display your name or your group name as needed. Click Next after that.
- Copy and paste your script into this box (files cannot be added here). No, that should remain at No, as we haven't signed the script yet. Additionally, we want this to operate at the system level as we are requesting BIOS. Finally, it's best to leave it at Yes because 32-bit vs. 64-bit shouldn't matter for our questions. Click Next after that.
- Check that everything is in order now, and then click Create.

Policy for compliance

With the script, we can now create the policy:

- Click on Create Policy under the Policies tab.
- From the drop-down menu, select Windows 10 or later, and then click "Create."
- After entering the information under Name and Description, click the Next button.
- The settings that we previously discussed are now visible. This time, Custom compliance is the sole setting we are making.
- Pick the script by clicking the blue button that reads "Click to select" after you've clicked "Require" in the "Custom compliance" section.
- Once your script has been selected from the list, click Select.

- Kindly select your JSON. You'll notice that it completes the script (this is a read-only box) as well as the search parameters. Proceed by clicking Next if you believe everything is in order.
- Choose Next once you've adjusted your non-compliance activities.
- Click Next because this is where we're not going to set any Scope tags.
- The goal of assigning at the user level is to prevent problems, just like with other policies. In this instance, Intune-Users will be utilized. When you're done putting up your task, click Next.
- Reviewing your policy and clicking "Create" is the last step.

All of it is required to configure our unique Windows compliance policy through the user interface.

Restricting Access Based on Compliance with Conditional Access

Before using compliance policies, one more thing must be completed. Certain mobile devices are locked down by our non-compliance settings, but most of the time we only inform consumers that their device isn't compliant, so they continue to use it. We do not want company data to be accessible on devices that do not adhere to our standards, such as unprotected or infected devices. We must first put up a conditional access policy technique in order to accomplish that. Please ensure that this breakglass account is established prior to the establishment of this policy. We can avoid including it in any restricted access policies in this way. In the event that a policy malfunctions and prevents others from entering, this will allow you to enter the setting.

How to go about it...

- Select Conditional access under Endpoint security to get started.
- To create a new policy, click.
- After naming the policy, select "0 users and groups."
- Select "All Users" from the Include list.
- You can omit your Break Glass account by clicking the "Exclude" tab. Consider your IT staff. To get them back in compliance with the regulations, they could have to employ these machines. The list of roles that are likewise prohibited in this situation will now include the position of Local Device Administrator.
- Select "No target resources" by clicking on it.

- Click All cloud apps in the Include tab; nothing should be accessible to these PCs.

We also do not want this policy to exclude anyone. In the future, however, you may want to consider excluding the Microsoft Intune Enrollment program if you wish to permit device registration in scenarios where a conditional access policy would typically prohibit it, such as location-based scenarios. Because they are not enrolled in MAM in any manner, personal devices that are not enrolled in it should not be blocked from using it. If we do, they will not comply. We shall utilize device-based filtering under certain conditions in this case.

- Under Filter for devices, choose 0 conditions, and then click Not configured.
- Make Device Ownership Equals Company the new rule. By doing this, the policy will be restricted to use on corporate-owned devices only. We created an additional policy here to mandate app security on our BYOD devices. Instead of replacing MFA, each of these measures provides an extra degree of security on top of it. Select "Done":

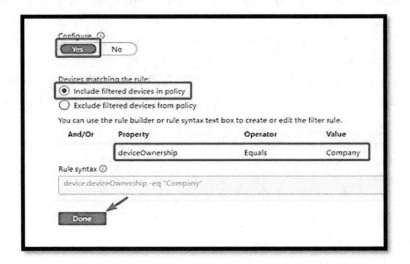

- Select 0 controls from the list of access controls.
- As this is a "allow" policy rather than a "block" policy, choose "Grant access". Next, choose the checkbox labeled "Device must be marked as compliant."
- If you set more than one setting here, you can specify if the condition is any or all of the options. Click Select once everything is configured.

- We can leave that option unconfigured as we don't require any session controls.

The final consideration is the state of the policy, which varies based on your surroundings. You'll receive calls to your IT help line if you set this to On because many non-compliant devices may prevent users from accessing corporate data. So, until you can resolve the issue, set it to "Report-only" and monitor who gets barred. After the majority of your devices have complied with the guidelines, activate the settings and increase security.

- In this instance, the policy will be activated.

Practice Exercises

- Set Up Your Protocols for Compliance
- Personalize Templates for Notifications
- Set up and put into practice a custom compliance policy for Windows

CHAPTER NINE
ABOUT MICROSOFT 365 INTEGRATION

Working together with Microsoft Teams

The information, people, and resources on your team come together in Microsoft 365 with Microsoft Teams, enabling them to collaborate more effectively and actively. You may secure your Microsoft 365 data in the most thorough and varied ways if you purchase for the Enterprise Mobility + Security suite, which includes Microsoft Intune and Microsoft Entra ID P1 or P2 features including restricted access. To enable mobile devices to connect to Teams for iOS and Android, you should at the very least set up a restricted access policy. To ensure the security of the teamwork experience, you should also set up an Intune app security policy.

Using Microsoft Intune, manage the Teams collaboration experiences on iOS and Android.

Utilize Conditional Access

Businesses can ensure that users of Teams for iOS and Android devices can only read content that is relevant to their jobs or studies by implementing Microsoft Entra Conditional Access policies. To accomplish this, you will require a restricted access policy that targets every potential user. Note: In order to deploy app-based restricted access restrictions on iOS devices, the Microsoft Authenticator app must be loaded. The Android app for the Intune Company Portal is required.

Establish Intune app security guidelines

You can find out which apps can access and use the data of your company from the App Protection Policies (APP). With the many options provided by APP, businesses may customize the security to meet their needs. It's possible that some users won't notice the policy settings required to complete a scenario. Microsoft has included taxonomy into its APP data protection framework for managing iOS and Android apps, assisting businesses in prioritizing mobile client endpoint security. There are three different setup settings for the APP data protection system.

Every level advances from the previous one:

- Apps that are private, PIN-protected, and allow for selective deletion are ensured by enterprise basic data security (Level 1). This tier ensures that the authentication of Android devices is accurate. This is a basic arrangement that allows IT and users to become acquainted with APP while providing the same data protection restrictions as Exchange Online folder policies.
- Enterprise-enhanced data protection (Level 2) includes techniques to prevent app data breaches and minimal OS requirements. Most mobile users who receive data from work or school will require this setting.
- Better PIN setup, APP Mobile Threat Defense, and advanced data security features are added with enterprise high data protection (Level 3). This approach works well for those who are browsing content that carries a high risk.

For both iOS and Android apps, you need to define an Intune app security policy, regardless of whether the device is a part of a unified endpoint management (UEM) system.

These policies should, at the absolute least, take into account the following factors:

- They consist of all mobile apps for Microsoft 365, such as Teams, Office, OneDrive, Edge, and Outlook. This guarantees that users of any Microsoft program can safely access and modify work or school-related data.
- Every user has these assigned to them. This safeguards all users of Teams, regardless of whether they are using iOS or Android.
- Determine which level of the structure best suits your requirements. Since they allow them to manage data security and access standards, the majority of enterprises should make use of the settings under Enterprise enhanced data protection (Level 2).

Reminder: In order to safeguard apps on Android devices that aren't enrolled in Intune with Intune app protection policies, users also need to install the Intune Company Portal.

Apply the app's settings

Managers of unified endpoint management (such as Microsoft Intune) can modify the functionality of Teams for iOS and Android devices via the app settings. Apps can be set up via the Intune App Protection Policy (APP) channel or the Managed App Configuration channel for iOS devices or the Enterprise channel for Android devices. Devices that have enrolled can use both of these channels.

Teams for iOS and Android can be utilized with the following configurations:

- **Permit only accounts for job or school.**

Every setup scenario enumerates the particular requirements associated with it. For instance, you want to be aware of whether the configuration requires device enrollment or Intune App Protection Policies, meaning that it is compatible with any UEM service. Keys for configuring an app are case-sensitive. Use the appropriate case to ensure the setup functions.

Footnote: Microsoft Intune refers to app configuration provided through the MDM OS channel as a Managed Devices App Configuration Policy (ACP). Microsoft Intune refers to the app configuration supplied through the App Protection Policy channel as a Managed Apps App Configuration Policy.

- **Permit only accounts for job or school.**

We adhere to the data security and compliance guidelines of our largest and most regulated companies, which is one of the most significant components of the Microsoft 365 value. Certain organizations are required to monitor all internal conversations and ensure that company-issued devices are exclusively utilized for business-related correspondence. It is possible to set up Teams for iOS and Android on enrolled devices so that the app can only be used by one company account. This satisfies these requirements. This configuration scenario is limited to enrolled devices. But any UEM service works just fine. To learn how to set up these setup keys if you're not using Microsoft Intune, consult your UEM instructions.

Domain-less sign-in makes the sign-in process simpler

You can facilitate sign-in to Teams for iOS and Android by pre-filling the domain name for users on shared and controlled devices by implementing the following policies:

Name	Value
domain_name	A string value providing the domain of the tenant to appended. Use a semicolon delimited value to add multiple domains. This policy only works on enrolled devices.
enable_numeric_emp_id_keypad	A boolean value used to indicate that the employee ID is all numeric and the number keypad should be enabled for easy entry. If the value is not set, then the alphanumeric keyboard will open. This policy only works on enrolled devices.

Microsoft Teams notification settings

Notifications let you know what's happening or about to happen in your immediate surroundings. They appear on the lock screen or the home screen, depending on how the settings are configured. Use the options below to configure your alerts through an app security policy on the website.

Options	Description
Allow	Display actual notification with all the details (title and content).
Block org data	Remove title and replace content with "You have a new message" for chat notifications, and "There is new activity" for others. A user won't be able to **Reply** to a notification from a lock screen.
Blocked	Suppresses notification and doesn't notify user.

For Android and iOS devices to display the notifications

+ Log in to the company portal on the device as well as Teams. To ensure that Teams can reach you through your device's alert settings, set it to Show Previews > Always.

- Notify the user logged in on the device about the message and lock the device. Tapping on a message on the lock screen displays it without requiring you to unlock the device.
- **Lock screen notifications should appear as follows (screenshots from iOS are provided; Android users should see identical text):**
    - ➢ The Reply and other quick reaction options for alerts from the lock screen shouldn't be shown to you.
    - ➢ The sender's photograph is not visible, but the initials are correct.
    - ➢ The text should read "There is new activity" for all alerts except chat notifications, and "You have a new message" for all other alerts. The notification title should appear.

Syncing with the Office 365 suite

Windows 10 and Windows 11 users can use Microsoft Intune to install the Microsoft 365 app suite

Apps must be added to Intune in order to be given, watched, configured, or protected. Among the app types that can be used are Microsoft 365 apps for devices running Windows 10 and 11. Selecting this app type in Intune will allow you to install and manage Microsoft 365 apps on Windows 10 or 11 devices. Should you own the appropriate rights, you can also distribute and configure applications for Microsoft Project Online desktop software and Microsoft Visio Online Plan 2. In the Microsoft Intune control panel, the list of apps shows the numerous Microsoft 365 apps as a single item.

Prior to commencing

It's crucial to remember that in order to securely remove any.msi Office programs that may be installed on the end user's device; you must utilize the Remove MSI tool. If not, installing the Microsoft 365 apps that Intune offered will be impossible. They don't add up if there are many required or open-app assignments.

A later app assignment will overwrite any loaded app assignments that are already there.

- Only devices running Windows 10/11 Creators Update or later are able to utilize these apps.
- You can only add Office programs from the Microsoft 365 programs suite to Intune.
- The app suite installation attempt by Intune may fail if any Office apps are running at the time, potentially causing users to lose data from unsaving files.
- Devices running Windows Home, Windows Team, Windows Holographic, or Windows Holographic for Business cannot be installed using this method.
- It is not possible to install Microsoft 365 desktop apps from the Microsoft Store if you have already installed Microsoft 365 apps on a device that uses Intune. We refer to these as Office Centennial apps. Installing this configuration can cause files to be lost or damaged.
- There isn't a surplus of required or open-app assignments. Any loaded app assignments will be replaced by a subsequent app assignment. For example, if Word is present in the first set of Office programs and not in the second, Word will be deleted. There is no need for any Visio or Project tool to handle this circumstance.
- It is currently not possible to have several Microsoft 365 deployments. The item will only receive a single deployment.
- Office version: Select whether to provide them with Office in 32- or 64-bit versions. While a 64-bit version can only be installed on 64-bit devices, a 32-bit version can be installed on both 32- and 64-bit systems.
- Take the MSI out of end-user gadgets. Select if you wish to erase Office.MSI apps that are already installed on end user devices. Should end-user devices have any pre-existing.MSI apps, the installation will fail. It will uninstall all Office (MSI) programs from the end user device, not only the ones that were chosen for installation in Configure App Suite. End users will receive the identical

language packs from their previous.MSI Office installations when Intune reinstalls Office on their computers.

Choose the Microsoft 365 Apps

- Log in at the Microsoft Intune admin center.
- Choose Add from Apps > All Apps.
- In the Microsoft 365 Apps section of the Select app type box, choose Windows 10 and later.
- The procedures for adding Microsoft 365 apps are displayed when you select "Select."

Step 1: Details about the app suite

In this phase, you provide information about the app suite. This information helps users locate the app suite on the company website and helps them identify the app suite in Intune.

- **On the App suite information page, you have the ability to modify or verify the following values:**
  - ➤ **Suite Name:** The name of the app suite that appears on the business page is this. Make sure the names you pick for each suite are unique. Users will only see one app suite on the corporate website if there are two suites with the same name.
  - ➤ **App Suite Description:** Provide an explanation for the app suite. For example, you may compile a list of the apps you've decided to add.
  - ➤ **Publisher:** Microsoft is listed as the publishing company.
  - ➤ **Category:** You can select one or more of the pre-made groupings provided by the app, or you can make your own category. When navigating the company portal or website, this setting makes it easier for consumers to find the app suite more quickly.
  - ➤ Choose this option to have the app suite appear as a highlighted app on the company portal. This will help customers find the app suite more easily when they search for apps on the homepage of the firm.
  - ➤ **Information URL:** You can enter the URL of a website containing details about this application if you so choose. Users can view the URL on the company website.

- ➢ **Privacy URL:** You have the option to enter the URL of a website with details about the privacy policies of this app. Users can view the URL on the company website.
- ➢ **Developer:** The developer is identified as Microsoft.
- ➢ **Owner:** It looks that Microsoft is the owner.
- ➢ **Notes:** Under "Notes," you can add any notes you'd like to link to this application.
- ↓ To view the Configure app suite page, click "Next".

Step 2: (Option 1) Use the configuration designer to configure the app suite

By selecting a Configuration settings format, you can select a template for modifying the settings of an application. Several options for format selection include:
- ↓ Designer of configurations
- ↓ Put in XML information.

When you select Configuration Designer in the Add app pane, three additional configuration boxes will appear:
- ↓ Set up the app suite.
- ↓ Details about the app suite
- ↓ Properties

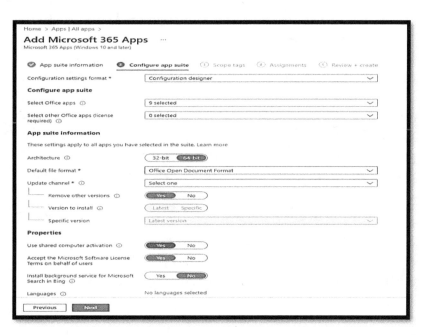

- **Navigate to Configuration App Suite page and select Configuration Designer.**
  - ➤ **Choose Office apps:** Choose the basic Office apps that you wish to distribute to devices by clicking on the apps from the dropdown menu.
  - ➤ **Choose more Office apps (licensing required):** You can grant devices access to additional Office apps that you are authorized to use by choosing the apps from the dropdown list. A few of these applications—such as Microsoft Visio Online Plan 2 and the Microsoft Project Online desktop client—are paid for.
  - ➤ **Architecture:** Select the Microsoft 365 Apps 32-bit or 64-bit version to attach. While a 64-bit version can only be installed on 64-bit devices, a 32-bit version can be installed on both 32- and 64-bit systems.
  - ➤ The Office Open Document Format or Office Open XML Format can be selected as the default file format from the list.
  - ➤ **Update Channel:** You can choose how Office updates are sent to your devices. Select from:

> ○ **Monthly**
> ○ **Monthly (Targeted)**
> ○ **Semi-Annual**
> ○ **Semi-Annual (Targeted)**

Once you've selected a channel, you can choose from the following:

- ➤ Other versions can be removed from users' devices by selecting "Yes." This option should be used if you wish to delete Office.MSI programs that are already installed from end-user devices. On end-user devices, the installation of.MSI programs won't function if they are already installed. It will remove all Office (MSI) programs from the end user's device in addition to the apps selected for download in Configure App Suite. The language packs that were previously installed on your end users' machines will be installed once more when Intune reinstalls Office.
- ➤ **Version to install:** Select the Office version you wish to install.

> Installing a specific version of Office on end-user devices for a selected channel is an option if you selected Specific as the Version to install in the preceding configuration.

Over time, the versions that are now in use will alter. As a result, when you perform a fresh deployment, some earlier versions might not be compatible with the available versions. Current deployments will continue to use the previous version, but the list of versions will be updated continuously for each channel. If a device updates its pinned version (or any other feature) and is published as ready, its reporting state will reflect "Installed" if it loaded the previous version prior to device check-in. The user will not be able to see it, but it will momentarily change to "Unknown" when the device checks in. When the user initiates the process of installing the latest version, the state will shift to "Installed".

> Use shared computer activation: If more than one person is using a computer, select this option.
> Approve the app end user license agreement automatically: If you wish to avoid requiring end users to approve the license agreement, check this option. Following that, Intune accepts the terms right away.
> Languages: Office comes pre-installed in any authorized language on the end user's Windows device. If you wish to expand the app suite's language options, use this option.

You can deploy additional languages for Microsoft 365 apps that are managed by Intune. Next to each language on the list is the Type of language pack (core, partial, and proofreading). Click Microsoft Intune > Apps > All apps > Add from the UI. Look for "Windows 10 and later" in the Add app pane, then select it from the list of available app types. From the App Suite Settings window, choose Languages.

+ To view the Scope Tags page, click Next.

Step 2: (Option 2) Use XML data to configure the app suite

If you select the Enter XML data option from the Setting format dropdown box on the Configure app suite page, you can use a custom configuration file to configure the Office app suite.

> **⎱ Enter the XML configuration.**

Remember that the Product ID may be O365ProPlusRetail or O365BusinessRetail (Business). However, the Microsoft 365 Apps for Business version app bundle can only be configured using XML data. Remember that Microsoft Office 365 ProPlus is the new name for Microsoft 365 Apps for Enterprise.

> **⎱ To view the Scope Tags page, click Next.**

Step 3: Choose your scope tags (if any).

With scope tags, you can control who has access to client app information in Intune.

> **⎱ Click Select scope tags to add scope tags for the app suite.**
> **⎱ To view the page containing your assignments, click Next.**

Step Four: Tasks

- Choose which group assignments for the app suite to remove, which are Available for registered devices, or which are Required.
- To display the "Review + create" page, click "Next".

Step 5: Evaluate and produce

- Review the numbers and settings for the app suite by going back.
- When you're finished, click Create to add the app to Intune.

It displays the Overview blade.

Details of deployment

The installation package will be downloaded by the end device from officecdn.microsoft.com when the Office Configuration Service Provider (CSP) applies the Intune deployment policy to the target machines. **There will be two new directories in the Program Files directory:**

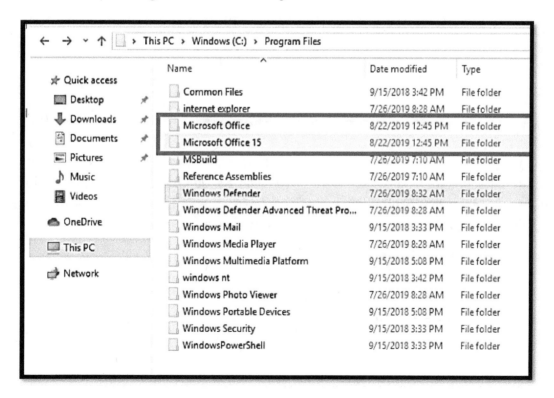

These files are stored in a freshly created folder located in the Microsoft Office directory:

The Microsoft Office 15 directory contains the files that initiate the Office Click-to-Run download. **Should the assignment type be required, the installation will start automatically:**

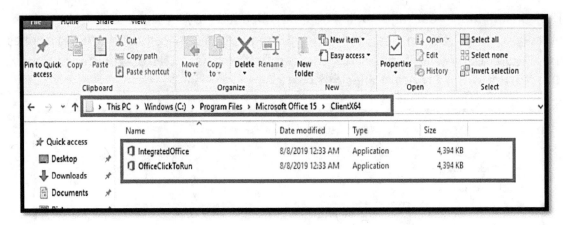

When the Microsoft 365 allocation is properly configured, the update will operate silently. The program files that were saved will be deleted after the installation is finished. When the assignment is set to "Available," the Office applications will appear on the Company Portal app, allowing end users to install them straight away.

Practice Exercises

1. Establish Intune app security guidelines
2. Explain the Microsoft Teams notification settings
3. Mention the steps for choosing the Microsoft 365 Apps

CHAPTER TEN
OBSERVING YOUR NEW CONFIGURATION

The best thing about modern device management is that a well-configured system can free up staff members' time to identify and address issues before end users do.

Applications license monitoring features

First, we'll examine application license monitoring. We will then go over the remaining features in the order that they appear in Intune:

The App Licenses

Licenses for apps are the first item on our menu. This is limited to use with store-based apps (Google Play Store, Microsoft, and Apple). You can select how many licenses to make available for each program when installing it with Apple Volume Purchase. You can order as many licenses as you need if your apps are free, but you may wish to restrict them if they are paid for. Any software that reaches its licensing limit will cease to be released, thus it's a good idea to monitor how licenses are being used. The options at the top include adding extra columns (the majority of which will be empty), refreshing, exporting to CSV, and—above all—beginning a VPP sync. It's useful to note that you may also remove the app by clicking the three dots. There is no way to alter the alphabetical order in which the apps are provided. To filter the list, you can utilize the free text field at the top. Check out the automation if you'd like to sort, which is far more beneficial. It gives you a similar panel with additional customization by utilizing the Out-GridView command. You will be directed to the application's information after you click on it.

Discovered applications

The next item on the menu is Discovered apps. Whether or whether Intune installed the apps, this report covers all programs and includes a list of all the apps that are available on devices under its management. Although it is a powerful tool, it can be challenging to maintain track of because each version serves as its record (a small tenant may have more than 1,000 entries). Sorting is not possible, but we may search, browse, and export using the button at the top. Clicking on an app will lead you to a website where you can view additional install data along with other details about that app. The script will allow you to arrange items in additional ways, similar to app licenses.

Install status of the app

The option for the app installs status for all apps across all devices is the next item on the list. You may Filter, Search, and Export this report just like you can with any other report from Intune. Of course, sorting by the columns is another useful feature of this blade. The name of the app will direct you to its informational main page. You will immediately be taken to the Device install status or User install status page if you click on Device failures or User failures. Before you start receiving support calls, check this frequently to identify any programs that are causing you problems or that are in the incorrect package. Sorting by Install failure will give you the best picture of what's wrong with your estate. You will see which user and device installations failed as a result.

Status of App Protection

Verifying the status of protected apps on both personal and work devices is a crucial task for any security team. Similar to the app install status, you can export, search, and sort based on the headers. As you can see, there are a lot of columns here, so pay attention to the bottom scroll bar. Near the bottom are the most crucial fields, such as Compliance state and App protection status. As these are MAM devices, click through is no longer available. When users are denied access to resources, monitoring your app protection status will assist you in identifying the issue, and restricted access will safeguard your company's data.

Status of App Configuration

The most recent report for a program's monitoring is App Configuration Status. This relates to any application setup guidelines you have set up for managed apps or devices (MDM and MAM). At the device level, it functions with iOS and Android smartphones alike. This report has the same search, refresh, and export options as other reports. You also have the option to sort by header. Once more, make advantage of the menu as there is a wealth of information here. Fortunately, the most of the significant locations are close to the start. For optimal user experience, even though this often won't have any serious security issues, it's still important to keep a watch on it.

Configuration of the tracking device

Now that we know how to track our apps, we can start looking at tracking the devices themselves, starting with the configuration profiles that are utilized on them. You can choose to use the New Devices Experience view, which is currently under test. We only utilized the New Devices Experience view because this will probably become the default. **Select Devices, followed by Overview, and then click the words located at the top:**

We will go over each of the three monitoring options for device setup one at a time. Navigate to Manage Devices and select Devices to locate them. Next, select Configuration. Following that, the updated version will lead you to the Monitor tab, where you can see our options, which we will now discuss.

Apps that are prohibited on certain devices

This option is compatible with all OS system device limitation regulations. It is possible to organize a plan for blocking specific apps, and the report will identify any device found to be running these apps. **Here, we have configured a macOS restriction profile to prevent users from utilizing Apple Calculator (while maintaining its functionality):**

The device is identified as having a forbidden app in the monitoring result:

 When you click on the row, the apps that have been found will be displayed. The typical Export button, a search option (which just searches for the user's email address), and a helpful sorting feature based on column names are located at the top.

Report on encryption

This is a crucial one to monitor, but ideally, Conditional Access and your carefully considered compliance standards will shield you from some harm. This prevents these devices from accessing M365 data, but in the event that an insecure device with locally stored files is misplaced or stolen, there remains a risk. This makes keeping an eye on your unencrypted gadgets a crucial task. Remember that this is limited to Windows and macOS devices; you won't be able to see any iOS or Android devices there. The fact that you can only search by device or username and that you cannot sort by column titles is inconvenient. This makes it more difficult to locate your unprotected devices in a large area; utilize the automation section's script instead. However, by selecting the filter icon at the top, you can focus on a smaller subset of the results. A helpful header called "Readiness" can tell you right away if a device isn't secured and if the issue lies with the policy or the device. If the device is not ready and the Trusted Platform Module (TPM) is not working, then the device should not be used remotely. Rather, it is advised to examine the hardware with your hands. We can now go on to our next report, which discusses certificate monitoring.

The Certifications

The final option for device setup in monitoring is certificates. This only matter if you are pushing certificates to your devices via Intune for purposes such as app packaging, login, and so on. Once more, the two most crucial headings—Certificate status and Certificate expiry—are located right at the conclusion. You might want to drag the headings to reorder them or use the Columns button to remove those that you don't need if your screen is smaller. You may search (including free text), export, and sort by column heading, but the filter button is no longer available. Sorting by expiration is the best option for general tracking. Use the search feature to locate items more quickly if necessary. We can review our certifications before moving on to the hidden assignment fails to report.

The Failures on assignments

Assignment failures are an additional monitoring option that isn't included in the other three. When you look at the device setup, this option examines failures at the policy level. Navigate to Devices and select the blue text labeled "Configuration profile status." You may easily verify whether of your policies are incorrect or don't function properly across all of your devices by doing this, which will open a new screen. To locate policies that have significantly failed, you can sort by column headers. Moreover, you can search by profile name. Additionally, you can limit by device, profile type, or profile source by using a more sophisticated filter. If you click on the name of the profile, you'll be redirected to another site where you can check which devices are experiencing issues with the profiles. In an ideal world, this report would be unambiguous; however issues with various gadgets will always arise. Examine the gadgets that are at odds first. These are issues with policy configuration or scoping, not device failures; that is, you have conflicting policies on the same device. Remember that even with all of its settings same, a policy can contradict itself. You can address the errors once the policies that conflict have been eliminated. If the amount exceeds one-third of your entire estate, there is typically an issue with the insurance (larger estates). Not the apparatus.

Compliance of Tracking Devices

Monitoring device compliance is just as important as monitoring device configuration. This is particularly crucial since it will be the most annoying problem for users if they are forced to utilize non-compliant devices. In order to access these reports, click

Devices and then Compliance. You can view the next six reports on the Monitor tab by following the next step. We will examine non-compliant devices first, followed by a review of the other available reports.

Noncompliant gadgets

The noncompliant devices are where this report begins. It displays all devices that don't adhere to any compliance plan on all systems, including Linux. If a device has multiple policies, one failure will render them all invalid. Use the search function to find a device name, device ID, login, user email, user ID, IMEI, or serial number. There's also the Export button and the standard sections. In addition to filtering by Compliance status, OS, Ownership type, and Device type, you can sort by the headings. The Device compliance panel itself will not appear when you click on a device; instead, a page with further information about that device will load. Keep an eye on this one if you have Conditional Access configured to prohibit non-compliant devices so you can address issues before the user gets blocked and calls to report them.

Devices lacking a policy for compliance

This is just another straightforward one that will display any devices on which there are no policies enforced. As soon as the general settings are correctly configured, the devices will be marked as non-compliant, which will assist you in determining the issue. If you have the option to label them as compliant, checking here is even more important to make sure that all of your devices are appropriately monitored and safeguarded. As of the time this was published, you could only export, select columns (which cannot be sorted), and perform a search. However, there are plans to improve things in the future.

Establishing compliance

This monitoring option verifies the configurations for each and every one of your compliance policies, including those that weren't created by Microsoft. It provides you with the precise policy settings that are causing the devices to violate the rules in addition to the initial list of noncompliant devices. To sync the results if this is your first start, you might need to click the Sync report option at the top. It is possible to export the displayed data and search or sort using the headers. More details, including the devices that aren't compatible due to the setting, will appear when you click on any of the rows. You may rapidly determine whether an issue is with a device or a setting by sorting by non-compliant devices. The time in the Compliance settings is the basis for the Is active setting. It could be in the top few categories, depending on the value you have selected.

Adherence to policy

As of right now, we are able to see both non-compliant devices and the settings causing them to be that way. But this merely provides information on the settings; it doesn't explain the policy they are a part of. "Policy compliance" is a menu option that displays each compliance policy along with the quantity of devices that are either non-compliant, compliant, or in an error state. When you view the report for the first time, you can once more perform a first synchronization. When it's finished, you can download the information, search, and arrange the titles. Sorting by non-compliance and errors is the best technique to handle devices that should be compliant. You will be directed to a page listing all the devices that comply with a policy when you click on its name.

Policies that are not in compliance

This is still being tested as of this writing, and it is essentially the same as the previous option. The sole distinction is that it only displays items that are incorrect or noncompliant because it doesn't mention anything that complies. You can sort the devices by platform and it displays a wide variety of gadgets. As usual, you may also search by policy name, export, and sort by heading. Upon selecting a policy, you will be directed to a list that, unlike the previous choice, only displays the devices that are experiencing issues. This option is preferable to the previous one for daily management as it reduces the quantity of data and allows you to concentrate on the sections that are important to view.

Report on Windows health attestation

The Windows health attestation report represents the final option for device compliance monitoring. This report examines the configuration of the device's attestation settings and is only compatible with Windows. This can be used to quickly determine whether BitLocker or Secure Boot may be compromised due to hardware or software issues. Observe the toolbar located at the bottom of the screen. Additionally, you can eliminate any sections that don't relate to your circumstances by using the Columns button. The outcome is really simple. There's a filter that can be applied even though there's no way to sort by headers or perform a search:

Select device type:
☐ Devices that support health attestation

Select data point status:
☐ BitLocker not enabled

☐ Secure Boot not enabled

☐ Code integrity not enabled

☐ Early launch anti-malware driver is not loaded

You are limited to viewing it here since you are unable to click on any of the results.

Tracking Device Registration

Now that our devices are compliant and configured correctly, we can verify that they have enrolled, but that won't be of any assistance. For this reason, we must make advantage of the options for tracking and registering devices. These are particularly useful for searching for errors and assisting in their correction when users are using self-enrolling devices. In order to get these reports, click Devices and then Enrollment. This will take you to the Monitor panel, where our options are displayed. We will now go through these in greater detail. We will examine unsuccessful enrollments first. After that, we will review each of the submitted reports.

Failures to enroll

We start by looking at the enrollment failures report, which displays all unsuccessful enrollment attempts made on all platforms using all authorized signup methods. It also includes highly useful information regarding faults. Here, you should focus on the powerful filter first. The platform, error type, registration type, and entry date and time can all be examined. This will greatly simplify the process of identifying any spikes or failures that occur frequently. Exporting the outcomes as a CSV file is an additional choice. You can also choose to show for All users or just one individual (Select user), which makes this option unique. This is a really useful tool for people who are

172

experiencing difficulties with enrollment. Not only is it not possible to sort by name, but the robust filter ought to eliminate the need for it. Additionally, a graph is displayed, which is useful for routinely monitoring enrollment failure rates for any abrupt drops that could be the result of firewall modifications or outages.

Incomplete registrations for users

Only iOS and Android devices that were enrolled through the Company Portal are eligible to use this section. Zero Touch, Android for Work, and Apple Business Manager Enrollments are not covered. A graph of incomplete enrollments is displayed, indicating that the user may have closed the enrollment screen or the enrollment period may have expired. By default, this should be empty, but you should still monitor it in order to assist any users that may be listed. At the top is an additional powerful filter. Sorting is possible based on the operating system, the date and time, or the registration stage at the moment of cancellation or timeout.

Deployments of Windows Autopilot

The final option displays a list of all successful and unsuccessful Autopilot launches over the previous 30 days; however it is only compatible with Windows devices. Like the other reports we looked at, it also includes another powerful filter. Data cannot be downloaded, however it can be found and sorted by name. You'll need to employ automation for that. The Autopilot device information appears when you click on a device. Since users usually set up Autopilot, it is always beneficial to keep an eye on these events. Deploying an unconfigured device is the last thing you should do. To assess how the person is doing and whether anything can be done to improve things, you can also take a look at the entire time.

Tracking Changes on Various Platforms

In most cases, it's imperative that you keep your devices updated with the most recent security patches. Updates can occasionally be problematic for devices, even though Intune offers solutions to handle this for you. We can check them to see if any updates are available for Windows, iOS, and macOS (but not for Android yet). To get these reports, navigate to the Devices section in the Intune menu. Each has a unique location, which will be covered in its report. We'll start this section by discussing Windows updates. After that, we'll discuss iOS and macOS updates.

The Windows upgrades

In Devices, choose Windows 10 and subsequent upgrades.

Following that, this provides you with an overview of the following:

- **Update the status of your ring device:** This displays the devices that are experiencing issues with the update ring policies overall, rather than with a specific version.
- **Errors in feature update devices:** This displays the number of devices inside your policies that are experiencing issues with feature update deployment.
- **Failures with expedited updates:** The same as previously described, but for updates that happen fast. This one is one that you should closely monitor, as fast updates are typically for serious security issues.
- **Driver update failures:** If driver updates are enabled, this will display all devices whose drivers have failed.

You can get the report below by selecting any of the reports and clicking the three dots in the top right corner:

If necessary, you may then click on rows in the report to get additional details. In the report, there is an option to export your information. Once you have a general understanding of the land, use the individual reports to identify any issues and take corrective action. Don't begin with policy errors. A device may not be receiving updates if a policy is not being applied to it. Faster updates are the most crucial factor to consider when they have been resolved.

Status of iOS updates

To reach this option, navigate to Devices and then select Apple Updates. Lastly, select the iOS update status by clicking. Along with a list of your iOS devices that cannot be installed, you will notice the same style that you are accustomed to seeing here. Apple only displays devices with issues since it doesn't report on devices that are operating properly. In addition to downloading, there is a powerful filter that may examine the installation state as well as a range of dates.

The complete list of choices is as follows:

Both a free-text search and header sorting are available. Since C-level executives frequently use iOS devices, there are a number of things that could go wrong with an update, including receiving a call, so this is something to always keep an eye on.

The macOS update status

Devices | Apple Updates | macOS update status you may locate this one at macOS Update Status. Upon clicking it, we are redirected to a report screen with a few fewer features but a similar appearance to the iOS screen. Although the filter restricts the update status options, it does allow you to define the minimum and maximum OS versions. Along with a search box that searches through the most important items, there is the typical Export button. But you are unable to sort the headers by clicking on them. Although there isn't as much information as for Windows and iOS, it's still sufficient to identify malfunctioning devices and fix them.

Keeping an Eye on Device Activity

As an Intune supervisor, particularly in a larger organization, you must monitor who performed what because there are potentially dangerous buttons on the panel. Suppose by accident someone clicks "Wipe" on the incorrect device and you have to document the incidence in an incident report. Fortunately, all of these Device operations are logged. To access these logs, navigate to Devices, then Overview, and lastly click the Device Actions box. This screen will detail every action that has been done on all devices, along with what was done, when it was done, and by whom. **Although you'll have to utilize the automatic script to search or sort by labels, it does feature a strong filter that contains every operation that can be performed on any device:**

Only viewing is possible (or exporting, if you select the Export button). This tool cannot be used to drill down. Although you should hardly ever need to complete this report, consider it your insurance coverage.

Analyzing Audit Records

We covered the topic of directly on-device monitoring in the previous section. While these activities can have a significant impact, they are less likely to result in major issues because they only impact one device at a time. Any change, elimination, or creation of policies greatly increases the possibility of larger-scale issues. To search for these kinds of modifications, we must go through the audit logs. Once you reach the Audit Logs page, you will see a screen that is similar to a report. Once more, a powerful filter option at the top allows you to perform actions like sorting by activity. However, bear in mind that this is a large list without an integrated search feature, so be sure to use it wisely. You can locate the individual who made the change by using the search box. Not by any of the other headers, but you can sort by date and activity as well. If you select "Export," just the content that is shown on the screen will be sent; no additional data will be available for you to copy. You can view additional information about the changes made, including the new and old values, by clicking on a row. This is especially useful if you need to reverse a change but don't have a backup or restoration tool to get the previous value.

Practice Exercises

1. Explain Applications license monitoring features
2. Track Changes on Various Platforms

CHAPTER ELEVEN
UNDERSTANDING POWERSHELL SCRIPTING OVER INTUNE

OVERVIEW

The scripting engine of Intune is a helpful tool that isn't always apparent. Platform scripts and remediations, formerly known as proactive remediations, are two types of scripts that can be executed on devices one once or continuously. PowerShell has become so strong with Windows 10 and 11 that devices can now accomplish about anything with a script. With Intune, we can utilize PowerShell scripts to change registry keys, copy files, set features not yet in the settings library, and even execute a script to remove Windows garbage for a cleaner build. Platform scripts are executed as setups to automate configuration settings and do other tasks required for device setup. Remedials, on the other hand, are scripts that are infinitely rerun, but their logic only executes when necessary. We will cover writing PowerShell scripts and Remediations in addition to learning how to utilize them. You will also receive some sample scripts to get you started. This will discuss using scripts to deploy applications in addition to patches and platform scripts.

Scripts for Platform Deployment

Since the first option has been in Intune longer than the others, we will start with it. Platform scripts on the device only need to be executed once. They can be executed as either a user or the system. They operate in 32-bit mode by default when they are first deployed, although this can be modified. It is crucial to keep in mind that the configurations for system/user and 32/64-bit will differ. Scripts performed when the User or Device setup indicates "Preparing apps" when Autopilot is operating. This phase does not have a name. If you see this time-out issue, it can be the result of a PowerShell script that failed and failed to return a success code in a timely manner. To view a script's output and determine what went wrong, obtain the script ID from the Intune website's address bar. **The following location will include the output, under a subkey with the ID:**

```
HKLM:\Software\Microsoft\IntuneManagementExtensio n\Policies
```

For greater completeness and ease of finding the output, logging ought to be included directly into the script.

Launching off

In this scenario, we will use a little script to deploy a registry key and remove an installed Windows AppX application. **In your chosen editor, create a new PowerShell script and enter the following code:**

```
Get-AppxPackage -allusers -Name
Microsoft.BingNews | Remove-AppxPackage -AllUsers
$Search =
"HKLM:\SOFTWARE\Policies\Microsoft\Windows\Window
s Search"
If (!(Test-Path $Search)) { New-Item $Search
}
If (Test-Path $Search) {
Set-ItemProperty $Search AllowCortana -Value
0
}
```

This will remove Bing News and prevent Cortana from appearing in the search box.

Once you've written your script, do these things to deploy it:

- Go to Devices in the Intune gateway, click on Windows, and then click on Scripts and Remediations.
- If nothing else is chosen, you will be taken to Remediations. At the top, click on the Platform Scripts tab. Then, click on Add.
- As always, give your script a Name and a Description. You will not be able to see the script's content in the gateway after adding it, but you can download and decode it through Graph if you need to. Because of this, it is important to be careful in your comments and keep a copy of the source files. After you've set these up, click Next.
- **On the first page of script settings, choose the script you added. After that, we have a few choices:**

- ➢ **Run this script using the logged-on credentials:** This can be set to Yes to run the scripts in the user's context and let them get to the user's data. Your users can't do anything else, though, unless they have administrative rights.
- ➢ **Enforce script signature check:** If you set this to "Yes," the script will only run if it has the right signature. This should usually be set to No for scripts that you make yourself. To keep things safe, make sure you sign each script before you share it.
- ➢ **Run script in 64-bit PowerShell host:** If you don't change this, any registry keys you write will go to WOW6432Node and files will go to Program Files (x86). If you change this to "Yes," the script files and results will be written in the main places.
- ✦ For the last script to work, it needs to run at the System level and in a 64-bit host because it is writing to HKEY Local Machine (HKLM). Since our script isn't signed, the signature check setting needs to be set to "No":

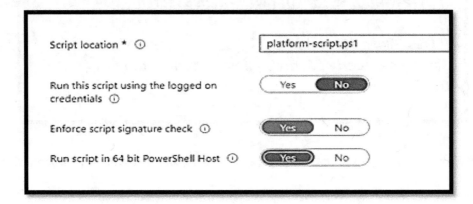

- ✦ Click Next once everything is configured.
- ✦ Click Next again; Scope tags are not needed for this.

The next step is to implement the script. Send it to a device group to enable it to operate during the Device phase of Autopilot. Send it to a user group so that it runs during the User phase. Because the script's purpose in this instance is to clean the device, we will execute it in the device context to ensure that it is finished before a user signs in. Click Next once you've configured.

- ✦ Finally, check that everything is configured correctly on the Review + Add screen before clicking Add.

You've finished creating, uploading, and adding your PowerShell Platform Script to Intune.

Starting the Configuration of Remediation Process

Platform scripts come extremely handy in situations where you wish to run something only once, such as during device setup. But given PowerShell's immense capabilities, you might wish to run a command more than once or view the results directly in the shell. This is the role of remediation, formerly known as proactive remediation. They operate with a monitoring and remediation setup, so while you can schedule them to run at a specific time, the script will only execute when necessary. There are two scripts in remediation: one for detection and another for remediation. Given that it informs the remediation script whether it must run or not, the detecting script might be more significant than the remediation script. The exit code is provided by this key. If the exit code is 0, the device complies with the inspection; hence no further action is needed. The remediation process begins when the exit code is 1. As long as the two exit codes are set, you can add anything you want to the scripts. To this approach, we will add a Remediation that, in most cases, should function well and clear up the disk if it runs out of space. Initially, we need to write two scripts: one for remediation and the other for detection.

Using the program of your choosing, write the following PowerShell scripts:

```
Detect.ps1:
$storageThreshold = 15
$utilization = (Get-PSDrive | Where {$_.name - eq "C"}).free
if(($storageThreshold *1GB) -lt $utilization){ write-output "Storage is fine, no
remediation needed"
exit 0}
else{
write-output "Storage is low, remediation needed"
exit 1}
Remediate.ps1:
$cleanupTypeSelection = 'Temporary Sync Files', 'Downloaded Program Files',
'Memory Dump Files', 'Recycle Bin'
foreach ($keyName in $cleanupTypeSelection) {
$newItemParams = @{
Path   =
```

```
"HKLM:\SOFTWARE\Microsoft\Windows\CurrentVersi
on\Explorer\VolumeCaches\$keyName"
Name = <StateFlags0001>
Value = 1
PropertyType =        'DWord'
ErrorAction    =       <SilentlyContinue'
}        @newItemParams | Out-Null
New-ItemProperty
}
Start-Process -FilePath CleanMgr.exe -
ArgumentList '/sagerun:1' -NoNewWindow -Wait
```

Only the C drive's free space is checked by the detecting script. If it is less than 15 GB, it sends Exit code 0, initiating the remediation process. Another item to consider is the data that is sent along with the exit code. When you wish to check on the status of the device later on, having a good write-output will be helpful because the detection output is visible in the Intune dashboard once it has been run. After the correction, the temporary files, downloaded apps, memory dump files, and the trash can (if applicable) are removed using the disk cleanup tool. An exit code is not required for the remediation script.

How to proceed...

Now that you have your scripts created, add them to Intune by following these steps:

Navigate to Devices and select Windows to access Scripts and remediations. Click "Create." "Remediations" will appear at the top of the screen. As in the last section, add the values for Name and Description. This is a blank space where you can additionally add an author; the name of the logged-in user will show automatically. While adding a thorough description is a good idea, remediations can be viewed on the website once they have been added, if needed. Click Next once you've configured. You can include your Detection and Remediation scripts on certain displays. The context can be set in the same manner as PowerShell scripts: system, signing, 32-bit or 64-bit. In this instance, we require system context, 64-bit, and unsigned.

✦ Click Next once you've configured:

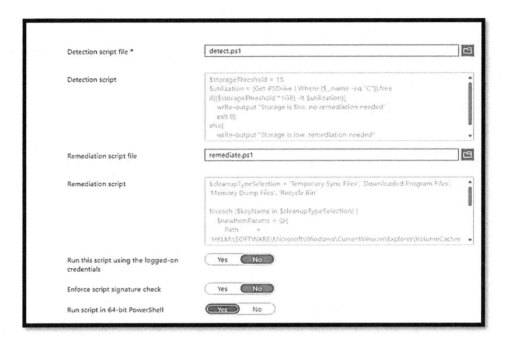

Scope tags are not required for such a site-wide cleanup, so proceed by clicking Next. Give the Remediation the work it needs to do now. You will be able to add All Users or All Devices as well. Once your group has been selected, click the "Daily" text. This will provide a menu where you may select the duration of the cleanup. There are three options available: Once (with a predetermined date and time), Hourly and Daily (where you may choose how many days and what hour). Since the devices in this scenario won't be much impacted by the detecting script, we'll execute it every hour.

✦ Click Next once you've configured:

Once you're satisfied with how everything appears, click Create. It is evident that the Version is marked as "No Version." There was an unchangeable text box on the first screen. As you make modifications to the scripts, it will continue to rise. We may investigate scripting the site now that our remediation has been implemented, allowing us to swiftly implement additional scripts.

You'll find additional information.

As previously mentioned, remediations provide us with additional elements beyond timing that are absent from Platform scripts. Let's examine this.

Observing the result

Rather of requiring you to visit the device physically, you can view the script's results in the shell. This is a very helpful yet hidden function.

The actions you need to take are as follows:

Navigate to Devices and then Windows in the Intune interface to reach the Scripts and Remediations page. Click on Remedials and Scripts. In your list of scripts, click the script you wish to view. Proceed to the menu on the left and select Monitor. Click Device status after that. You will find other options if you click on Columns. To fit on the screen, the standard status is shrunk. Click Apply after checking the boxes next to the outputs for the pre- and post-remediation detections.

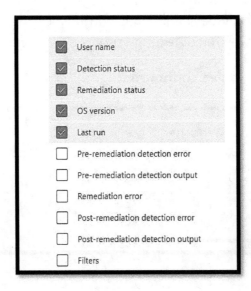

Now, the detecting script's results will be displayed, both before and after repair. This outcome will only be as good as your recognition script if write-output is set to that. You ought to consider this when drafting your scripts. Now that we know how to view the results, we are free to consider conducting remediation whenever we choose.

Performing remediation actions as needed

Another helpful option that might assist you in completing remediation quickly is run remediation on demand. When you need to quickly apply security updates or diagnose a device issue, this is quite beneficial. You might include a list of any frequent errors in the detecting script so you know where to begin. Subsequently, you might perform a remediation using regular procedures to address issues.

To execute remediation on demand on a device, follow these steps:

- Go to Devices, select Windows, and then select your device from the list to launch it whenever you'd want.
- Select "Run remediation" by clicking the three dots (...) now.

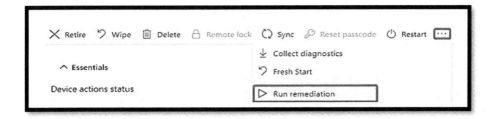

A list of the tenancy's implemented remediations will be visible to you. Once you've decided which remediation to perform (you can only choose one), click perform remediation. You can perform a cleanup on multiple devices simultaneously with Graph.

Making Use of Personalized Detection Scripts in Applications

Keep in mind that your detection script requires a standard output (STDOUT) and an exit code (0) when creating it. An exit code of 1 or omitting the STDOUT will result in the installation being reported as unsuccessful. Prior to searching the STDOUT, the script must send something out.

Because of this, the following code will function and indicate that the installation is finished:

```
Write-output "App found"
Exit 0
```

Lastly, we have the ability to utilize and execute a distinct detection script:

- You must include the script in order to use a custom detection script, regardless of whether you do so during packaging or after deployment. Navigate to Apps and then Windows to reach post-deployment. When you locate the app in question, click on it.
- Click on Edit next to Detection rules in Properties now.
- Select the dropdown option that says "Use a custom detection script" and then find the detection script you created.

Design note: System and user context cannot be selected. The fact that custom detection scripts only execute in the system context—even while the application is executing at the user level—is one vexing aspect of this. To access files or registry keys in the user context, you must use your script to identify the user who is currently logged in and add that user to c:\users\ or HKCU\. A method in the GitHub project returns the username and SID of the user who is presently logged in.

- Select the appropriate 32- or 64-bit configuration. Because you will frequently be searching the Program Files directory for files or registry keys, this is crucial for programs. Make sure the script asks for the correct location.
- Lastly, execute the script silently and enable or disable the Enforce script signature check. If your scripts aren't signed, set this to No. The line that reads "run script silently" is not something you should be concerned about. Additionally, unsigned scripts will continue to operate in the background while they hijack the system.
- After completing the setup, select Review + Save.
- Once you're satisfied with how everything looks, click "Save."

This is the whole recipe for utilizing and configuring a custom detection script. We can now examine a few real-world examples.

Scripts for application detection examples

These are some illustrations to help you understand how app detection scripts function. When you can view a script that is already executing, it is frequently easier to completely comprehend the output requirements.

The 7-Zip data can be easily verified using this script:

```
$Path = "HKLM:\SOFTWARE\7-Zip"
$Name = "Path"
$Type = "STRING"
$Value = "C:\Program Files\7-Zip\"
Try {
$Registry = Get-ItemProperty -Path $Path - Name $Name -ErrorAction
Stop | Select-Object - ExpandProperty $Name
If ($Registry -eq $Value)
{ Write-Output "Detected" Exit 0}
Exit 1}
Catch {Exit 1}
This script uses file detection for the following app:
$File = "C:\windows\system32\notepad.exe"
if (Test-Path $File) {
write-output "Notepad detected, exiting"
exit 0
}
else {
exit 1
}
```

PRO TIP: We will discuss several applications that go beyond this, since in practice you would likely use the GUI tools to make these kinds of discoveries. This sample script will confirm the creation and activation of a service.

This will assist if your app requires a service in order to function:

```
$service = get-service -name "MozillaMaintenance"
if ($service.Status -eq "Running") { write-output "MozillaMaintenance detected
and running, exiting"
exit 0
}
else {
exit 1
}
```

If you want to be certain you have the most recent version but are skeptical of
the application's provider versioning, you can check out when the file was last
modified:

```
$filedate = (Get-Item
"C:\Windows\System32\notepad.exe").LastWriteTi
me
if ($filedate -gt (Get-Date).AddDays(-1)) { write-output "Detected"
exit 0
}
else {
exit 1
}
```

That brings us to the end of setting detection scripts using the UI and some samples.

Now let's see how to automate this procedure.

Using Scripts for Custom Requirements in Applications

PowerShell also allows you to use bespoke requirements scripts. Much of this is
covered by the essential rules, but you may want to go one step further. For instance,
you may state that an application is exclusive to a particular company's hardware.
When you are updating installed apps, there is one situation in which they are really
helpful. Since the user installed these, when an update is pushed to them, the user
must download and install the most recent version from the company website (if the
rules are configured correctly to detect when a reinstallation is necessary). This is

```
```

absolutely not a good idea, particularly if you are using a zero-day hack. In this scenario, you might provide the necessary app to each user and then establish a rule stating that the app must first determine whether it is already installed on the device before being installed. These function more like compliance scripts than remedial or detection scripts. Since Intune reads the scripts output, which needs to fulfill the condition specified in the application requirements rule, we don't need an exit code.

Starting Off

For the sake of this example, we will stipulate that the application is only compatible with hardware manufactured by ACME, the firm that we founded expressly for this purpose. To install and launch the necessary script, follow these steps: First and foremost, we must write our script. **In the preferred editor, create a new PowerShell script by utilizing the following code:**

```
$Manufacturer = Get-WmiObject -Class Win32_ComputerSystem | Select-Object - ExpandProperty Manufacturer $Manufacturer
```

All that is involved in this is retrieving the maker's name from the machine's WMI and returning it. An app has to include this right away. Navigate to Apps, select Windows, and then search for the concerned app. After clicking on it, select "Properties."

- Select Edit next to Requirements now.
- Click + Add at the bottom.
- Locate the drop-down "Requirement type" menu and select "Script."
- When you select the script we recently created, the Name column will be automatically filled in, but you can edit it if needed.
- You have options for system and user context, 32- and 64-bit versions, and whether or not the script needs to be signed.
- Telling it what data to seek for right now is necessary.

You have to make the appropriate decision out of the available options. If you don't, even if the device satisfies your needs, your requirements script will fail:

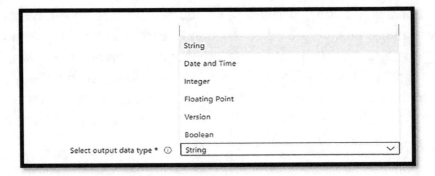

| Select output data type * ⓘ | String ∨ |

String
Date and Time
Integer
Floating Point
Version
Boolean

If you're not sure which one you need, type the variable followed by in your script
.gettype().
This would look like this in our case:
$manufacturer.GetType()

This will provide you with details regarding the outcome and the desired name, which in this instance is String:

```
PS C:\Windows\system32> $manufacturer.GetType()

IsPublic IsSerial Name                                    BaseType
-------- -------- ----                                    --------
True     True     String                                  System.Object
```

To check if this code finds a numeric value, run it:

- *$test = 1*
- *$Test.gettype()*

An integer number will be the response:

```
PS C:\Windows\system32> $test.GetType()

IsPublic IsSerial Name                                    BaseType
-------- -------- ----                                    --------
True     True     Int32                                   System.ValueType
```

- Choose the appropriate data type from the dropdown menu.
- Choose your operator, which can be Equals or Not Equal to for a string. With the other kinds of information, you have more options.
- Since we are looking for a single response, we will set this to Equals. Lastly, we must set the desired value, which in this instance is ACME:

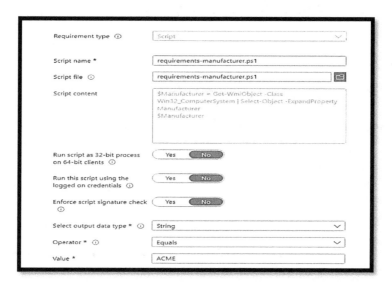

- Press OK.
- On the Requirements page once more, click Review + Save.
- Verify everything is in order, then select "Save."

All that's needed to include a custom requirements script is that. Let's examine a few actual situations.

Samples of scripts with customized specifications

Use cases for customized requirements scripts in application deployment are demonstrated by the following examples.

This script will identify the manufacturer and provide it back:

- *$Manufacturer = Get-WmiObject -Class Win32_ComputerSystem | Select-Object - ExpandProperty Manufacturer $Manufacturer*

This script will determine whether an installed application is present.

```
$File = "C:\windows\system32\notepad.exe"
if (Test-Path $File) {
write-output "Notepad detected"
}
else {
write-output "Notepad Not Detected"
}
```

You would be searching the GUI for a String data type with an Equals operator and a Notepad value that was identified in the requirements configuration.

This script will search a device for a specific hotfix:

```
$hotfixid = "KB5030219"
$hotfix = Get-HotFix | where-object HotFixID -eq $hotfixid
if ($hotfix) {
write-output "Hotfix detected"
}
else {
write-output "Hotfix Not Detected"
}
```

We require the Hotfix detected string for this one.

Practice Exercises

1. Discuss Scripts for Platform Deployment
2. Explain Configuration of Remediation Process
3. Make Use of Personalized Detection Scripts in Applications

CHAPTER TWELVE
TENANT MANAGEMENT

OVERVIEW

All renters have access to Tenant Administration's options, which span a wide range of subjects from user experience to administrative duties. As an Intune supervisor, you should be aware of all of your options in order to serve your users well and complete your daily tasks as soon as feasible.

Assessing the Connectors You Use

We'll start out by discussing something crucial that you should be aware of: connections from third parties, such as Apple iOS Device Management and the Apple VPP connector. There are many options available, but not all of them will be helpful in every circumstance, so pay attention to the ones that are important to you. Here, we shall study the many types of connections. On the Intune website, navigate to Tenant Management and select Connectors and Tokens.

This will take you to a brand-new area with tons of choices. Let's now examine what is available:

- **Enterprise Windows certificate:** If you are utilizing your code-signing certificate with MSIX packages, you submit it here to your tenant. This page contains a crucial date that indicates when the certificate will expire after it is added.
- **Microsoft Endpoint Configuration Manager:** This is where you can view the Intune connection status and the time and date of its most recent successful sync if you are utilizing Co-Management with Configuration Manager.
- **Connectors for Windows 365 partners:** This enables estates running Citrix or VMware with Windows 365 to add a connection and then monitor its progress. To view this screen, a Windows 365 license is required.
- **Windows information:** This location contains two Windows file settings. The first is to enable the transmission of diagnostic data, which is required for Autopatch among other purposes. The other option is a proof of licensing. When you select "Yes," Intune will recognize your license type as either

Enterprise, Education, or AVD (E3, E5, F3, F5). This will enable you to use tools like Remediations that are exclusive to that SKU.

- If you are responsible for managing Apple devices, you should be aware of Apple VPP Tokens. These are used to purchase and manage apps, as well as to view and refresh their expiration dates. In the event that you need to add a paid program to Intune quickly, you may also find the sync option here.

- **Managed Google Play:** Here you can see the current state of the Managed Google Play Connector and optionally apply a scope tag to newly installed apps for role-based assignments.

- **Chrome Enterprise:** For configuring and monitoring your synchronized ChromeOS devices from your Chrome Enterprise domain.

- **Over-the-air firmware update:** Upon writing this, this option allowed you to link Intune and Zebra Lifeguard, however it was limited to Zebra devices.

- **Microsoft Defender for Endpoint:** Here you may adjust cross-platform preferences for the entire tenant and monitor the health of your MDE connector. Remember that MDE requires the appropriate licensing.

- **Mobile Threat Defense:** You can enroll in and monitor the performance of third-party security solutions by selecting the Mobile Threat Defense option. Additionally, Windows MAM requires it.

- **Partner device management (JAMF):** This option allows you to establish a link between your macOS devices and JAMF compliance with Conditional access so that you can use JAMF compliance and JAMF to control your devices.

- **Management of partner compliance:** This is similar to JAMF; however it supports more platforms, including VMware, Blackberry, and MobileIron. It also has cross-platform choices for iOS, Android, and macOS.

- **TeamViewer connector:** This connector will function with Intune if you utilize TeamViewer for online help.

- **ServiceNow connector:** To utilize this one, you must have a license for either Intune Suite or Remote Help. By setting up the link, the Troubleshooting and Support window for Intune users receives information about ServiceNow issues directly.

- **Certificate connectors:** To enable device authentication, upload your NDES and SCEP certificates here.

- **Derived Credentials:** Select this option to configure certificates for use on all systems having Smart Card authentication.

Including Filters

If you want to use the assignment for All users or All devices, but just for specific users, filters are an excellent (and faster) solution. At the time this was developed, it was also the sole method available for adding device filters to user assignments. As of this writing, filters are limited to iOS and Android apps and devices. You must utilize a Dynamic Entra Group in order to conduct searches based on users. To use them in the assignment, you have to construct filters. This will be covered in this section.

There are the following filter choices available to you:

The Controlled applications

- App version
- Device management type – unmanaged, Apple Business
- Manager, Kiosk, Android Enterprise, and so on
- Device manufacturer
- Device model
- Operating system version

The controlled devices

- Device name
- Manufacturer
- Model
- Device category
- Operating system version
- Is rooted (iOS, Android)
- Device ownership – personal or corporate
- Enrollment profile name
- Device trust type (Windows) – hybrid or cloud-only
- Operating system SKU (Windows)

Now that we are aware of their purposes and the alternatives that are available, we can construct our filters.

Take the following actions to construct your first filter:

- Navigate to Tenant Administration and select the desired filters. Next, select Managed devices or Managed apps by clicking Create. In this instance, a device filter will be employed.
- After selecting the Platform characteristic that the filter will apply to and filling out the Name and Description sections, click Next.
- To add the searches your rule requires, use the rule builder located on the Rules panel. In this scenario, set Property to manufacturer, Operator to Equals, and Value to ACME to obtain only devices manufactured by ACME. **The Edit button next to Rule syntax allows you to make manual changes to the rule as well:**

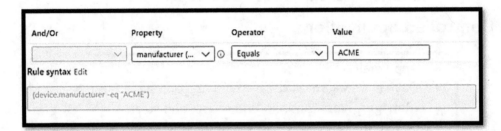

After you've set the rule, you can click Preview to see which devices it will find. This is a nice technique to double check that the filter is configured correctly before utilizing it during assignment. When you accept the rule, click the Next button. Scope tags are covered later, so for now click Next. Finally, check that everything is in order, and then click Create.

Intune Roles Configuration

We configured our environment with the Intune Administrator position, but you may wish to assign other roles to the various property managers so that they have only the necessary permissions to perform their duties. For this, you may either build a custom role with the desired rights or utilize one of the built-in roles. Here, we will cover how to configure a specific job in PowerShell as well as the GUI.

- **After selecting Tenant Administration, select Roles.**

Attention! Before creating a role, select "My permissions" to view the permissions you now have in the tenant. Return to "All roles" and select any pre-existing role by clicking on it. This will direct you to the job page. You may view the rights that have been granted to the person by clicking Properties. You can then assign them to managers by selecting Assignments.

- To create a custom role, click All roles, then + Create, and finally select Intune role.
- After entering your role's name and description, click the Next button. A minimal role that can reset the LAPS password, sync, and modify the BitLocker keys is being developed.
- Select the rights that the task you're creating requires from the rights page then click Next.
- We require the following options in this scenario: Rotate BitLockerKeys, Sync devices, Reboot immediately, and Rotate Local Admin Password. Under "Remote tasks," you can locate them. Click the "i" icon to find out more about a particular permission if you're unsure about what it signifies.

Attention: You may want to utilize scope tags at this point in order to grant certain access to specific devices. For instance, you may choose to restrict the administrator's ability to perform tasks to the computers in that office and not to all of the tenant's PCs. We will discuss scope tags in the upcoming recipe.

- We're making this tenant-wide in this instance. Click Next once you've configured.
- Finally, confirm that every setting is correct before clicking Create.
- Now that we have achieved our goal, we must contribute. Once you have clicked on the newly created role, click Assignments.
- Select + Assign.
- After entering the assignment's name and description, click "Next."
- Select the Entra group that this position belongs to now. Everyone in the group will then be assigned a role. Once finished, select Next.
- You can instruct these administrators to exclusively deal with a specific user group by using the Scope Groups interface. You can designate a specific set of devices or people that you wish to grant access to, or you can select "All Devices/All Users" to grant them access worldwide. Only if the selected group is selected will the administrators be able to carry out tasks against members of that group. Once finished, select Next.
- Next, let's examine scope tags. Scope tags are less significant than scope groups because this method is limited to acts that occur on devices. To ensure that various administrators can only make changes to their own set of rules, you may want to restrict access to specific roles that allow users to see or

modify policies. This is the place, in this instance, to provide the scope tag that is utilized to create the policy.

- Click Next once everything is configured. As usual, check that everything is in order before clicking Create.

Utilizing Scope Tags

We shall first discuss the differences between scope groups and scope tags.

- When an administrator creates a scope group under an Intune role, it notifies them of the devices or people they can act on on behalf of roles that have actions configured. They resemble Entra ID's administration units in those managers can be prevented from viewing every device and user belonging to a renter.
- Tenant objects can be equipped with scope tags, which let you to control exactly who can view what and how. For instance, you may designate a certain area of your policies with a scope tag, making it changeable only by a select group of managers. Giving local managers some autonomy, but limiting it to their own tools and procedures, might be advantageous for larger organizations with several management teams. The scope tag in iOS apps is derived automatically from the VPP token.

When you have a large number of computers dispersed throughout several locations, scope tags are an essential component of your role-based access control (RBAC) strategy of least privileged access. Especially with group tags, they function flawlessly. You have the option to apply group tags to your computers when enrolled in Autopilot. After that, you may make an Entra group and assign it to the scope tag using that group tag. Now that we understand their purpose and how they operate, we can build our first scope tag.

To create a new scope tag, follow these steps:

- Under Tenant Administration, select Roles.
- From the menu on the left, select Scope tags and then click + Create.
- Click Next after entering your scope tag's Name and Description.
- Selecting the groups you want this tag to go with is all that's left to accomplish. In this example, we are using a static group with devices from a remote office. Click Next once you've configured.

🔸 After ensuring that your scope tag is configured correctly, click "Create."

Customizing the Experience for End Users

🔸 Under Tenant Administration, select Customization.

In case different user groups have different demands, we can adjust the default settings here or, at the bottom of the page, build up multiple policies with group assignments. This might be helpful for a single renter who manages several subsidiary businesses. Since we just want to alter the standard settings in this instance, click Edit next to Settings.

There are several of these settings, so we will go over them one by one:

🔸 **Identifying:** This is not too difficult. Simply add your logos for both light and dark backgrounds, select company names and colors, and decide whether to display the logo alone or in conjunction with its name.

🔸 **Support information:** These are the details displayed in the Company Portal's hotline. You can provide the hours when assistance is available, your contact information after hours, and a physical address if you welcome walk-ins in the "Additional information" area.

🔸 **Configuration:** Here's where you define the capabilities and limitations of Company Portal:

🔸 **Enrolling a device:** Select whether to allow the "Enroll" button to function automatically.

🔸 **URL for Privacy Statement:** A publicly accessible link to your statement.

🔸 **Notice about privacy:** You have the option to modify the privacy warning. For iOS and iPadOS, you may accomplish that here.

🔸 **Types of devices:** It is possible to prevent users from selecting a group on their own if categories have been established.

🔸 **App sources:** App providers have additional apps that will be displayed on the Company Portal. You can add a great deal of apps to your Office site, including any Enterprise apps that are available in Entra and any co-managed Configuration Manager apps. The first two alternatives have the potential to quickly make the Company Portal appear crowded, so proceed with caution.

🔸 **Conceal features:** Once you've chosen the options you want your users to not view, click "Hide." On Windows and iOS/iPadOS devices, you can conceal the Remove and Reset buttons to prevent users from unenrolling their devices. As a result, there will be an increase in complaints as people will click buttons carelessly.

🔸 Click Review + Save once your settings are how you want them to be. Verify everything is in order, then select "Save."

Sending Out Organizational Communications

Important information can be displayed via organizational messages on end-user devices that are limited to Windows.

Three locations may display this kind of message:

🔸 Taskbar messages: these seem as normal toast alerts and are located directly above the toolbar.
🔸 Notification area messages: These appear in the notification area and are compatible with various communications, including Teams messages and email notifications.
🔸 Messages from the Get Started app: After licensing, the Get Started app's messages only need to be viewed once. They appear in the app called Get Started.

Before continuing, please confirm that you are authorized to use group messaging. One of these licenses is required:

- Microsoft 365 E3
- Microsoft 365 E5
- Windows 10/11 Enterprise E3 with Intune Plan 1
- Windows 10/11 Enterprise E5 with Intune Plan 1

With these settings, you can send several message types. Now that we know what a group message is, we can set one up.

How to proceed...
🔸 Choose Organizational Messages, then Tenant Administration. After selecting Message at the top, select + Create.
🔸 In the pop-up window, select the message type and theme, and then click OK. In this instance, we will build a Taskbar message with an important move.

Since the message isn't there, we must include a link to it online. It might be a news article or a link to a private page.

- Give your message a name and select the language you want to use. A link and a logo are also options. Click Next: Schedule after that.

Please be aware that the "Get Started" app message requires two messages.

- Here, you can choose the start and end times of your campaign as well as the frequency of message delivery. When using Get Started, your only option is Repeat frequency, which also offers the Always On option and indicates how long the message will be displayed. Click Next: Scope tags after completing the setup.
- If you need to provide others permissions, add scope tags here; if not, click Next: Assignments.
- The Assignments tab is the only place where you may assign to users or user-based groups, so make sure everything is configured properly there. It will only go after people who are part of a mixed group. You also have the option to send the message to every user if it's intended for the entire organization.
- Click Next: Review + Create once everything is configured.

Setting up personalized Notifications

Organizational messages are limited to Windows devices, as was previously mentioned. Both iOS and Android devices can receive personalized alerts. These will appear in the alerts section of the device. If you are utilizing this method to submit any private information, please verify your settings again since these might appear on a lock screen depending on how your security is configured.

To create and send a personalized message, simply adhere to these simple steps:

- Select Custom Notifications under Tenant Administration.
- After selecting a Title and Content for your message, click Next.
- As tasks are needed, assign them. Again, this is exclusive to users; "All Users" is not an option here. Once finished, select Next.
- Once you're certain that everything is correct, click Create.

Creating the Terms and Conditions

When enrolling a device, users should accept corporate policies, particularly if they are utilizing Bring Your Device (BYOD) or are doing so from home. The two ways to accomplish this are through the Terms and Conditions in Intune and the Terms of Use in Entra Conditional Access. Although terms of use are far more flexible and powerful, we will discuss both of them here to provide you with a complete understanding. Now that we've seen our alternatives, let's learn how to set them up. We'll start by reviewing Intune's terms and conditions, which are essentially a short set of guidelines that the user must accept.

Establishing the terms and conditions

- Navigate to Terms & Conditions after Tenant Administration. Click the + Create button.
- After entering the title and brief description of your insurance, click the Next button.
- Enter the actual Terms & Conditions, the Summary of Terms, and the Title of the policy now. These are just plain text; for images, links, and other content, we require the terms and conditions in Entra.
- Click Next once the steps have been completed.
- If you need to grant access to others, add your Scope tags. In that scenario, simply press Next.
- Let's examine this term's task. Here you should follow user assignments as much as possible to maximize your catch rate. If necessary, you can also provide to All Users. Select Next.
- Once you're certain that everything is correct, click Create.

Regarding the Intune terms and conditions, that is all that has to be done. Now let's examine those that Entra provides.

Setting Up the Terms of Use for Entra

Even if these are Entra settings, we can access them via the Intune website. Go to Endpoint Security to reach Conditional Access.

- Navigate to the Manage menu, select Terms of Use, and then select Add New Terms.
- Add your PDF after selecting a Name, Title, and Language.
- **We have a few choices here:**
  - ➢ Demand that users extend the terms of use: Every user is required to read the Terms of Use.
  - ➢ Demand permission from users on all devices: Users have two options: ask them each time they use a gadget, or get their consent all at once.

- Consents that expire: "Expire consents" signifies that any prior consent must be revoked and these guidelines must be followed immediately.
- Days until re-acceptance is necessary: When does a user no longer need to re-accept
- Lastly, you have the option of Create new policy to implement these rules or create conditional access policy later, where you can amend an existing policy in the Grant access area.

In this instance, we'll employ an existing tactic:

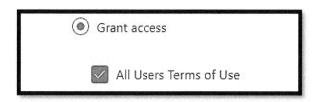

- In the moment, select "Create." If you chose to create a new policy, you will be redirected to the familiar Conditional Access Policy screen, where you may make any necessary adjustments.

Setting Up Multiple Admin Approvals

- Select Multi-Admin Approval by going to Tenant Administration.

All of the requests that are pending processing (All requests), all of the requests you have submitted (My requests), and the established policies (Access policies) are all visible to you.

- Click + Create after selecting Access Policies.
- Decide if your policy applies to scripts or apps, and give it a name and description. Click Next after that.
- Select an Approvers group from the resulting screen. There ought to be administrators in this group who can approve requests. Once finished, select Next.
- Finally, check that everything is in order, and then click Create.
- We will now examine their application. When you install a new application or script, you will be prompted to provide a business rationale. We have a "Submit for approval" button in place of a "Create" button.
- This is the Multi-Admin Approval request view screen.

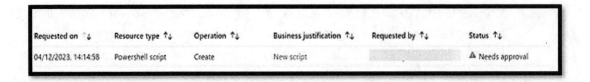

Requested on ↑↓	Resource type ↑↓	Operation ↑↓	Business justification ↑↓	Requested by ↑↓	Status ↑↓
04/12/2023, 14:14:58	Powershell script	Create	New script		⚠ Needs approval

- After logging in as an approver and selecting "Business justification," a flyout detailing the request's details—including what was put in the script and why it was submitted—will show up.
- In the flyout, type a few notes before selecting "Approve request" or "Reject request."
- Subsequently, the requester needs to finish it on the Multi-Admin Approval website. This will add the script or application and prepare it for delivery. When you click the Create button, information can be obtained from the request's data. After that, this data is returned to Graph.

Confirming Your Version as a Tenant

- Click on Tenant Status after going to Tenant Administration.
- **You may view details about your tenant, including their version and position, in the first tab:**

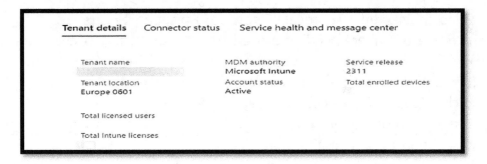

- On the Connector status tab, the list of configured connections will appear rapidly. In this scenario, you can use the previous method (Reviewing your connections) to learn more if you uncover any issues.
- Last but not least, the Service health and message center section will display any significant issues with Microsoft, any occurrences in your tenant that require your attention, and any communications. Messages typically address revisions, additions, or other issues.

Using the Troubleshooting Tools in Intune

- After selecting Troubleshooting, select Support. Then select Troubleshoot from the menu.
- Choose a person from the list, and all of their details will be processed right away.
- To make sure there are no straightforward issues, such as a user who isn't authorized or is blocked, we must first verify the User status.
- The user's entire information, including devices, rules, compliance, apps, and more, is summarized on the Summary screen.
- **Use of the following tabs is possible:**
  - ➢ **Devices:** Every device owned by the user, including those that aren't working properly with Entra or Intune.
  - ➢ **Groups:** The Entra groups that an individual belongs to are referred to as "Groups."
  - ➢ **Policy:** The guidelines that the individual has been provided.
  - ➢ **Applications:** The number of devices that the user can use to run the cross-platform apps, as well as those that the user has access to.
  - ➢ **App protection policy:** This refers to the user's present status and the app security policies that have been granted to them.
  - ➢ **Updates:** The regulations for updates installed on the devices of the users.
  - ➢ **Enrollment limits:** This person is subject to the limits and limitations specified under Enrollment Restrictions on the platform. By comparing it to the Devices tab, we can determine whether the user has surpassed their enrollment limit and is unable to enroll any additional devices.
  - ➢ **Diagnostics:** The outcomes of any requested testing.

Go to the device in question and press the "Collect Diagnostics" button to request diagnostics. A ZIP file containing all of the machine's crucial data will be emailed out after a while.

Putting up Notifications for Enrollment

Follow these steps to configure registration alerts for your users:

- Go to Devices and select Enrollment to get started. Click on the site's tab to configure the notifications there. Every site must have its own policy.

- Click + Create Notification after selecting Enrollment Notifications.
- After entering the notice's name and description, click Next.
- On the Notification Settings page, you may select the type of message to deliver. Either a push notification or an email notification, or both, may be sent.
- **All that is required for a push notification is the following information in the text and title:**

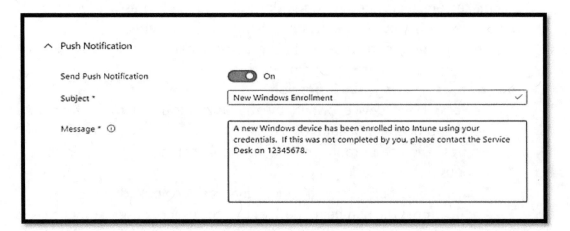

- **There are several options available to you for an email notification:**
  - ➢ You have the ability to alter the email's Subject and Message in addition to adding HTML if you activate the raw HTML editor.
  - ➢ One may include a heading.
- Additionally, you can provide the company name, your contact information, and a link to the company portal, which allows users to view the devices they have enrolled. The Tenant Administration modification settings are where all of this data is obtained. The option to put device information to the bottom is one really useful feature. In this manner, the user can view the device that was enrolled and determine whether any questions need to be answered in order to report it.
- Click Next once you've configured.
- If you would like to allow someone else to get the notifications, add a value to the Scope tag. If not, click Next.
- Assignment needs to be completed at the user level because the device won't be accessible until after registration. Thus, send to all users or select a subset of users. Click Next after that.
- Once you're certain that everything is correct, click Create.

Setting up Device Limitations

You can modify the device limit limits and device platform restrictions settings on this page. We'll start by looking at device limitations.

Device limit limitations

You can restrict how many devices you utilize by doing the following:
- Select Devices, then Enrollment.
- After choosing a platform, select Device limit restriction.

This is where you can add new limitations or modify the global default restriction. The highest number of queries is executed first when running the restrictions queries in numerical order. As soon as it locates the policy that pertains to the individual, it ceases scanning the others. If you need to implement various limits for distinct user groups, create additional policies. However, all it takes to have a broad technique is to alter the standard policy. To give ourselves additional authority in this case, we will be adding a new policy.

- To create a restriction, press +.
- Name the policy and provide a brief summary.
- Select a limit by clicking on Device Limit. This could include one to fifteen devices.

Design note: Keep in mind these guidelines for tidying up your gadget. If someone receives a new computer and the device limit is set to 1, you will need to manually remove the old computer before they may add the new one. If you have turned off your personal devices, it shouldn't be harmful to have this number greater because the devices will all still belong to the company.

- Click Next once everything is configured.
- To assign this policy to someone, add a Scope tag value here. If not, click Next.
- On the Assignments screen, assign the appropriate value to the policy. It is the default assignment, thus you cannot select "All Users." Rather, you must select a user group here. Once finished, select Next.
- Verify that your limitation limit and assignment are correct in the final step before clicking Create.
- The device's limits have now been fully configured. Now let's examine the limitations on device platforms.

Platform limitations for devices

There is more specificity in what we can and cannot accomplish on our platform. You have two options: either modify the universally applied default policy, or design unique policies for every platform. In this instance, we wish to discontinue BYOD enrollment on all platforms, so we will alter our standard approach.

Follow these steps to configure device platform restrictions:
- Select Devices, then Enrollment.
- Click Device platform restriction after selecting a platform.
- Select the text in blue that reads "All Users."
- To edit the Platform settings, select the Edit text next to it under Properties.

You have complete control over the platforms; operating systems, individual devices, and manufacturers (exclusive to Android) you wish to accept. If you decide to block users based on version, be sure to periodically check the settings because older versions are no longer supported and newer versions are released. If you don't, you may find yourself allowing everything through or preventing new devices. We will **cease supporting Android Device Administrator as well as all individually owned devices since its support is about to expire:**

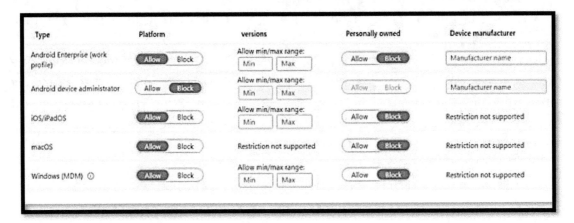

Type	Platform	versions	Personally owned	Device manufacturer
Android Enterprise (work profile)	Allow / Block	Allow min/max range: Min Max	Allow / Block	Manufacturer name
Android device administrator	Allow / Block	Allow min/max range: Min Max	Allow / Block	Manufacturer name
iOS/iPadOS	Allow / Block	Allow min/max range: Min Max	Allow / Block	Restriction not supported
macOS	Allow / Block	Restriction not supported	Allow / Block	Restriction not supported
Windows (MDM) ⓘ	Allow / Block	Allow min/max range: Min Max	Allow / Block	Restriction not supported

- After completing the setup, select Review + Save.

There are no assignment or scope tags present because these regulations are already established at the tenant level. If you wish to grant access to others or need different settings for distinct groups, create separate policies to overlay the baseline.

- Make sure everything is in order before clicking "Save."

Creating Policies for Quiet Times

- To configure Quiet Time regulations, go to Apps and then Quiet Time.
- After selecting the Policies tab, select + Create Policy.
- Select the desired Policy type number from the drop-down menu, then click Create.
- After giving your insurance a name and a description, click "Next."
- The first thing you can do in this situation is grant the person the ability to modify the settings. Leave this option to Yes if you have no strict needs.
- In the Certain Hours option, you can program alerts to sound just during specific hours of the day. Align these hours with the times you anticipate your employees will be in the office. Remember that they have the right to alter these at any time. To disable alerts on the weekends, remove the checkmarks from Saturday and Sunday in this area.
- In the "Allday" area, select the days you have off, such as Saturday and Sunday. Set it to "Require" and "Configured," and it ought to select those days on its own.
- Click Next once you've configured.
- If you would like to grant access to another person, add a Scope tag value. If not, click Next.
- When thinking about your assignments, take the firm into account as a whole. Make sure the workers who work on call, such as your IT staff, are not covered by the policy. It may be advisable to leave them out because some executives work longer hours and don't want to always having to manually adjust the settings.

If you have diverse shift times, think about creating separate policies to accommodate them. In order to maintain track of which users, based on their shift schedules, are in certain groups, you would most likely need to integrate your HR system.

- When you have finished configuring your assignments, click Next.
- Once you're certain that everything is correct, click Create.

When you create a Date Range policy, the Configuration parameters are the same except that you can only select a date range.

Practice Exercises

1. Discuss how to Assess the Connectors You Use
2. Discus the filter choices available
3. Explain Intune Roles Configuration
4. Set Up the Terms of Use for Entra
5. Discuss the Troubleshooting Tools in Intune

CHAPTER THIRTEEN
INTUNE SUITE: GETTING STARTED
How to Use and Deploy Remote Assistance

With remote help, you can receive support for Windows, macOS, and Android. Unregistered devices can be connected, and it offers complete control with customizable Intune roles and adaptable role-based access control (RBAC). There are several requirements in order to use Remote Help. We'll speak about configuring the policies and RBAC in this section. On your devices, though, you must already have the apps installed. We will now discuss configuring an RBAC role to permit Remote

Help use and permission on the property for specific administrators.

- To enable remote help, navigate to Tenant Administration and select Remote Help.
- After selecting Settings, select Configure.
- Make sure Enable Remote Help is set to Enabled from the drop-down menu. Here, you may also enable or disable chat and enable Remote Help for devices that are not enrolled.
- Once everything is configured as you desire, click Save.
- **Now we may prepare for our new role:**
  - ➤ The next items you should click are roles and tenant administrations.
  - ➤ Select the Intune role by going to create.
- After entering your name and a brief description, select "Next."
- **Select your access for the role by scrolling down to the Remote Help app In the role list. One of these options is yours:**
  - ➤ **See the screen:** basic view-only accessibility
  - ➤ **Elevation:** Enables the administrator to raise the machine's UAC.
  - ➤ **Unattended control:** This can operate without the end user's permission.
  - ➤ **Assume total command:** Rather than only being able to observe the computer, this option allows the administrator to run it.

You may want to create different roles at different admin levels.

- Click Next once everything is configured.

- If you would want to assign the roles to a certain business unit, you can add your scope tags on the following screen. Once finished, select Next.
- Finally, check that everything is in order, and then click Create.

Examining Microsoft Tunnel for the Management of Mobile Applications

Using MAM, you can get apps on an unmanaged Android or iOS device to connect to a VPN server. The features of the Tunnel VPN are enhanced by the Microsoft Tunnel for MAM. As a result, your on-premises system's Microsoft Tunnel access needs to be active and connected.

Follow these steps to configure Microsoft Tunnel for your mobile apps:

- Select App protection policies by going to Apps.
- Either draft a new policy or amend an old one.
- On the Data Protection page, scroll to the bottom and select the option to "Start Microsoft Tunnel connection on app-launch" set to True.
- Click Save or Create to save your changes, depending on whether you were making changes to an already-existing policy or starting from scratch.

The final step in configuring Microsoft Tunnel for MAM is this.

Evaluating Distinctive Devices

Advanced Endpoint Analytics is another component of the Intune Suite and consists of three parts:

- **Identification of anomalies in a device:** This function looks for patterns throughout your estate using machine learning and notifies you of any potential issues.
- **Personalized scopes for devices:** By adding scope tags to the Endpoint Analytics Reports, you may do this to allow different groups of managers to have varying rights. You could, for instance, allow a business team to view reports solely for the devices they own.
- **Improved device timeline:** This extends each device's historical events to provide you a better understanding of what has been happening.

The anomaly detection feature of Azure Automation can then be used to automatically send email or Teams alerts whenever issues are discovered. We can now examine the peculiar behavior of our device by knowing what the parts are.

- Go to Reports and select Endpoint statistics to get started.
- Click on Anomalies at the very top of the main screen.
- This is where all the weird stuff your gadgets have discovered is shown. By default, it sorts them according to intensity, but you may adjust it to any column.
- More details, including the devices impacted and any ties (device association groups) between those devices and the identified issue are displayed when you click on a title.

Device anomaly detection is an excellent tool for proactive device support. It may also lend additional weight to any issues that should be brought to the attention of a hardware vendor.

Configuring Privilege Management for Endpoints

Giving end users increased access to specific apps without giving them complete control over the device is possible using Endpoint Privilege Management (EPM). For instance, this can be necessary to elevate a business app or enable certain tool usage on devices for your employees. EPM can be configured to either elevate automatically or require approval beforehand.

How to proceed...

We will first go over how to configure EPM in the user interface:

- Locate and click on Endpoint Privilege Management under Endpoint Security.
- We must first create a settings policy. Click Create, select Windows 10 and later, and then select Elevation settings policy to accomplish this. After that, click the "Create" button.
- Click Next after naming and describing your policy.
- To begin with, we must activate the EPM on this screen. Next, we can select whether diagnostic data to report on: controlled endpoint elevations only, diagnostic data and all endpoint elevations, or diagnostic data only. It is also

possible to set a Default elevation response (None, reject all requests, or need approval from the user).

⁜ After everything is configured to your liking, select Next:

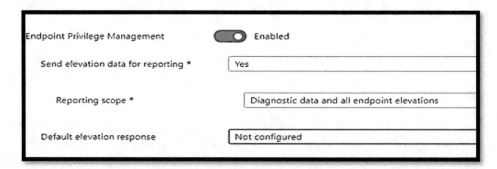

⁜ If you need to assign permissions to a certain set of managers, add your scope tags on the following screen. If not, simply select Next.

⁜ As needed, provide the policy. In the event that scope tags are not being used, this setting has an impact on the entire lease. Applying it to all users or all devices makes sense. Once finished, select Next.

⁜ Finally, check that everything is in order, and then click Create.

⁜ We can now add our first rule to allow an application to level up because EPM is now configured at the tenant level:

⁜ Under the Endpoint security > Endpoint Privilege Management menu blade, select Create Policy. Select Windows 10 and later from the pop-up option that displays, then select Elevation rules policy. Click Create after that.

⁜ Give your coverage a name and a description. You may wind up with several policies for your different EPM regulations, thus it will be beneficial to follow good name practices in this situation. Click Next after that.

⁜ **You can add multiple apps to the "Configuration settings" screen by clicking the "Add" button. You'll notice that something already exists there; to modify this one, click + Edit instance:**

- Give the Rule a name and an explanation in the fly-out.
- You can select in Elevation conditions if the user must authenticate with Windows credentials or provide a business explanation, or if the program will accept itself. It is important thinking about because these are useful for reviewing.
- Regarding tasks for children, you have additional options. You may force people to follow your rules, or you can force them to accept or reject them right away. If you raise the Command Prompt application, for example, and the user wants to open Notepad, you can select the context in which Notepad opens.
- Now, let's speak about the file metadata that Windows and Intune utilize to determine whether or not the program can be raised. Here, there are two ways that you can set the program.
- Get-filehash -path "path to executable" is a PowerShell script that you may use to obtain the filehash.

Alternatively, you can send a certificate that the file is able to utilize.

An export of a certificate can be accomplished with the PowerShell function below:

- Get-AuthenticodeSignature -FilePath "path to executable"

You can use the same license for several apps from the same developer by selecting the Reusable Settings option. Additionally, a File name value must be entered here. If you'd like, you can additionally include the numbers for the internal name, Product name, File path, Minimum version, and File description.

- After everything is configured, select Next, then Save.
- On the Scope tags screen, allocate if necessary, and then click Next.
- As tasks are needed, assign them. Here, abide by the least privilege approach, which suggests minimizing assignments, particularly if child processes are permitted. Click Next once you've configured.
- Finally, check that everything is in order, and then click Create.

Practice Exercises

1. Explain how to Use and Deploy Remote Assistance
2. Discuss Microsoft Tunnel for the Management of Mobile Applications
3. Explain the process of Configuring Privilege Management for Endpoints

CHAPTER FOURTEEN
EVALUATING TECHNICAL REQUIREMENTS FOR REPORTING

OVERVIEW

We will now continue to examine the available pre-made reports. Along with demonstrating how to use Log Analytics for more sophisticated Windows Update reporting, we will also walk you through exporting the data for usage in Power BI and Azure. Getting a point-in-time (PIT) snapshot of your situation through reporting is essential in any Intune scenario, particularly if the executives of the organization request it. This section explains the reports that come with Intune and demonstrates how to run them either automatically or manually.

How to Look Through Reports on Device Management

To view the device management reports, click the Reports item in the menu. Device settings contain all of them. We can examine each report individually now that we have them. We will review the data contained in the numerous reports that are now available.

Examining the conformity of the device

The device compliance will be examined using the subsequent procedures:

- Go to Device Compliance and select the Reports option at the top to view device compliance reports. We will first go over the capabilities of each of the following reports, and then we will discuss how to execute them. With the exception of device compliance trends, all of the reports will be run in accordance with the requirements.
- **Compliance of devices:** This displays a list of every device along with its compliance status. This study will be of interest to all responsible parties due to its practicality. It can be exported; however clicking on it to view the devices that don't comply is not possible. There are some useful built-in filtering and search features.

- **Trends in device compliance:** This simple graphic illustrates the evolution of device compliance over the previous sixty days. Only the option to filter exists. Click-through and exit are not available.
- **Devices and settings that are not in compliance:** This is the report of non-compliant devices and settings. It is typically the most helpful and provides more information than the Device compliance report you just saw. The device name is displayed, followed by the precise compliance policy setting or settings that are causing the non-compliance. In the event that you have a custom policy, this can examine every configuration. It also indicates whether something is incorrect or whether the configuration is just off. It includes capabilities for searching, filtering, and sorting based on titles.
- **Devices without a policy for compliance:** This report is rather straightforward; it simply lists all of the devices for which there are no compliance policies. It is usually a good idea to check this; especially if you have devices setup that isn't listed as compliant (it will tell you what they are set to and how to modify them). This should always be empty. In addition to filtering by OS and device owner, you can sort and find by device name. For a basic report, this ought to be more than sufficient.
- **Configuring compliance:** The compliance settings for all platforms and rules are displayed in this report, along with the percentage of each setting that complies and does not. You have the option to sort all fields in addition to searching and filtering, and you can click through to discover whether devices are compliant or not for each setting. This report might assist you in identifying patterns throughout the entire estate, particularly if you discover a large number of noncompliant equipment and wish to investigate potential patterns.
- **Policy compliance:** This report is comparable to the previous one, but it examines device compliance and non-compliance per policy at the policy level rather than focusing on specific settings. Once more, you may use this to identify the policy that is suddenly blocking a large number of devices for breaking the rules. This feature makes it easier to locate the report where a specific setting is located in a farm with a large number of policies. As with the others, you can search, filter, and sort by column.

All you need to do to run these reports are clicking the Generate report (or generate again) button, with the exception of Device compliance trends. The report may take a few minutes to complete, but the website will notify you when it completed. All you need to do is click the "Refresh" button to launch the Device compliance trends report. Our reports on device compliance have been reviewed and updated.

Verifying the settings of the device

To see how the policies are working, we can now examine the device setup report:

- Click Reports, then Device Configuration, and lastly the Reports tab at the top to access this report. Next, select Profile configuration status by clicking.
- If you have previously run the report, press Generate again, or Generate report again.
- **You will receive this message as soon as it is generated:**

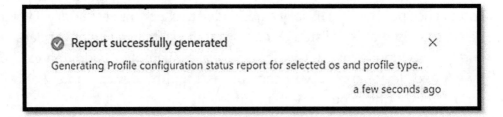

- An inventory of every profile for every operating system is displayed in this report. - It also keeps track of how many times each profile has been flagged as Conflict, Error, or Success.

In addition to exporting, you may search for a profile by name or arrange the results by any title. OS and profile type filters are also available. Sorting policies that contradict or include errors is a fantastic technique to identify trends in the data. Successful people are less of a concern.

TIP: You cannot dig down into this report because you are unable to click on any of the rows. All you can do is view it. That concludes the device configuration process. We are now able to examine Group Policy analytics.

Analyzing the metrics for Group Policies

Group policy analytics are employed with this report. All that is displayed are the settings as they are at the moment and the outcomes of every loaded group policy. A list of the settings that were discovered and whether or not they are ready to be imported into Intune will be displayed on the Summary screen when it initially appears.

Create your report by according to these instructions:

- To access it, select Reports and then Group Policy Analytics. Once there, select Group Policy Migration Readiness from the Reports menu.
- Once you are in the report, click Generate or Generate again if you have previously done so.
- When the report is finished, it includes the usual Export button, a helpful summary, and a fairly powerful filter:

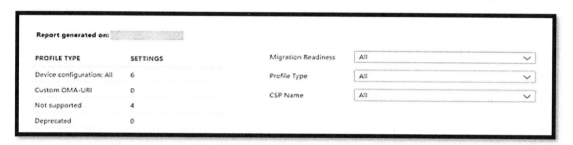

You can view nearly everything by sorting by each title. While clicking through is not feasible at this time, this report explains what can and cannot be moved. To do any additional tasks, you would need to return to the Devices page for Group Policy Analytics. Even though it's never a good idea to load a lot of settings at once, this report will at least highlight which parameters require examination and may need to be adjusted or configured in another manner utilizing PowerShell scripting, custom policy, or policy ingestion.

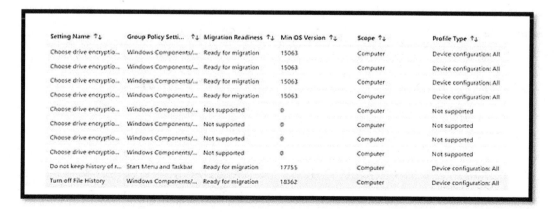

We can examine what is available for co-managed devices now that we have reviewed the Group Policy analytics data.

Devices connected to the cloud

Only organizations using Configuration Manager that wish to investigate co-management can benefit from the Co-Management Eligibility and Co-Managed Workloads reports. To view these reports, navigate to Reports | Cloud Attached Devices on the Intune website, and then select the Reports tab. We may now examine the contents of these reports.

Eligibility for Co-Management

This study explains the current state of cloud-connected devices and if co-management is possible. To run the report, click Generate report or Generate again. When this is executed, it will provide basic device information along with each device's eligibility. Similar to the other reports, you can search, sort, filter, and export the headers.

Jointly Managed Tasks

When configuring co-management, you may select which tasks are handled by Configuration Manager and which are handled by Intune. This report will identify all of your devices along with the tasks that are assigned to them when you run it. If you encounter issues, this is an excellent tool for solving them. As with the previous report, choose Generate Report or Generate Again. This report, along with the Co-Management Eligibility report, has a powerful filter that enables you to rapidly search for particular variables. Use the categories instead, as you can only discover and sort by device name and ID. That concludes our discussion of the contents of device management reports and their usage. We may now examine the process of automating these.

Examining Endpoint Security Reports to Gain Knowledge

We'll examine the crucial security reports next. Even if you don't personally examine them, you may have security teams or a security operations center (SOC) that needs to monitor these. If everything goes according to plan, a compliance policy will cover everything that is being observed here. But reports come in handy whenever something goes wrong. By selecting Reports and then Endpoint Security, you may locate every endpoint security report that is discussed in this section. Once we've located the Reports menu in the user interface, we can review each report.

Examining Microsoft Defender Antivirus

Click Microsoft Defender Antivirus in the Endpoint security reports area, and then select the Reports tab. You can access our two reports by doing this. Here, we'll go into greater detail about each of them.

Status of antivirus agents

Everything you require to know about the protection software on each of your devices is included in this report. It is possible to promptly identify any potentially dangerous tools, identify the damaged portion, and resolve the issue. To create the report, click Generate report or generate again. You ought to have a helpful map that displays the status of your devices after executing the report. If not entirely green, then it ought to be green. There is the ability to group by header, a straightforward search tool, and an effective filter.

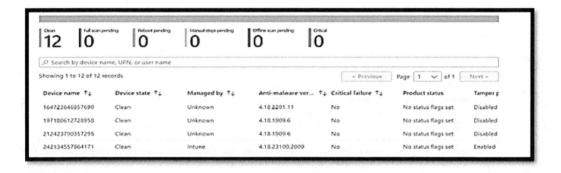

FOOTNOTE: There is a large scroll bar at the bottom and a lot of information to comprehend. Make sure everything is inspected, particularly if a gadget is generating error reports.

Discovered malware

A list of all the devices that are infected or have previously been impacted is displayed in this report. Additionally, the type of malware and the frequency of discovery are displayed. Click Generate report or Generate again, just like before. Use the filter, search, and sort by header options after running it. A helpful graph that displays the current state is also available. Because it allows you to monitor infected or persistently violating devices, this report is rather significant. It makes sense to look at firewall reports after reviewing antivirus findings.

Looking over firewall reports

You may view the functionality of Windows Firewall across all of your devices in the firewall report. The paper is helpful and easy to read. Follow these steps to create the report:

- To view this information, select Firewall, and then click MDM Firewall status for Windows 10 and later. As you can see, there are no tabs in this report.
- Select "Generate report" or click "Generate again."

You will get a screen similar to the one you previously saw once the report has been prepared. It will feature an all-state map, a robust filter, and the ability to search and sort by any field. As a matter of fact, you'll just need to filter or sort the ones when the firewall is disabled. The outcome will be the same in either case. We have followed these procedures to create and review computer security reports. At this point, we can consider automating them.

Evaluating Endpoint Analytics Reports to Improve Performance

Endpoint analytics is a veritable data gold mine that provides you with information about your estate as well as a comparative analysis with other similar-sized enterprises. Since the endpoint analytics reports are simply display-and-export reports, we won't instruct you on how to run them. Rather, we will discuss the functions of each report and how you might use them. Next, we will construct a single automatic script that will allow us to swiftly and simply extract the data from any of the reports.

- To see these reports, navigate to Reports and select Endpoint Analytics.
- Verify that "Connected" is selected under the Intune data collection policy setting by clicking on Settings.

Now that we know where to look, we can examine what all of our endpoint analytics reports have to offer.

Initial performance

This set of studies looks at the initial performance, from pressing the button to having a functional screen. After that, it evaluates this against an industry standard to show you how well your setup and gadgets compare.

Here is where you may learn more about the following topics:

- **Tenant-wide model performance:** every model (minimum of ten devices).
- **Device performance:** This is an excellent way to assess how much performance improves with a Solid State drive because it, along with the model performance, also indicates the type of drive.
- This test compares the SSD/NVMe (driver/nonvolatile memory express) to a clunky spinning hard disk. In addition to identifying drives that are beginning to fail, this can assist with business cases.
- **Startup processes:** An inventory of all the processes that have been discovered, accompanied by the quantity of devices discovered and their startup times.
- **Restart frequency:** This one is particularly useful as it displays the frequency of computer restarts over the last 30 days along with the reasons behind them. This is a good spot to check if you released any driver or application updates to see if any unexpected reboots could be connected to those. Additionally, you may want to look into Advanced Endpoint Analytics' Anomaly Detection.

Now that we've examined startup performance, we can turn our attention to application reliability.

Application dependability

These reports examine crashes that occur within apps, all the way down to the application level. The dependability number in relation to the baseline and the last 14 days' worth of spam are displayed on the first screen.

The reports include the following:

- **App performance:** A summary of every app discovered, together with the number of devices using it, its duration of use, and the number of crashes it has

223

experienced in the previous 14 days. The fact that this report displays the frequency of app usage makes it useful. Thus, an application that crashes frequently but is widely used is not as harmful as one that crashes frequently but is not used very often.

- **Model performance:** This evaluates how well each program functions on every device model to look for trends in crashes that might be related to hardware issues. For your more resource-intensive apps, such as CAD or graphics software, this is quite beneficial.
- **Device performance:** This delves even further into the specifics of the machine and displays the health of the device in addition to a list of all software crashes for each machine. This one may come in handy when someone remarks on app crashes or device performance. One device's much lower statistics than those of other devices may also indicate a hardware malfunction.
- **Performance of OS versions:** A helpful report for updating OS. Prior to deploying to the larger estate, evaluate this's performance once it has been deployed to the test and pilot rings to look for any obvious evidence of performance loss. Similarly, a noticeable improvement in performance could encourage people to update.

We'll now review reports that allow you to work from anyplace.

Work from any location

Whether your devices are Autopilot built or Intune connected (or co-managed), the majority of these reports concern how they are managed in the cloud. Nonetheless, a significant study that examines all of your devices' hardware requirements indicates how prepared they are for Windows 11.

The reports are as follows:

- **Model performance:** a summary of each model's count together with the outcomes of cloud management and Windows compatibility. It's simple to determine which kinds are incompatible with Windows 11 and how many devices will require replacement in the process. The Windows report contains precise data.
- **Device performance:** Every device performs the same as it did in the last report. That's definitely less helpful now, though, because the upcoming reports will only examine individual variables.

- **Windows:** A crucial study that examines every device discovered and identifies those capable of running Windows 11. In the event that there is a problem that can be resolved more rapidly, it will indicate whether it passed or failed and provide an explanation for why. To view the crucial columns, make sure you scroll all the way to the end.
- **Cloud identity (also known as Microsoft Entra Hybrid Joined or Microsoft Entra Joined):** This will display the devices together with the level of control they possess. It is probably less helpful than other reports.
- **Cloud management:** Two examples of control tools for the devices displayed here are Intune and Configuration Manager. The approach for compliance is also displayed. In a split situation, it can be a rapid way to obtain data or do basic repairs.
- **Cloud provisioning:** This displays your devices together with the Autopilot-related data. It does provide a little bit more detail than the Device Enrollment screen and has filtering, which could be helpful.

The Work from Anywhere reports come to an end with this. We are now able to review resource performance reports.

Performance of resources

Windows 365 Cloud PCs are the subject of these two reports. They allow you to monitor the performance of the devices you have been provided and inform you if you require an upgraded license to keep up with the device's requirements or a reduced license to save costs if the devices aren't being used frequently.

The available reports are as follows:

- **Model performance:** ratings for CPU and RAM for every kind of hardware. If you notice that one variety is experiencing more issues than the others, you might need to enhance licenses for the entire farm.
- **Device performance:** This looks at how well each device is working so you can relicense as necessary and find any devices that may be having issues or aren't being used sufficiently. As you can easily scale up again if necessary, this is the one you should monitor the most to keep your costs down. It is usually advisable to start with a lesser specification to determine how well users can handle it. This is especially true for Windows 365, which will significantly enhance web-based app speed and operates on the Microsoft network.

Remote connection establishment

This evaluates how well your Windows 365 devices function when interacting with the cloud PC from a host computer. It examines the average speed, the total rate, and the speed of the last connection.

It contains the following reports:

- **Model performance:** This illustrates the time it takes for cloud PCs to log in and out. If a certain model is significantly impacting the user experience, pay attention to the sign-in time as the RTT shouldn't fluctuate much at the device level.
- **Gadget performance:** Every gadget is examined here. For instance, if a person needs to log into multiple apps, their computer might need to be speedier. Here, the RTT is more helpful since it may indicate that the host computer is experiencing network connectivity issues.

Using Power BI with Intune Data Warehouse to Provide Enhanced Analysis

Anyone who has ever used Power BI will attest to its incredible power as a reporting tool. With Intune, you can customize what can be done right out of the box and add a ton of other functions. It's fantastic that Power BI can be utilized with Intune Data Warehouse, and there are even pre-configured tools to assist you in getting started.

How to proceed...

- From the Reports menu, select Data Warehouse.
- Although you can manually import data by clicking on the URL on this screen, we'll utilize the pre-configured template in this instance.
- Click the Get Power BI app link for the time being.
- In the Intune Compliance (Data Warehouse) app box, click Get it now. This will direct you to Power BI, which will appear in your list of apps shortly after that:

- Select the recently added app.
- Select Compliance Overview by clicking. Don't worry, samples are being used.
- Select "Connect your data."
- As there are no parameters in this application, click Next on the Connect to Intune Compliance (Data Warehouse) screen.
- Select the desired privacy level, and then click Sign in to establish a connection.
- When prompted, confirm your identity in the pop-up box (you might need to accept pop-ups).
- In a minute, your data will reflect the same information.
- Now that your data is linked, you can edit it as needed.

Keeping an eye on Windows Updates with Reporting Tools

The most popular and helpful reports in Intune are most likely those related to Windows Updates. This is due to the fact that monitoring Windows Update progress is essential to maintaining the safety of the entire farm. First, we'll look at the built-in reports. For even more control, we'll include Log Analytics in the following section. Because there are a number of additional choices required to generate these reports, the inputs cannot be automated. To get the same outcome, the same amount of text boxes and clicks would be required. For this reason, we won't be discussing automating them in this part. However, if you find this intriguing, you may import and export it using the same POST methods as many of the other reports.

- On the Intune website, select Reports, followed by Windows updates, and then the Reports tab.
- There are multiple reports in this folder; we will start by discussing how to run each report before discussing its contents.
- Choose from the available reports. In this instance, the Windows Feature Update Report will be utilized.

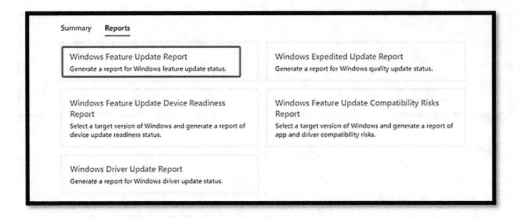

To select what to report on, click the blue text on the right side of each report. Here, we must click the update ring on the appropriate profile. After selecting your option, a "Generate report" button will show up. Press it. When the report is prepared for viewing, you will be notified.

Having mastered the art of running reports, let's examine what they display:

- **Windows Feature Update Report:** When delivering feature updates like 22H2, the Windows Feature Update Report will display the update's status for every device in the selected policy or ring.
- Similar to the previous report, the Windows Expedited Update Report only displays Quality updates (if they are configured because they require additional licensing).
- **Windows Feature Update Device Readiness Report:** Additional licensing and license checking must be enabled for the Windows Feature Update Device Readiness Report. You can select an OS version after it's switched on, and it will inform you when your devices are prepared to get the update. This report is particularly useful for planning updates.
- The Windows Feature Update Compatibility Risks Report is an additional resource that is highly beneficial for update planning. This one will display a list of all the tools and programs that are incompatible with the selected operating system. The same licenses and other prerequisites apply as previously.
- **Windows Driver Update Report:** This will show you how the selected driver is installed throughout your estate if you are utilizing the new driver update capability.

Now that we know what's in the built-in Windows update reports, we can look at using Log Analytics to improve this.

Increasing the Reporting Capability of Windows Updates

By employing Log insights to obtain additional data, alter it, and provide real-time insights, we can take things a step further. Great reports are included with Intune. In order to finish this section, we must first construct an Azure Log Analytics area.

- Navigate to https://portal.azure.com and look for workspaces for Log Analytics.
- Click "Create."
- After deciding on the subscription type you desire, select an existing Resource group or create a new one.
- After naming your space, select Review and Create.
- If everything seems good, click Create.
- When you return to the Azure website, click Monitor.
- Proceed to Workbooks and select View after that.
- Scroll down to find Insights, then select Windows Update for Business Reports.
- Select "Get Started."
- Click Save Settings after making your selections for your subscription and the previously created area.
- Click Save to confirm.
- When this is finished, you'll be informed.

After a few days, you can edit and export the data from the file.

Moving Diagnostics to Azure for In-Depth Examination

Finally, it should be noted that this portion also makes use of Azure, but it does so to store Intune logs and diagnostic data in a few distinct locations, as indicated below:

- A Log Analytics workspace
- Azure Blob storage
- An event hub
- A partner solution

In this instance, we would use a Log Analytics area because it offers more functionalities than Blob storage.

Getting ready

This one will require a Log Analytics workspace, so if you launch it and then forget about it, be sure to set up a cost alert. In the Azure portal, select Log Analytics workspace and press create new. Name your workspace; in this case, we built an area called intunealerts within the rg-loganalytics resource group. With that in place, we can now set up the data to export to our desktop.

Follow these steps to configure the diagnostics for export:

- Return to the Intune console and select Diagnostic Settings after selecting Reports.
- Select the "Add diagnostic setting" option.
- The following information can be added to your workspace: You can select what to transmit to the area on the next screen. Please note that there are fees for data, so determine the amount of data you require and compare it to the potential expenses.
  - **Audit Logs:** These keep track of any additions and modifications made to the Intune website, such as the inclusion of new policies or the removal of outdated ones.
  - **Operational Logs:** Registration of users and devices, along with noncompliant devices
  - **DeviceComplianceOrg:** Provides information on device compliance and compiles a list of noncompliant devices.
  - **Devices:** Device status and inventory
- After selecting the reports, check Send to Log Analytics workspace and select the previously created workspace.
- After you're done, click Save.
- After some time, your logs will appear under Logs in Log Analytics.

This concludes the Configure Intune Diagnostic Data Exports section.

Practice Exercises

1. Explain how to Look Through Reports on Device Management
2. What is Application Dependability?
3. Discuss the process of using Power BI with Intune Data Warehouse to Provide Enhanced Analysis
4. Explain the ways of increasing the Reporting Capability of Windows Updates
5. Mention the steps to configure the diagnostics for export

CHAPTER FIFTEEN
WINDOWS APP PACKAGING

Overview

We will now discuss the various application types available and how to configure them in your system. Applications are essential for using Windows devices, and ensuring that they are packed correctly will guarantee a positive end user experience.

Putting applications in order

All kinds of apps have the same assignment options, thus we also need to consider them.

We have three options for what we can do:

1. **Required:** This will cause an installation. It will only show up in the Company Portal under Installed Applications.
2. **Available for enrolled devices:** For devices that have been enrolled, this shows the app in the Company Portal so users can do it themselves.
3. **Uninstall:** This gets rid of the app.

Installing and removing unnecessary programs from the estate should generally be done through Microsoft Entra groups. Assignments, though, are dependent on the app. This gives you additional alternatives after release, and since the group is already organized and ready to go, it's really useful if you need to rapidly remove an app. You can also specify an installation deadline, a restart delay, and whether to display or conceal install/uninstall alerts during assignment. Consideration should also be given to the human versus device environment, particularly when opening Win32 applications.

The Microsoft Store Integration: How to Use It

We'll start by examining the Microsoft Store integration. This connects directly to the Winget store source and no longer makes use of Microsoft Store for Business. Additionally, this is how Windows apps like Calculator and Notepad are used and updated. **FOOTNOTE:** Updates for Store apps installed via Intune will continue to be sent, even in the event that end users are unable to access the Windows Store due to security precautions. Thankfully, this modification has also simplified the process of opening an application!

How to proceed...

- To start, click Apps and then Windows.
- Click "Add."
- From the drop-down option, select the Microsoft Store app (new). Another name for it is the Microsoft Store app. Click Select after that.
- Click Search when the Microsoft Store app is open.
- Look through the fly-out to find the app you wish to utilize.

Please Note: Intune will only search for apps with a kid-friendly rating because it is frequently used in schools. This implies that not all apps will be displayed. **Locate these apps in the online Microsoft Store and note the App ID, indicated by the red rectangle in the following image:**

Go to Intune and search for that ID:

- Since we will require the Company Portal later on for the experiment, we will keep things simple in this instance. Click "Select."
- By the way, the type will be displayed as UWP. Applications for the Universal Windows Platform come in a variety of forms, including APPX, MSIX, and others. This is just a typical store app.
- Several Win32 applications can also be deployed in this manner rather than being combined into a Win32 intunewin package.
- You will now be able to fill in the details (except from the logo, which is still pending at this writing). Click "Select image" and upload a logo to add one.
- If the customer chooses to self-service install, here is what they will see, and you have the ability to modify any of the data here.

Among the options available to you, these three stand out as crucial:

- Make this the highlighted app in the company portal: This will cause the app to remain on the Company Portal home screen's Apps page.
- Install behavior: If you would want to pause ESP until this program is installed, please adjust this to System. If not, User will function properly.

KEEP IN MIND: Choose your users and systems carefully during the deployment process because putting them in the same app can cause havoc with your environment.

- **Category:** Grouping your apps could make it easier for users to select the best one to use if you have a lot of them.
- Click Next after you're certain of the data.
- Click Next on the Scope Tags page.

Examine the assignment at this time. We're going to make this app a must-install for the Intune Users group since we want every user to have it. Click Next once you've configured. Finally, check that everything is in order, and then click Create. We have now launched a Microsoft Store app using the user interface.

Starting the Packaging Process into MSIX

MSIX is a comparatively new package format. It functions by monitoring an application's installation, recording any modifications to the disk, registry, and other locations, and then compiling all of these changes into a single file that the user may load. One benefit of MSIX is that, in a multi-user environment, it may be used as AppAttach on Azure Virtual Desktop settings to allow users to access apps without needing to install them on the host computer. NOTE: Modifications made to an MSIX package can be undone by the end user. Programs using databases should not be packaged since any modifications made will be lost if they are undone. Client-server applications are OK, but not ones with databases integrated in.

Launching off

The following has to be fulfilled for MSIX packages to function:

- **Certificate for code signing:** All things need to be signed before they can be shipped. Either purchases a public code signing certificate that will be instantly recognized by all devices, or use Intune or a certificate authority (CA) to generate a self-signing certificate that you can then distribute to your devices. Go to Tenant Management and click on it to locate connectors and tokens in Intune.
- Select your cert, and then distribute it using Windows Enterprise Cert.
- **Packaging apparatus:** You will need a virtual machine if you wish to package on MSIX. To avoid having to go through any additional processes that wind up adding to your final bundle, this should be as explicit as possible. In order to easily use backups and checkpoints again for the subsequent package, ensure sure they are activated as well.

Quick Create can be used to set up a Windows 10 or 11 computers with Hyper-V. It will accomplish the following tasks:

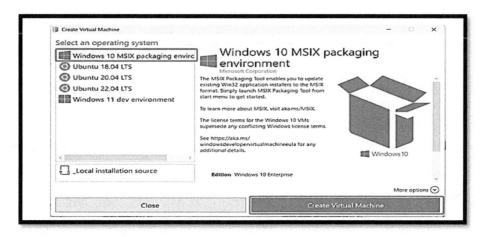

We can start the section now that the four requirements are met. We will package the application first, and then we will examine the deployment process.

The Packaging process

Now that we have a packaging machine and a license, we can begin the packaging and deployment process. We'll use Notepad++ in this instance. Follow these steps to get your first MSIXL ready.

- Select Application Package after launching the MSIX Packaging Tool.
- Click Next after selecting Create package on this machine.
- Your machine will undergo a few checks. Click "Disable selected" next to the marked item to uncheck everything that has been advised for the best packing experience. Next, click this:

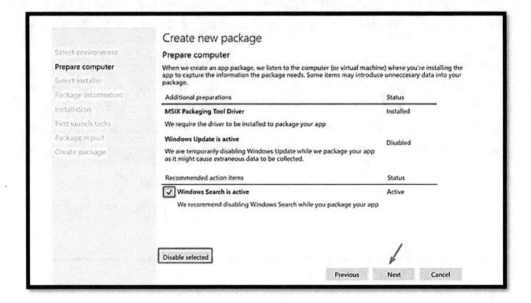

- You can enter the installation instructions on the next screen if you are aware of them. In this instance, however, we will start a fresh install from scratch; therefore we will leave the installer boxes empty.
- We shall sign our application here. Point to the generated certificate, select Sign with a certificate (.pfx), and type the password.

It is imperative that you complete the Timestamp server URL field. When your existing ticket expires, you will need to renew your products with a new one if you do not fill this out. As long as the certificate was valid at the time the app was created and signed, you can select a date server, and the application will continue to function even after it has expired. **Click next after entering the data as displayed in the image below:**

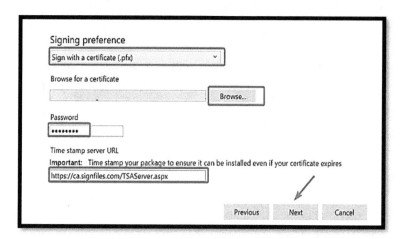

+ The next screen, under "Package information," is where you have to enter the product information. Generally, an app's name, operating system, and version are appropriate beginning points for names (Notepad++_x64_8.5.8_001, for instance). Enter the name, display name, and description of the package. These are going to appear in the business portal. Select a version and a name for your Publisher. Click Next after that.
+ On the box that reads "Create new package," install your app. Click "Restart machine" if you need to restart it. When the computer boots up again, the sequencer will load once more.
+ Turning off automatic updates whenever possible is a good idea because users can undo a package that will erase any updates.
+ Click Next once you've configured.
+ The screen that follows displays the executables that were located. The main launcher will detect any changes made during the initial run and have the ability to disable certain features such as updates and hints and tips.
+ Additionally, you can remove any executable stubs that you do not want customers to view, such as uninstall.exe.
+ If any are missing, you can manually add them here by clicking Browse. When you're finished, click Next.
+ Given that this is the final tracking phase, you must affirm that you still wish to observe the device. Click "Yes," then proceed.

- Any services that the sequencer discovered here can be excluded. When you're finished, click Next.
- In the end, select the package's saving location and press "Create." If you need to look at the files and registry keys or make more modifications, you may also access the package builder from this page.

Deploying the MSIX file is the next stage.

Implementing our MSIX suite

Now that the software is packed, we can release it to Intune:

- Navigate to Apps, then Windows in Intune.
- Click "Add."
- After selecting the Line-of-Business app, hit "Select."
- Select the MSIX file that you created in the preceding phase by clicking Select app package file. Click OK after that.
- If necessary, you can edit any information and upload an image before clicking Next.
- Click Next on the Scope Tags page.

Since this software is simple enough for users to operate on their own, we will establish needed and Uninstall groups to assist users in determining whether or not they require the program. Everyone will subsequently be able to join these groups. You can switch between downloading as a gadget and as a human at this point as well. Click Next when you've finished configuring your assignments.

- Finally, check that everything is in order, and then click Create.

The section on packing an MSIX application has come to a conclusion. We can examine Win32 apps as our next topic of discussion.

About Win32 application packaging

You should read this section carefully because the primary method of deploying your software will be through Win32 packaging.

Launching off

Before we package, we should tidy up our application source code so that when the time comes to upgrade that amazing and strange program in two years, we can simply figure out what's what. NOTE: Make sure the directory only contains source files, as the package tool will collect all the files in the Source directory you give it. For instance, you'll be perplexed as to why an application that weighs only 2 MB when packaged looks to be 45 GB if you point it at your Downloads folder! The package tool creates intewin files, which are basically encrypted ZIP files that are published to Azure Blob storage with a manifest. Upon selecting "install," the software package is downloaded, decrypted, and launched on your machine.

Although it's entirely up to you, the following method of folder organization works well:

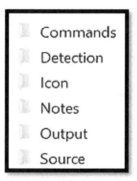

The Source folder contains additional files, launcher and configuration files, and raw files. The output will contain the intunewin file. The rest ought to be rather obvious. Remember to keep a copy of any source files you use, as once you add them to Intune, you cannot remove them. It's time to examine the various installation creation methods now.

Make a direct call to MSI/Exe

We could instruct Intune to launch the file during installation if we just packaged the executable or MSI file on its own:

```
msiexec.exe /i myinstaller.msi /qn myinstaller.exe /silent
```

This is acceptable; however you are unable to modify anything either before or after the installation. Remember that if the MSI was created that way, Intune might install it in the user context. This will be shown by the context being grayed out. If you wish to execute one of these in the system context, you will need to modify the MSI or figure out a way to wrap it.

The Script in batch

While PowerShell is far more modern and capable, a batch script can still be used for packing. It's okay if doing something helps you feel better. For now, this will work just fine, but in the long run, PowerShell or the PowerShell Application Deployment Toolkit (PSADT) would be a better option.

Write an installation batch script. Here is the file you need to install after packaging:

As an illustration:

```
rem Delete file
del c:\temp\myfile.txt
rem Stop Service
net stop myservice
rem Install App
my-installer.exe /verysilent /allusers /noreboot
rem Delete Shortcut
del %public%\desktop\myshortcut.lnk
```

For those that use batch scripts, these are some useful pointers.

When a command window appears, type SET to view a list of the machine's settings. Just as we did with the public user environment, %public%, you may link to these within%. It is not necessary to append a backslash when discussing the current directory:

```
%~dp0myinstaller.exe
```

Simply rename your batch script to install.bat or any other appropriate name, and then replace the install command in Intune.

A PowerShell script

Installation is made even better with PowerShell scripts, which provide you more control over the system. Additionally, doing complex tasks with them is simpler. Right now, anything is conceivable. You may examine the circuitry below and add programming.

In this instance, for a PowerShell script to launch an MSI, the code below needs to be executed:

```
$MSIArguments = @(
"/i"
('"{0}"' -f $filelocation)
"/qn"
"/norestart"
"/L*v"
)
Start-Process "msiexec.exe" -ArgumentList $MSIArguments -Wait -NoNewWindow
```
  - You can, of course, add or remove features for apps that don't have an MSI when you use PowerShell.

We'll use DotNet as an example here:
```
  - Enable-WindowsOptionalFeature -Online -FeatureName 'NetFx3' -Source .\sxs\ -NoRestart -LimitAccess
```
This is what the installation command in Intune would look like:
```
  - powershell.exe -ExecutionPolicy Bypass -file myinstaller.ps1
```

About PSADT

With its many additional functions, PSADT (https://psappdeploytoolkit.com/) is an extremely strong PowerShell tool that may be utilized to enhance the process even further. Run a specific file in the user context while the others run in the system context, add tasks before and after installation, or check to see if any programs are open and ask the user to close them if they are. **NOTE:** You must utilize the ServiceUI application from the Microsoft Deployment Tools (MDT) toolkit if you want users to be able to interact with your app after deployment through Intune.

Toolkit for Deployment Tools (MDT)

The install code for software that is packed with PSADT and enables user interaction would be as follows:

```
.\ServiceUI.exe          -Process:explorer.exe          Deploy-
Application.exe
```

After discussing the various installation methods, it's time to discuss packaging an app.

How to proceed...

Now that we have the source files, we must package them using Microsoft's IntuneWinAppUtil and launcher. This provides us with the intunewinfile by opening and bundling the source files.

Take the following actions to package your program in the Intunewin format:

- We must load the app first. We are going to use 7-Zip to make things easier. We will be prompted to name the source folder in a message.
- Point it at the Source folder, which was created earlier and contains the setup file and software media.
- Next, provide the application file's (setup file's) name.
- Giving IntuneWinAppUtil instructions to place the intunewin file (in the Output folder) is the final step.
- Once the program has been packed, we need to find out how Intune can determine that the download was successful.

Application recognition

Get the detection type to inform Intune that the download was successful before adding anything.

We can do the following actions to locate our sensor and then configure it in Intune:

Windows Sandbox is typically useful as a test system to find a file or registry key that may be used to identify an object.

Additionally, you may use this PowerShell script to rapidly obtain the product code for an MSI application:

```
$path = "PATH TO MSI"
$comObjWI = New-Object -ComObject WindowsInstaller.Installer $MSIDatabase =
$comObjWI.GetType().InvokeMember("OpenDatabase
","InvokeMethod",$Null,$comObjWI,@($Path,0))  $Query = "SELECT Value FROM
Property WHERE Property = 'ProductCode'" $View =
$MSIDatabase.GetType().InvokeMember("OpenView"
,"InvokeMethod",
$null,$MSIDatabase,($Query))
$View.GetType().InvokeMember("Execute",
"InvokeMethod", $null, $View, $null)
$Record =
$View.GetType().InvokeMember("Fetch","InvokeMe thod",$null,$View,$null) $Value =
$Record.GetType().InvokeMember("StringData","G etProperty",$null,$Record,1)
write-host "Your MSI code is $Value" - ForegroundColor Green
```

You can use the MSI code obtained from this script for both detection and uninstallation.

Now that we have the file, we must add it to Intune.

- Click the Apps link on the Intune website. Next, select Windows.
- Then click Add.
- Click Select after selecting Windows program (Win32) from the drop-down menu.
- The blue text that reads "Select app package file" should be clicked.
- Now select the Intunewin file that we previously created, and then press OK.
- We need to add a publisher at the very least and a name, description, version, and image at the very best because, because we packed an application, it will only fill in the path. Click Next once you've completed these forms.

We can make some changes on the next screen. Start by filling in the Install and Uninstall directions according to the app's packaging. This could be a file path, a PowerShell script, or a batch file. If the application is an MSI, both fields ought to be filled up automatically.

- Additionally, you can decide how long the process should continue for before failing and stopping. This is more effective for larger or more intricate tasks. For 7-Zip, the standard 60-minute option will function as intended.
- Apps that users install on their own via the Company Portal are eligible for allowable uninstall. If users select "Yes," they will also be able to remove the app independently.
- You must select System as the installation action for this application. However, some apps might be designed with users in mind, so adjust as necessary.
- If it needs to restart, you can also instruct it on what to do.
- Add any odd return codes the program may have here in the final step. The standard codes will function just fine most of the time.
- When you're finished, click Next.
- Setting the system requirements is the next step in getting the program installed. If a device does not fulfill these requirements, the software will not proceed further.

You can configure additional details at the device level, like RAM and CPU speed, for more complex applications like CAD software. If you want to take it a step further, you can even add your own requirements script. For instance, you may utilize the Windows Management Interface (WMI) to inquire about the device chassis and then inquire here if you only want to install on laptops (for a VPN client).

- Since we've supplied you a 64-bit version of 7-Zip, all we need to check is that the PC meets that requirement. Click Next once you've configured.
- Establishing the recognition rule is the next stage. Intune will utilize this to verify that the program is installed correctly.

Here are some things we can do:

- **MSI:** Any straight MSI file will have this automatically filled in. It is also possible to add a globally unique identification (GUID) for MSI. This will determine whether the ID already exists.

- **File:** Use the name, date, version, or size fields to search for a specific file (useful for updates). You could try pointing it to the executable file. Pay attention to the 32/64-bit option. On 64-bit computers, if you select "Yes," it will appear in the 32-bit context, such as Program Files (x86).
- **Register:** Search for a specific key, term, version, or number in the register. For both 32-bit and 64-bit, it is same.
- The requirements script you can use this script to search for nearly anything, including a functioning service or a combination of many methods. The script must exit with an exit code of 0 to indicate that it was successful in order for this to function.

This instance demonstrates this:

```
$service = get-service -name
"MozillaMaintenance"
if ($service.Status -eq "Running") { write-output "MozillaMaintenance
detected and running, exiting"
exit 0
}
else {
exit 1
}
```

- For 7-Zip, we will use a File Rule type with the right path and file set to check for the presence of the 7z program.
- Click Next when we're done setting up the detection.
- The next section will talk about Dependencies and Supersedence, so we can press Next on these two for now.
- On the Scope Tags page, click Next.
- It's time to give the application to someone. For better control, we will set Available for registered devices to All Users (or All Devices) since this is free software. However, we will make sure that Required and Uninstall are set to specific groups. After setting up, click Next:

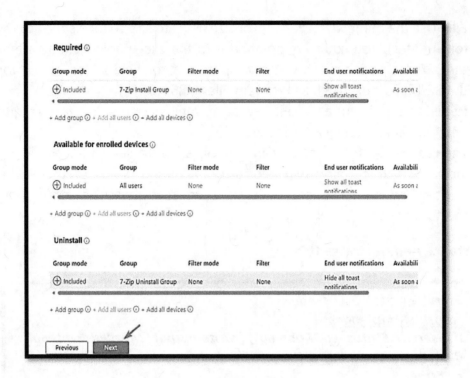

Handling Dependencies and App Supersedence

We'll examine application supersedence and application dependencies in this part. Since automating involves switching between existing programs, we won't discuss it here. Rather, we will discuss how to put things up and why you would utilize them.

The Supersedence of other applications

Upon the release of an updated app, you have many options:

- To make it function with the current version, get a fresh copy of the IntuneWin file and modify its search parameters.
- Create a new application and reassign the tasks.
- Utilize the superseding application.

You have the option to simply upgrade or to uninstall the previous version before downloading the new one. It will everything still function perfectly. It's also simpler to manage because you won't have to stress about assigning the same task again or managing several programs.

The Dependencies

One issue with Autopilot and Intune is that they lack the ability to arrange apps in a hierarchy similar to Configuration Manager. As a result, you could never be confident that, should a program need to start, the necessary engine (.NET, Java, VC Libraries, etc.) would be installed in a timely manner. Prior to dependencies, in order to use the install script, you had to install the app after bundling the two into it. This was effective, but whenever you updated one of the apps, you had to repackage the other one as well, even if the changes were little. This is where dependence is useful: you select the required code or application and add it as a dependent to the main application. After that, Intune will see if the application has already loaded. If not, the main program will be launched after the dependency has been installed.

Launching off

To continue this part, you will need the following:

- The identical supersedence application in two distinct forms
- An application that relies on something

We can now look at how these parameters are created, starting with application supersedence.

Setting up the supersedence of an application

In this instance, we'll utilize 7-Zip and update from version 19.00 to 23.00. **Follow these steps to configure application supersedence in the application setup:**

- Click Windows after selecting Apps.
- Locate your application by going through the list. Older versions can be swapped out with new ones. In this instance, 7-Zip 23.00 is required. Apply pressure to it.
- Click Properties.
- "Supersedence" should be found; select "Edit."
- To add the app that it will replace, click "+Add".
- Locate the app you wish to use in the fly-out and click Select.
- Set Uninstall to Yes if you must delete the previous version of the app entirely in order to load the updated version. Once all is in order, select Review + Save.
- In order to ensure that the changes are saved, click "Save" one again.

This can also be configured at the time of the original application release if you are certain that the new version doesn't require any more testing. You can verify that the new version is bug-free prior to release by configuring it after it has been released. Now that we have discussed supersedence, let's look at how to configure application dependencies.

Setting up an application's dependence

Although it is not necessary, we will be adding the Visual C++ 2013 Redistributable package as a dependency for our latest 7-Zip 23.00 version.

To configure our app's reliance on other apps, take the following actions:

- Click Windows after selecting Apps.
- Locate and click on your app (in this example, 7-Zip 23.00) from the list.
- Click Properties.
- Scroll down to Dependencies and click Edit.
- Selecting "+ Add" will display a menu with an application list.
- Find your app in the list, select it with a click, and then select "Select."

Here, you may select whether you want to install the app manually or whether you want it to install automatically when the parent app is installed. In most cases, it is automatic to choose the superior option. Once you have finished configuring everything, click Review + Save.

- You will be prompted to confirm any supersedences you have put up here. Click Review + Save once again since we already know these are correct.
- Lastly, to validate your modifications to the program, click Save.

What do application dependencies and supersedence mean? Now that we are aware of them, we can arrange for tenant applications to be submitted.

Using Office Programs

Microsoft 365 Apps is another term for the Microsoft Office Suite of Apps. It's perhaps among the most crucial apps that you should have on your gadgets. Because of this, we need to make sure they are set up correctly, consistently, and ideally forced on the Enrollment Status Page (ESP).

Starting off

The Microsoft 365 apps can be installed in Intune in three distinct methods. Compared to the other two, one of them is far more dependable. The best method to achieve it is to encapsulate it as a Win32 application using the Office Deployment Tool (ODT). We shall talk about this in this part since we will then have control over how it is delivered during the ESP. We also know that it will be installed using the Intune Management Extension (IME), which prevents conflicts between programs. Before we look at how to launch as a Win32 application, we should have a look at the other alternatives available on the website.

These involve typing XML or utilizing the graphical user interface (GUI) with setup creator options:

- Click Windows after selecting Apps.
- After selecting Microsoft 365 Apps for Windows 10 and later, click Add. Press the Select button.
- In the first screen, select "Next." The "Configure app suite" screen will appear as a result.

With the Configuration Designer tool, you can quickly build up your application package without having to package any apps or modify any XML. Although it is a quick way to start the apps, you are unable to decide which apps—like Skype for Business—should not be loaded. This is not something you can really control. When you switch to Office Customization Tool, you can use distinct XML created by the tool. As we will do for the Win32 software, enter XML data. If you utilize the built-in Microsoft 365 application configuration, there's a potential it will clash with a different version. This is as a result of its installation functioning more as a plan than an application. It is also outside your control to deal with detection, particular requirements, supersedence, and dependencies (which come in handy if you have programs that install Office products).

How to proceed...

Now that we've looked at the approaches we shouldn't use, let's learn how to install, package, and run a program as a Win32 application.

To utilize Office as a Win32 application, take the following actions:

- The first thing we need to do is set up our XML file. This will specify the languages to be used, the components to load, and other details for the Office Deployment Tool. To do that, navigate to the Office Customization Tool.

Here, you can select the Office version to use, the products to uninstall, the language packs to use, and more. In order to prevent customers from downgrading after installation, the update channel you choose here should preferably match your Broad Ring. This is because we will be configuring the update channel using Intune in the next section. If your program has unique needs, you may also specify which version to install.

- Since this would be executing in the system context nonetheless, it is advisable to leave Show installation to user set to No in the Installation settings. Additionally, if you are launching during Autopilot, confirm that Shut down running apps is set to Yes. If an application is currently executing, timeout issues may arise. If you are launching after the initial setup, it could be best to use PSADT and instruct customers to close the apps themselves as you have no idea when they will be installed.

A notice that reads, "Uninstall any MSI versions of Office," is located in the "Update and upgrade" option. This will remove any Office applications that were discovered. If you're installing the entire suite, this usually won't be an issue, but if you're installing individual apps, like as Project or Visio, ensure sure this is set to No. Everything will be deleted if it isn't, with the exception of the installed software. Change first by going to Licensing and Activation. Inherently Say "yes" to the EULA. Your end users won't have to accept it on their own in this way.

Regarding licensing, we mostly have three options:
- **User-driven:** Every user receives a license, and they are only allowed to install up to five times before the Office site requests that they take down any installed content.
- **Shared Computer:** This option is most effective in settings like hospitals or hot desks where staff members have access to a variety of devices. When a device is in "Shared Computer" mode, it will not consume one of the five user licenses. If you choose to utilize this option, confirm that it is permitted by your rights.
- **Device-based:** When a machine has several unlawful users, the machine itself is licensed. This calls for a unique permit.

In Application Preferences, you can configure anything that can be managed by Group Policy or Intune Policy. While this is sufficient for one-time settings, you will have greater flexibility and be able to make changes without needing to re-package apps if you use Intune policies.

- When you're done modifying the parameters, click Export.
- After choosing the desired file style, click "OK," and save the XML.
- Now that we have our XML file, we need to figure out how to use it to get the Office apps in front of users. This will be accomplished using the Office Deployment Tool. By launching the downloaded software file, you can organize the files into a folder.

It is now necessary to establish the Win32 folder structure. The Office Deployment Tool has an XML file and a setup.exe file that you may download and place in the Source folder.

Additionally, create a uninstall.xml file containing the following details:

```
<Configuration>
<Display Level="None" AcceptEULA="True" />
<Property Name="FORCEAPPSHUTDOWN" Value="True" />
<Remove>
<Product ID="O365ProPlusRetail">
</Product>
</Remove>
</Configuration>
```

- Wrap it with the IntuneWinAppUtil tool, select setup.exe to launch the installation, and store the file intunewin in the Output folder.
- Now that we have our IntuneWin file, we can add it to Intune. Navigate to Windows under Apps on the Intune website.
- After selecting "Win32," click "Add," then "Select." Select your intunewin file by clicking the folder icon, then click OK.

Since this is a Win32 application that opens from a file, all fields must be filled out. The icon is a part of this. Click Next once you've configured. We must now explain how to install and uninstall.

> For your install command, you need the following: *setup.exe /configure Configuration.xml*
> For the uninstall command, you need this: *setup.exe /configure uninstall.xml*

- Click Next after making any other changes.
- Make sure to use the most recent version of Windows in your estate combined with the 64-bit version of our program. Click Next after that.
- Office programs install the Click-To-Run program first, which downloads the files, making it more difficult to set detection criteria. Now that we know the Click-To-Run utility is broken, we will search for a registry key.

We have configured the following registry keys:

> *Key Path:*
> *HKEY_LOCAL_MACHINE\SOFTWARE\Microsoft\Offi ce\ClickToRun*
> *Value: LastScenarioResult*
> *Detection: Exists*

- We don't want to link it to a 32-bit program because we're delivering the 32-bit version. If we do, it will attempt to establish a connection with WOW6432Node but be unsuccessful in doing so. On 64-bit clients, set Associated with a 32-bit app to No.
- After everything is configured, select Next and then OK.
- There are no Dependencies, Supersedence, or Scope tags associated with this app because it is an essential app required throughout the estate. On all three screens, click Next.
- When viewing assignments, you have the option to Deploy to a Group, All Users, or All Devices. Without a doubt, you should install this on every device. Once you've selected the group, click Next.
- After verifying that everything we configured is accurate on the Review + Create screen, click the Create button.

The section on installing Microsoft 365 apps has come to an end. Let's investigate the process of updating the apps.

Bringing Office Applications Up to Date

Now that our Office applications are live, we must ensure that they remain current. It's best to use the same ring strategy that we did for Windows updates because these are important apps. In this manner, you can look for issues pertaining to the firm and major UI modifications that may require sharing with the organization. The optimal method for handling Office updates will be covered in this article. We will discuss how to set them up after taking a closer look at the two primary options. Using the Office Admin site is one option for the Office portal. Using Policy Management, you can adjust any Office policy setup parameter here. Version releases and updates can also be managed using the Cloud Updates menu. This is a wise decision, however because it's separate from the Intune portal, there's an additional gateway to manage and a greater possibility of issues as the same configuration might be made twice.

Configurations database

Using the Settings catalog, we can make changes to any ADMX-backed settings directly on the devices. We can also use the update groups we currently have or start new ones. We will carry this out in this section.

Updates from the office

- Select Windows from the Devices menu, then click Configuration Profiles. This recipe uses the Settings library in the same way as all the others.
- Tap Create at the top. Select New Policy after that. Select Windows 10 and later next.
- Lastly, select the Settings catalog from the resulting window. Finally, select "Create."
- Give the name and description of your new page. Select names for the rings that take into account the fact that most of the time you will require at least three distinct profiles for them. Click Next after that.
- On the Settings screen, click Add Settings. In the list that appears, select Microsoft Office 2016 (Machine). Select the Updates option. The most recent Office 2016 policies are compatible with all Microsoft 365 products.
- By choosing the machine policies, which write the keys to HKEY Local Machine (HKLM) instead of the HKEY Current User (HKCU) hive, users are unable to alter the frequency of their updates.

- **To update, we require these two configurations:**
  - ➤ Turn on Automatic Updates Put it in the enabled state.
  - ➤ **Update Channel:** Verify that it is activated. Align Channel with the ring that is being configured.
- In the options section, you can also modify the Update Deadline if necessary.
- After selecting the appropriate channel, press "Next."
- After the Scope tags page, click Next to move on to the following page.

Assign the application now. You may wish to place some heavy Office app users in one of the earlier rings for Office updates, as the collection of users and devices may differ, in order to identify any issues before they are rolled out to the entire estate. If users in your organization, such as IT personnel, frequently switch between computers, you may want to use device groups to prevent Office versions from upgrading and downgrading when different users log in. Just be cautious when adding and removing groups so as not to mix up device and user groups.
- When you have finished configuring your assignments, click Next.
- Once you're certain that everything is correct, click Create.

Office update settings in the user interface are now finished.

Protection for Windows Applications

The need for application protection has increased since more people are using their personal devices to view work-related information. As of this writing, Windows Mobile Application Management (MAM) is a new functionality that is limited to the Microsoft Edge browser. This approach involves configuring MAM and adding conditional access controls to prevent personal devices from accessing non-Microsoft Edge content. First of all, remember that personal devices are not eligible to register for Microsoft Intune. Should they do so, they will circumvent the limitations on access.

Follow these steps to configure Windows application protection:
- Encouraging all tenants to use MAM is the first step. This only has to be done once.
- Go to Connectors and Tokens under Tenant Administration. Next, select "Mobile Threat Defense."
- Provide a connection method for the Windows Security Center.

PRO TIP: When it is utilized, it will update, so don't worry if it reads "not available".
- Next, select App Protection Policies by going to Apps.
- Select "Windows" from the "Create New" menu rather than "Windows Information Protection."

- After naming and describing your policy, click "Next."
- On the Apps screen, click the blue + Select Apps text and select Microsoft Edge. Click Next once Select has been selected.
- Configure your settings for data protection. You can decide, for instance, whether to prevent printing and whether to permit data to be moved into and out of the program. Click Next after that.
- On the Health Checks panel, you can further secure the data. For instance, you can specify minimum program versions and decide how many days after creation to erase the data. The minimum operating system versions can be adjusted under "Device conditions" to prevent any unauthorized Microsoft installs.

PRO TIP: You may wish to include the "Disabled Account" health check setting here. In this manner, you can guarantee that any former employees cannot log in using their personal devices.

- When you're finished configuring everything, click Next.
- On the Scope group's page, select Next as this is a global rule.
- As tasks are needed, assign them. Remember that the group must contain users because this is happening at the user level and applies to devices that aren't registered for Intune or Entra ID. All users with a valid Intune license might be added to a dynamic group, however at this time, selecting all users is not an option. Click Next once you've configured.
- Once you're satisfied with how everything looks, click Create.
- Now that the Intune side is complete, we must implement more security for restricted access.
- Go to Conditional access under Endpoint security.

We need to prevent non-company owned devices from being used for anything other than the web app, which is why we are enforcing compliance. This policy only applies to BYOD devices, thus even though you should follow this procedure on all devices, we will additionally employ a device filter to exclude company-owned devices. Select All cloud apps and All users (apart from your Break Glass account) first. No data should ever leave our protected system. Make sure that the device platforms are set to only Windows since this is a Windows-only setup. **We want other sites to be exempt from this policy:**

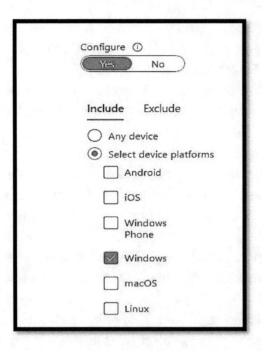

We want to allow the computer to pass in this instance. We will make sure that remains secure in the upcoming plan. **Thus, everything should follow this guideline, with the exception of the browser:**

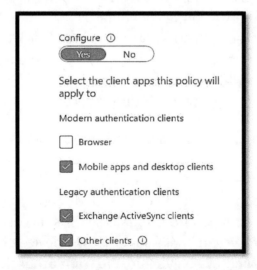

As previously stated, we will exclude business devices by applying the filter displayed in the following image:

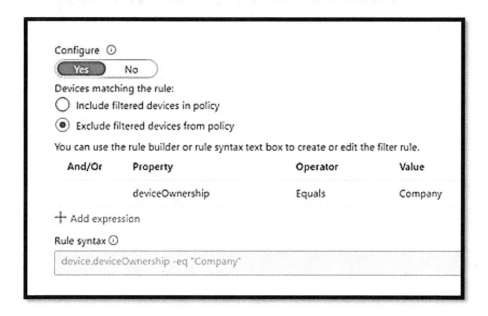

device.deviceOwnership -eq "Company"

Configure ⓘ

[**Yes** ｜ No]

Devices matching the rule:

○ Include filtered devices in policy

◉ Exclude filtered devices from policy

You can use the rule builder or rule syntax text box to create or edit the filter rule.

And/Or	Property	Operator	Value
	deviceOwnership	Equals	Company

+ Add expression

Rule syntax ⓘ

device.deviceOwnership -eq "Company"

Next, we must mandate compliance, which will instantly disable any gadgets that are not business property. Go to Grant access and select "Require device to be marked as compliant" to accomplish this.

◉ Grant access

☐ Require multifactor ⓘ
   authentication

☐ Require authentication ⓘ
   strength

☑ Require device to be marked ⓘ
   as compliant

This has prevented us from accessing anything without using a browser. Our goal with the second restricted access technique is to prevent browser access. Again, we want to reach every user, every cloud app, and every Windows device. This policy will not work if you select any other option; it should only be used on browsers.

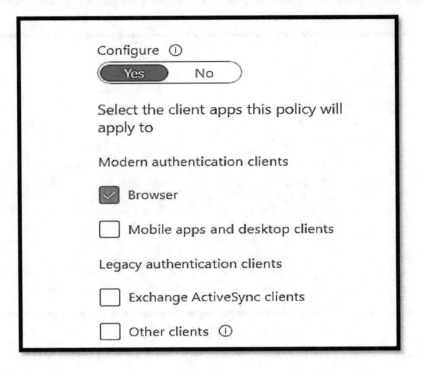

Again, avoid corporate devices using the same filter. The most crucial need is that we provide an app protection policy in the Grant access section.

You can also use Conditional Access App Control in the Session settings to prevent downloads (preview) as an additional safety precaution.

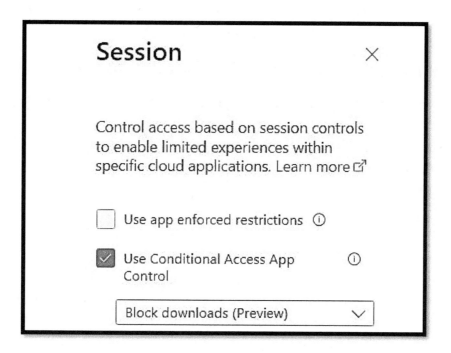

We have now secured our data on personal devices using the Edge browser, and we have prevented any other means of access on Windows.

Practices Exercises

1. Explain the usage of Microsoft Store Integration
2. What do you understand about Win32 application packaging
3. Discuss the steps to utilize Office as a Win32 application
4. Explain the ways to bring Office Applications Up to Date
5. What are the steps to configure Windows application protection?

CHAPTER SIXTEEN
UNDERSTANDING TROUBLESHOOTING
Frequent Problems & Fixes with Intune Troubleshooting

Despite Microsoft Intune's abundance of capabilities, there is always a chance that you will encounter issues with its utilization. Here are some strategies for resolving issues you may encounter:

Device enrollment issues

The difficulty of joining devices with Intune is a prevalent issue. A user may experience issues if their Azure AD join settings are incorrect, security policies are changed, or limited access restrictions are implemented. Tools like logs, Intune support files, and the Intune device troubleshooter can help you swiftly resolve these issues.

Issues with Mobile Device Management

Handling of smart devices might be an additional issue. For instance, conflicting configurations may prevent the implementation of IT compliance requirements or the synchronization of registered devices with the Intune service. You can take proactive measures, such as reviewing the Event logs and verifying the tenant status, to address certain Intune issues.

Application Security Guidelines Inaccurate setup

Application security policies frequently lead to issues because they are misconfigured or poorly understood by users. Improper handling or protection of data might impact a service's functionality. IT specialists who review application setup policies and make changes to the Intune site's settings can resolve these issues with Intune.

Problems with Performance and Connectivity

The Intune service may have trouble connecting and operating as intended if there are network issues or system overloads. Utilizing Intune's integrated state tracking and reporting features can assist you in identifying these issues. Regular system updates and performance checks can resolve these kinds of issues.

Difficulties with Reporting and Compliance

Companies may also encounter difficulties reviewing the gathered data or reporting compliance due to incomplete or erroneous data in the system. Monitoring, assessing, and resolving these issues is feasible using Microsoft Intune's dedicated reporting and inspection tools.

Issues with Authorization and Authentication

Inaccuracies in authentication and permission frequently result from improperly configured access policies or outdated passwords. Frequent inspections, evaluations of IT guidelines, and password modifications will eliminate these issues and facilitate Intune troubleshooting.

Advanced Microsoft Intune Troubleshooting Methods

Once you've mastered the fundamentals, you can utilize some more sophisticated methods for Intune troubleshooting. Fixing Intune issues that won't go away can require going the additional mile.

Making Use of the Troubleshooting Portal for Microsoft Intune

The Troubleshooting Portal for Microsoft Intune is an effective tool that every IT professional should be able to use. You may view all of the information about your gadget in one location by visiting the website. The website displays issues with device registration, policy rollout, or compliance policies to help with improved Intune troubleshooting.

Logging and Reporting Diagnostics

Diagnostic reporting and logging are additional crucial components of Intune troubleshooting. Diagnostic logging reveals critical information about the operation of the system and highlights areas of failure. In this instance, it ought to be evident from the log if users have recently modified security settings or experienced issues with entry rules. Additionally, it can display any discrepancies between the current statuses of registered devices and your expectations for their behavior. On the other side, reporting prevents issues by taking action before they arise. Reports can be customized to prioritize high-priority areas such as current device management, allowing you to address issues before they negatively impact user experience. One way to monitor issues with Microsoft Edge would be to schedule a daily check-in report. This would alert you to potential issues with Intune early on.

Frequent Upgrades and Updates for Systems

As with any other system, Microsoft Intune requires regular upgrades and adjustments to function properly. Updates often improve the program's speed, safety, and functionality by fixing flaws that have previously been discovered. You can reduce the amount of time and anxiety you spend troubleshooting Intune if you stay up to date with these modifications. Consider creating a plan for finding and applying system updates. Microsoft frequently shares information on its official websites and social media pages to ensure people are informed about the most recent Intune troubleshooting techniques. You will switch from the Intune interface to the improved Microsoft Endpoint Manager Control center as part of this.

Resolving some Intune Windows device enrollment issues

Error hr 0x8007064c: The device has already been registered.

A cloned image containing enrollment data, persistent account certificates, or prior enrollment are some possible causes of an enrollment failure with the error message "The machine is already enrolled" and error hr 0x8007064c.
Take these actions to fix the problem:
Resolution:

1. **Access MMC:**
   - Press the Windows key and type "Run" to open the Run dialog.
   - Type "**MMC**" and hit Enter.
2. **Add/Remove Snap-ins:**
   - In the MMC console, go to "**File**" and select "Add/Remove Snap-ins."
3. **Select Certificates:**
   - Double-click "Certificates" and choose "Computer account" > "Next," then select "Local Computer."
4. **Navigate to Certificates:**
   - Expand "Certificates (Local Computer)" and select "Personal" > "Certificates."
5. **Delete Intune Certificate:**
   - Locate the Intune certificate issued by Sc_Online_Issuing.
   - If found, delete it.
6. **Delete Registry Key:**
   - Check if the registry key exists: HKEY_LOCAL_MACHINE\SOFTWARE\Microsoft\OnlineManagement and delete it along with all subkeys.
7. **Re-Enroll:**
   - Attempt to re-enroll the device.
8. **Additional Steps:**
   - If the issue persists, search for and delete the registry key: KEY_CLASSES_ROOT\Installer\Products\6985F0077D3EEB44AB6849B5D7913E9 5.
9. **Re-Attempt Enrollment:**
   - Retry the enrollment process.

Error 8018000a: There is already an enrollment for this device

Encountering the error code 8018000a and the "Something went wrong" message. The message "The device is already enrolled" suggests that the device has previously been linked to Microsoft Entra ID or enrolled in Intune by a different user.

Take these actions to fix the problem:

Cause:
- Another user has already enrolled the device in Intune or joined the device to Microsoft Entra ID. This can be confirmed by checking Settings > Accounts > Work Access for a message similar to "Another user on the system is already connected to a work or school. Please remove that work or school connection and try again."

Solution:
1. **Sign Out and Sign In with the Other Account:**
   - Sign out of Windows and then sign in using the account that has already enrolled or joined the device.
2. **Remove Work or School Account:**
   - Navigate to Settings > Accounts > Work Access.
   - Remove the work or school account associated with the device.
3. **Sign Out and Sign In with Your Account:**
   - Sign out of Windows and sign in again using your account.
4. **Enroll or Join the Device:**
   - Proceed to enroll the device in Intune or join the device to Microsoft Entra ID using your account.

This phone is not authorized to use this account.

- **Error:** "This phone is not authorized to use this account. Verify the information you submitted, try again, or get assistance from your employer."
- **Cause:** An invalid Intune license was used by the person who attempted to enroll the device.
- **Resolution:** Give the user a current Intune license, and then enroll the device.

It appears that the MDM Terms of Use endpoint is not set up properly.

- MDM Terms of Use Endpoint Error Inaccurate setup
- **One of the following is usually the cause of an error message stating that the MDM Terms of Use endpoint is incorrectly configured.**

> **Cause:**
> 1. **User License Issue:**
>   - The user attempting to enroll the device lacks a valid Intune license or an Office 365 license.
>   - This scenario triggers an error message stating, "Looks like we can't connect to the URL for your organization's MDM terms of use."
> 2. **Incorrect MDM Terms and Conditions URL:**
>   - The MDM terms and conditions URL within Microsoft Entra ID is either empty or does not contain the correct URL.
>
> **Solution: To resolve this issue, you can implement one of the following methods:**
> 1. **Assign a Valid License to the User:**
>   - Go to the Microsoft 365 Admin Center and assign either an Intune or a Microsoft 365 license to the user.
> 2. **Correct the MDM Terms of Use URL:**
>   - Sign in to the Azure portal and navigate to Microsoft Entra ID.
>   - Select "Mobility (MDM and MAM)" and click on "Microsoft Intune."
>   - Choose "Restore default MDM URLs" and ensure that the MDM terms of use URL are set to https://portal.manage.microsoft.com/TermsofUse.aspx.
>   - Click "Save" to apply the changes.

Something was not right

Seeing error number 80180026 usually happens in the following scenarios when trying to connect a Windows 10 PC to Microsoft Entra ID:

> **Cause:**
> - MDM automatic enrollment is enabled in Azure.
> - The Intune PC software client (Intune PC agent) is installed on the Windows 10 computer.
>
> **Solution:**
> To resolve this issue, you can utilize one of the following methods:
> 1. **Disable MDM Automatic Enrollment in Azure:**
>   1. Sign in to the Azure portal.
>   2. Navigate to Microsoft Entra ID > Mobility (MDM and MAM) > Microsoft Intune.
>   3. Set MDM User scope to None.
>   4. Click "Save" to apply the changes.
> 2. **Uninstall the Intune Client:**
>   - Uninstall the Intune PC software client agent from the affected Windows 10 computer.

An error occurred: "The Software Cannot Be Installed, 0x80cf4017"

If the error number 0x80cf4017 appears along with the message "The software cannot be installed," it usually means that the client software is not up to date.

Error: "The Account Certificate is Not Valid and May be Expired, 0x80cf4017"

When the error code 0x80cf4017 appears along with the message "The account certificate is not valid and may be expired," it is also a sign that the client software is out of current.

Practice Exercises

1. Mention some Frequent Problems & Fixes with Intune Troubleshooting
2. Discuss the Advanced Microsoft Intune Troubleshooting Methods
3. **Resolve the Intune Windows device enrollment issues below:**
   ➤ Error hr 0x8007064c: The device has already been registered.
   ➤ Error 8018000a: There is already an enrollment for this device
   ➤ An error occurred: "The Software Cannot Be Installed, 0x80cf4017"
   ➤ Error: "The Account Certificate is Not Valid and May be Expired, 0x80cf4017"

CHAPTER SEVENTEEN
COMMON QUESTIONS (INTERVIEW QUESTIONS AND ANSWERS ON INTUNE)

Overview

Design Note: These should be viewed as Intune FAQs, or Frequently Asked Questions, instead of Intune Interview questions. If you read through each question and the links that go along with it, you will find all the information.

How can I register for a free trial account of Microsoft Intune?

Creating a Microsoft Intune tenancy is a prerequisite for registering for a free trial account. If you haven't had access to the Intune gateway before, you can use it for free for 30 days. Using the same account you used to view the sample, whether it be from work or school, you may login in and add Intune to your contract. If not, you can create a fresh Intune account.

What details are needed to complete the Microsoft Intune free trial sign-up form?

To get a free trial of Microsoft Intune, participants must provide their email address, name, corporate phone number, size, nation or region, and domain name that your organization or corporation uses.

What should I do once I've completed the Microsoft Intune free trial sign-up form?

Following the completion of the sign-up form, you will need to select "Next," provide basic account information, pick a domain name and username, create a password, verify your phone number using the code supplied to your mobile device, and, if prompted, provide your tax ID or PAN registration number.

After successfully opening a trial account for Microsoft Intune, what can I do?

Once you've successfully created a Microsoft Intune trial account, you can access the Microsoft 365 admin Center, set up your property, add users and groups, grant licenses, control users and groups, view information about your contract, and begin the process of managing contemporary endpoints. In order to initiate the modern endpoint control procedure, you may also assist users and other devices and, if necessary, add apps.

Intune Version Upgrades are managed by whom?

What Intune does is provide software as a service, or SaaS. The hardware of Intune servers is updated or upgraded by Microsoft. Installing updates, configuring infrastructure and other tasks are not concerns for Intune Manager. These are managed by engineers from Microsoft.

Does Intune need the installation of a server?

Unlike on-premise systems, Intune does not require any computer hardware to function. Microsoft is in control of all computer technology and design because Intune is software as a service (SaaS) product. However, the server architecture may be required for the distribution of certificate profiles in order to provide additional capabilities, such as an NDES connection, among other things. Again, though, these are not Intune sections.

Which decisions about architecture and design are optimal?

The solution to this issue is becoming more elusive. Like the majority of device control applications, Intune consists of a client and a computer. The computer is run by Intune Service. The client side is divided into two sections.
- Windows MDM Client (system-integrated)
- Agent for Intune Management Extension (IME)

On-premise device control platforms like SCCM have quite different architectures and design choices than Intune (the cloud). The SaaS option should be taken into consideration while making decisions on style and strategy.
- There are no decisions to be made about the placement of Intune servers or the construction of the essential Intune infrastructure elements. This has

previously been resolved by Apple. Their PCs and Azure Datacenters are dispersed throughout all areas.

+ Network connections to Intune services via the Internet and on-premises require decisions. In this scenario, administrators connect to Intune services from the on-premises network, and endpoint devices connect to the cloud.

Organizations may require a separate network for the purpose of registration in order to add both new and existing devices to Intune control via Windows Autopilot/ADE.

+ How to create authorized registration alternatives for the business needs to be decided. What if we asked you whether you only wanted to support enrollments using Windows Autopilot, Android Device Admin, or Apple ADE?

+ Make design choices for programs, regulations, Windows updates, third-party app updates, and certificate distribution strategies with Intune. Techniques for repackaging (IntuneWin) and packing (MSIX), among other things.

+ The strategies for using Delivery Optimization (DO) for content distribution on home networks and on-premises. Utilize Intune to configure the device control life cycle as well.

+ Determining how to integrate Intune with existing systems such as SCCM, ServiceNow, and others was one of the most significant design choices.

Which kinds of devices are Intune-manageable?

Every day, more and more device platforms are added to the list that supports Intune. **The following categories of device platforms are available for enrollment:**

Windows

Android

iPad/iOS

macOS

Linux

Where can I find out if Intune service is available?

To find out the current status of the Intune, navigate to the Intune Tenant Admin–Tenant status tab in the Intune admin site.

Where can I get the details of the Intune Version?

The Intune portal (also known as "Intune admin") is where you can learn about the various Intune versions. By selecting Tenant Administration from the Intune Portal, you may find the Service Release number.

In the context of Intune, what is device enrollment?

There are various methods of enrollment. "Device enrollment" refers to adding desktops and mobile devices to an organization's mobile device management (MDM) solution, such as Intune. Every operating system has a separate procedure for configuring a device. Every registration method would offer a unique user experience and setup. The device receives an MDM certificate during the registration procedure. Use this certificate in order to communicate with the Intune service.

Can we use Intune to administer a server operating system?

No, handling servers is not intended for Intune. It is a device management solution for endpoints. It's unlikely that Intune will support servers very soon. However, because Windows 10 and 11 are multi-session operating systems that resemble server OS, Intune can manage VDI tasks that are executed on them.

Which alternatives are available for integrating people and devices with Intune?

It's difficult to respond to this query once again because it's unclear what it wants. Never hesitate to ask for further details if necessary.

You can discuss the following prerequisites for user training:

+ The user needs to be identified using Azure AD.
+ Intune Licenses (Azure AD P1 for Conditional Access) are required for the user.

Additionally, respond to the following queries regarding adding devices to Intune:

- Co-Management of Windows Devices is a device option available to devices that are already connected to Intune.
- Windows Autopilot is an additional method for adding devices to Intune.
- By using automatic enrollment, Windows Azure AD Joined Devices can also be configured.
- Intune Group Policy Enrollment can also be used to add hybrid AD connected devices.
- Both Apple and Android permit the joining of Apple and Android devices in various ways. Enrolling in a personal device differs from enrolling in a device controlled by the company.

Is there a way for Intune admin to revert to an earlier version?

This isn't how SaaS operates, in my opinion. The most recent version of the site that is functional must be used. It is NOT possible to go back to the previous version of the Microsoft Intune service. Therefore, the answer is no; after you have the most recent version of Azure, you can return. The Intune gateway is also compatible with this.

How do the Intune Device, Group, and User Discoveries function?

Once more, SaaS solutions like Intune don't care how Users, Devices, or Groups are located. This is because the solution integrates seamlessly with user accounts, groups, and Azure AD devices.

- There are no user and group items unique to Intune. Rather, it makes direct use of Azure AD users and groups.
- Though the Intune service has its own device objects that are closely related to Azure AD device objects, Intune also obtains its device identities from Azure AD.

What do Intune's collections and groups represent?

There is no such thing as an Intune collection, unlike SCCM groups. There aren't any stand-alone group items available for Intune. Intune makes advantage of Azure AD Groups (User and Device). Certain groups were only for usage with the Intune Silverlight site. However, a feature of Intune that relates to collections—sort of like a group in SCCM—is known as "Intune Filtering Rules." These rules allow Intune to prevent devices from being added to a program or policy.

Azure AD Groups can also be utilized for the subsequent rollout options:

> a) **Assigned/Static User AAD Groups**
> b) **Assigned/Static Device AAD Groups**
> c) **Dynamic User AAD Groups**
> d) **Dynamic Device AAD Groups**

Windows Auto Enrollment: What Is It?

All MDM companies, including Intune, AirWatch, and others, can use this service or solution from Azure AD. You can set up a policy in Intune to automatically add Windows devices that join or register with Azure Active Directory to Intune control. The auto-enrollment facilitates the management of company data on Windows devices used by your employees.

Does Windows Autopilot Take the Place of SCCM OSD?

In order to facilitate the Windows out of Box Experience (OOBE), Microsoft provides Windows Autopilot as a server as part of Endpoint Manager. However, this service is not the same as Windows Autopilot; it cannot be used to install any operating system on Windows devices; rather, Autopilot operates on top of the newly installed operating system on a device to facilitate the initial login process (OOBE). As a result, a new method for reinstalling operating systems on devices, etc., is required.

How can I set up Windows Autopilot to Onboard Devices?

There are three ways to add devices to Windows Autopilot. These are:

- Upload the Device Hash and add the Deployment Profile.
- Request from the sellers that the new devices be added to Autopilot services as part of the purchase transaction.
- Use the "Convert all targeted devices to Autopilot" option if the devices are already in tune.

The provided Autopilot scenario will execute when the specified devices launch the Windows out of Box Experience (OOBE) once more.

Where can you find out the current status of Windows Autopilot Sync using Intune Service?

After logging in to the Intune Admin (Intune) portal, proceed to:

- Navigate to Devices > Windows Enrollment > Enroll Devices.
- To check whether Windows Autopilot and MS Intune are in sync, navigate to the "Windows Autopilot Deployment Program" and select "Devices"!

You can manually sync Intune and Autopilot Service, or get more information about the sync by viewing the most recent successful and unsuccessful sync requests.

Where can I find the Cloud Attach Status and SCCM and Intune Sync?

With SCCM Cloud Attach, which facilitates the syncing of SCCM devices with Intune, helpdesk and other teams can manage devices from the Intune portal. Additionally, you can do remote tasks for SCCM clients from the Intune portal.

To check how SCCM Cloud Attach Sync is interacting with Intune, follow these steps:

- Go to the Intune Admin Center, log in, and select Tenant Administration.
- Click Microsoft Endpoint Configuration Manager after selecting Connectors and Tokens.

This page displays information about the latest successful sync date, the health of the link between SCCM and Intune, the name of the SCCM server, the site code, the site full version, the site mode, and the support ID.

Sync SCCM Database with Intune using SCCM Cloud Attach?

The "SCCM Cloud attach" architecture allows connections to be made whenever needed. It is untrue that Microsoft is transferring the whole SCCM database to the Intune service!

Which remote assistance solutions are available for devices that are managed by Intune?

Remote Assistance options are available through the Intune Admin Center portal. Microsoft's online help solution is called Online Help and is compatible with Intune, Azure AD, and other products. The Remote Help option is not part of the Intune service or license, but it does require a separate license. Another online help tool integrated into the Intune portal is TeamViewer, which also requires a separate license.

Which approach to creating Intune Policies is advised?

Again, this is a challenging Intune Interview question because the real answer is "It depends." There are multiple ways to create policies in Intune. Security policies that center on protection must be created using the Endpoint Security page; from this page, you can create and manage other security policies, such as Defender Antivirus, Encryption, Firewall, and more. Intune policies must be created using the Settings Catalog process for all the different kinds of devices, including Windows, iOS/iPadOS, and macOS.

Describe the Intune patching mechanism.

Windows Update for Business (WUfB) serves as the foundation for the entire Intune updating process. In order for Intune patching to function, a WSUS server is not required. Patching with Intune is simple and less involved than with SCCM. Instead of selecting and creating monthly patch packages, you can create policies for feature and quality changes. If you select the "Quality updates for Windows 10 and later" option, you can create policies for fast patch deployment. The policies in this section facilitate clients connecting to the cloud-based WUfB service and applying patches; the WUA server handles the update process on the client side.

What is the difference between the standard WUfB patching approach and the Windows Autopatch patching mechanism?

Microsoft released Windows Autopatch, a cloud service that automates changes to Windows, Microsoft 365 Apps for Business, Microsoft Edge, and Microsoft Teams. The Intune license does not include a Windows AutoPatch license, so if you don't already have the necessary licenses, you will need to purchase additional ones.

Windows Autopatch handles the following rings automatically:

- Modern Workplace Devices – Test
- Modern Workplace Devices – First
- Modern Workplace Devices – Fast
- Modern Workplace Devices – Broad

Which third-party program patching tool does Intune support?

Third-party app developers like PatchMyPC and ManageEngine can help get all the third-party fixes to the Intune portal automatically. Intune will soon be able to fix third-party apps. But, this will require an additional license; it is not included in the basic license for Intune. SCCM has a very basic built-in third-party repair option.

What are DLP policies, or Intune App Protection?

Combining DLP or app security policies with Mobile Application Management (MAM) solutions allows you to control only the business apps rather than the entire device. App security policies are guidelines that ensure that data belonging to an organization remains secure and under control in a managed app, even when Intune isn't being used for device monitoring. Intune App security policies are typically used with iOS and Android devices. The Intune App Protection Policy can be a list of things that you can't do or that are being watched. It can also help prevent data from shifting from work apps to personal ones.

Can Intune safeguard Enterprise App Data without requiring device management?

Yes, you can use DLP, MAM, or Intune App security policies to protect data from business apps. To use an Intune App security policy, an app must be wrapped with the Intune App SDK. Approximately 100 sellers have already added Intune App Protection policies to their apps in the Google Play and Apple Play shops. Examples of such apps include MS Office Apps, Adobe Acrobat, and more. With Intune App Protection Policies, you can control and safeguard data from apps without having to register iOS, Android, or Windows devices in MDM.

Is it possible to link Azure AD Device Groups with Intune App Protection Policies?

It is possible to add Intune App Protection policies to Azure AD Device Groups. However, it is not a good idea to give the device group an app security policy; instead, the Azure AD User groups should be assigned the Intune App security policies. This is because the purpose of the Intune App security policies is to "just" handle business apps and data, not the devices that users use.

Is device enrollment required to employ Intune or MAM app protection policies?

No, device enrollment is not required in order to use MAM or Intune app security policies. You may still assign these types of policies to users without having to enroll the device.

How does one go about automating the migration of AD Group Policies to Intune Cloud Policies?

Yes, you can move supported AD Group Policies to Intune Cloud Policies. Group Policy Analytics is a new tool from Microsoft that allows you to move on-premise group policies to policies in the Intune Settings Catalog. You can use Group Policy Analytics to examine your on-premises GPOs and determine how much management support you currently have. Click "Import" to begin the analysis, and click "Migrate" when you're ready to replace your old choices with new ones.

---

1. Export GPOs into XML
2. Import Group Policy XML to Intune
3. Analyze the policies to determine whether these GPOs are MDM-compatible or not
4. Migrate **GPOs** to **Intune Settings Catalog policies**

In summary

Microsoft Intune is a virtual super hero for companies that want to keep their computers, phones, and tablets safe and organized. It helps managers and IT professionals ensure that all workplace devices are secure and compliant. Businesses can use Intune to establish policies that restrict access to sensitive information, such as emails and company files, as well as to manage which apps are allowed on work devices and keep everything up to date and functioning properly. Intune can be compared to your company's friendly neighborhood watch, keeping an eye out for problems and ensuring that everything stays safe and organized. If you're in charge of technology at your company, Intune may become your new best friend!

INDEX

C

www.ingramcontent.com/pod-product-compliance
Lightning Source LLC
La Vergne TN
LVHW081517050326
832903LV00025B/1524